SOCIAL AND PREVENTIVE PHARMACY

PRINCIPLES AND PRACTICE

MURALIDHAR RAO AKKALADEVI

Made with ♥ on the Notion Press Platform
www.notionpress.com

Dedication

I dedicate this book to my mother, **Akkaladevi Saraswathi,** whose unwavering love and affection have always been a source of strength and inspiration for me. She instilled in me the values of hard work, determination, and a commitment to excellence.

I am grateful for her guidance, support, and unwavering belief in me. This book is a tribute to her, and I hope that it will serve as a lasting reminder of her influence on my life and work.

Dr.A.Muralidhar Rao

Hyderabad

10-03-2023

Contents

PREFACE

Pharmacy is a crucial field of healthcare, and its role in promoting public health cannot be overstated. As the world continues to face new and complex health challenges, it is becoming increasingly important to integrate preventive measures in pharmacy practice. The field of social and preventive pharmacy has emerged as a key player in this regard, as it focuses on the prevention of diseases and promotion of public health through the use of medications and other healthcare interventions.

This book, Social and Preventive Pharmacy: Principles and Practice, is aimed at providing a comprehensive overview of the principles and practices of social and preventive pharmacy. It covers a wide range of topics, from the basics of public health to the application of preventive measures in pharmacy practice.

The book discusses the concepts of health and disease, and the evaluation of public health. It also delves into the understanding of prevention and control of diseases, social causes of diseases, and social problems of the sick. The topics of social and health education, hygiene and health, and sociology and health are also covered.

Furthermore, the book provides insights into preventive medicine and the general principles of prevention and control of diseases. It includes specific diseases such as cholera, SARS, Ebola virus, influenza, acute respiratory infections, malaria, chicken guinea, dengue, lymphatic filariasis, pneumonia, hypertension, diabetes mellitus, cancer, and drug addiction-drug substance abuse.

The book also discusses various national health programs, their objectives, functioning and outcome. These programs include the HIV and AIDS control program, TB, Integrated disease surveillance program (IDSP), National leprosy control program, National mental health program, National program for prevention and control of deafness, Universal immunization program, National program for control of blindness, Pulse polio program, and more.

The final sections of the book cover national health intervention programs for mother and child, national family welfare program, national tobacco control program, national malaria prevention program, national program for the health care for the elderly, social health program, and the role of WHO in the Indian national program.

Overall, this book is an essential resource for pharmacists and healthcare professionals who are interested in social and preventive pharmacy and wish to improve their knowledge and skills in this field.

Dr. A.Muralidhar Rao

Social And Preventive Pharmacy :Principles And Practice

Dr.A.Muralidhar Rao

Published by Notion press

Notion Press, Inc.
800, West EI Camino Real #180,
California USA 94040

Notion Press Media Pvt Ltd,
#7, Red Cross Road,
Egmore, Chennai, Tamil Nadu 600008

Email ID: publish@notionpress.com

Phone Number: +91 44 46315631

I

Concept of Health and Disease

I. Introduction

A. Definition of Health and Disease

Health can be defined as a state of complete physical, mental, and social well-being, and not merely the absence of disease or infirmity. This definition was given by the World Health Organization (WHO) in 1948 and has been widely accepted as the standard definition of health.

Disease, on the other hand, is a condition that impairs normal functioning of the body or mind. It is often characterized by specific symptoms and signs and is caused by various factors, such as infections, genetic abnormalities, lifestyle choices, and environmental exposures.

The definition of health and disease has evolved over time and has been influenced by various factors, including cultural, social, and political contexts. The WHO definition of health, which was given in 1948, has been criticized for being too idealistic and difficult to achieve in reality. However, it remains a useful framework for understanding the complex and multifaceted nature of health.

Health is not just the absence of disease but also involves a state of physical, mental, and social well-being. This means that good health requires more than just the absence of illness or injury. It also involves a positive state of well-being and the ability to function at an optimal level in all aspects of life. Thus, health can be seen as a dynamic and ever-changing state that is influenced by a range of factors, including genetics, lifestyle choices, social and environmental factors, and access to health care.

Disease is a condition that disrupts the normal functioning of the body or mind. It can be caused by a range of factors, including infections, genetic abnormalities, lifestyle choices, and environmental exposures. Diseases can be acute, meaning they come on suddenly and are of short duration, or they can be chronic, meaning they persist over a long period of time. Some diseases can be treated or cured, while others are incurable and can only be managed to improve quality of life.

Public health is the science and art of preventing disease, prolonging life, and promoting health through organized efforts and informed choices of society, organizations, public and private, communities and individuals. It is a multidisciplinary field that encompasses a range of disciplines, including epidemiology, biostatistics, environmental health, health policy, and social and behavioral sciences. The goal of public health is to improve the health of populations and reduce health disparities by addressing the underlying social, economic, and environmental factors that contribute to disease and poor health outcomes.

B. Concepts of public health

Public health refers to the organized efforts of society to prevent and control diseases, prolong life, and promote health through collective action. It involves the study and application of various scientific and social principles to improve the health of populations.

Epidemiology: Epidemiology is the study of the distribution and determinants of diseases in populations. It involves the use of statistical methods to identify patterns and risk factors associated with diseases. Epidemiological studies provide important information for public health decision-making, such as identifying outbreaks, evaluating prevention strategies, and identifying vulnerable populations.

Health promotion: Health promotion refers to the process of enabling people to improve their health and well-being. This can include interventions aimed at improving health behaviors, such as promoting physical activity, healthy eating, and smoking cessation. Health promotion can also include creating supportive environments and policies that promote health, such as ensuring access to safe housing, education, and healthcare.

Health policy: Health policy refers to the decisions, plans, and actions that are undertaken to achieve specific health goals. This can include policies related to disease prevention and control, healthcare delivery, and health financing. Evaluating health policies can involve assessing their impact on health outcomes, equity, and cost-effectiveness.

Health systems: Health systems refer to the organizations, institutions, and resources that are involved in delivering healthcare services. This can include hospitals, clinics, public health agencies, and community organizations. Evaluating health systems can involve assessing their capacity to deliver high-quality care, to reach underserved populations, and to respond to emergencies.

Social determinants of health: Social determinants of health refer to the social, economic, and environmental factors that influence health outcomes. These can include factors such as income, education, employment, housing, and access to healthcare. Understanding social determinants of health is important for identifying and addressing health inequities.

C.Evaluation of Public health

Evaluation of public health involves the measurement of health outcomes and the assessment of the effectiveness, efficiency, and equity of public health interventions and policies. This includes the use of various methods, such as surveillance systems, program evaluations, and health impact assessments. The goal of public health evaluation is to provide evidence to inform decision-making and improve the quality and effectiveness of public health programs and policies.

Surveillance:

Surveillance is the systematic and ongoing collection, analysis, interpretation, and dissemination of health data for the purpose of planning, implementing, and evaluating public health interventions. It involves the monitoring of disease and health-related events to identify changes in trends or patterns, and to detect outbreaks or other emerging health threats.

Public health surveillance can be conducted at different levels, including local, state, national, and global. The data collected through surveillance can be used for a variety of purposes, such as:

Identifying and tracking disease trends: Public health surveillance is used to monitor the occurrence and distribution of diseases and health conditions within a population. This information is used to identify trends, patterns, and clusters of disease, and to track changes over time.

Detecting outbreaks and other health threats: Surveillance systems can detect outbreaks of infectious diseases or other health threats, such as bioterrorism or environmental hazards. Rapid detection of outbreaks is essential for timely public health interventions to prevent further spread of disease.

Monitoring the effectiveness of interventions: Surveillance data can be used to monitor the effectiveness of public health interventions, such as vaccination programs, disease control measures, and health promotion activities. This information can guide public health policy and decision-making.

Conducting research: Surveillance data can be used for research purposes, such as identifying risk factors for disease or evaluating the effectiveness of interventions.

Surveillance data can be collected from various sources, including healthcare providers, laboratories, vital statistics, and disease registries. The data is analyzed and interpreted by public health professionals to inform public health policy and practice.

The success of a surveillance system depends on the quality, completeness, and timeliness of the data collected, as well as the ability to effectively analyze and interpret the data. Continuous evaluation and improvement of surveillance systems is essential to ensure their effectiveness in protecting public health.

Program evaluation:

Program evaluation is a critical component of public health practice that involves the systematic collection and analysis of data to assess the effectiveness, efficiency, and impact of public health programs and interventions. It provides valuable information that can be used to improve the quality of services, identify best practices, and ensure accountability.

There are several steps involved in program evaluation, including:

Setting program goals and objectives: This involves defining the specific outcomes that the program aims to achieve and the indicators that will be used to measure progress.

Developing an evaluation plan: This involves identifying the data sources and methods that will be used to collect and analyze data, as well as the timeline and budget for the evaluation.

Collecting and analyzing data: This involves gathering information on program inputs, activities, outputs, outcomes, and impact using a variety of methods, such as surveys, interviews, focus groups, and secondary data sources.

Interpreting and reporting findings: This involves synthesizing and interpreting the data to assess program performance and identify areas for improvement, and communicating the results to stakeholders.

Using evaluation findings: This involves using the information obtained from the evaluation to make programmatic and policy decisions, improve program implementation, and adjust program goals and objectives as needed.

There are several approaches to program evaluation, including:

Process evaluation: This focuses on assessing the implementation of a program, including the extent to which the program was delivered as intended and the quality of program implementation.

Outcome evaluation: This focuses on assessing the immediate and intermediate effects of a program, including changes in knowledge, attitudes, behaviors, and health status.

Impact evaluation: This focuses on assessing the long-term effects of a program, including changes in morbidity, mortality, and quality of life.

Health impact assessment (HIA):

Health impact assessment is a process that evaluates the potential health effects of a policy, program, project or any other intervention on a population or community. The primary goal of HIA is to inform decision-making by identifying and addressing the health impacts of proposed policies or programs.

HIA is a multi-disciplinary approach that draws on expertise from various fields such as public health, environmental health, urban planning, and social sciences. The process typically involves the following steps:

Screening: The first step is to determine whether an HIA is necessary and feasible for the proposed intervention.

Scoping: This step involves defining the scope and boundaries of the HIA, identifying the population and health outcomes of interest, and determining the data sources and methods to be used.

Assessment: This step involves gathering and analyzing data on the potential health impacts of the intervention, including both positive and negative effects.

Recommendations: Based on the assessment, recommendations are developed to mitigate negative health impacts and enhance positive ones. These recommendations may include modifications to the proposed intervention, or additional measures to be taken to improve health outcomes.

Reporting: The findings and recommendations are compiled into a report that is presented to decision-makers, stakeholders, and the public.

Monitoring and Evaluation: The final step involves monitoring and evaluating the implementation and outcomes of the recommended interventions to determine their effectiveness and to inform future decision-making.

HIA has been used to evaluate a range of interventions, including transportation policies, urban development projects, and energy policies. It is a valuable tool for promoting health equity and social justice by ensuring that the health impacts of policies and programs are considered and addressed in the decision-making process.

Overall, health impact assessment is a crucial component of public health practice and helps to ensure that policies and programs are designed and implemented with consideration for the potential health impacts on the population.

Health equity assessment:

Health equity assessment is a tool used to measure the fairness in the distribution of health outcomes and social determinants of health across different population groups. It aims to identify and address health disparities and inequalities that are unjust and avoidable. Health equity assessment involves analyzing various factors such as social, economic, and environmental conditions, and their impact on health outcomes.

The assessment also evaluates policies, programs, and interventions to determine their effectiveness in reducing health inequities and improving health outcomes for disadvantaged groups. This includes examining access to healthcare services, education, housing, and other resources that contribute to health outcomes.

One of the main objectives of health equity assessment is to promote health equity by identifying and addressing systemic barriers that prevent certain groups from accessing the same level of care and resources as others. The assessment can be used by governments, healthcare organizations, and public health agencies to develop policies and programs that aim to reduce health inequities and promote health equity.

Overall, health equity assessment is an important tool in promoting social justice and ensuring that everyone has an equal opportunity to achieve good health. It recognizes that health is not just an individual responsibility but is influenced by broader social, economic, and environmental factors.

II. Understanding the concept of prevention and control of disease

A. Definition of prevention and control of disease:

Prevention and control of disease refer to the measures and strategies employed to reduce the occurrence, transmission, and impact of infectious and non-communicable diseases on individuals and populations.

B. Importance of prevention and control of disease in public health:

Prevention and control of disease is essential in maintaining public health and reducing the burden of illness and death in populations. It aims to reduce the incidence, prevalence, and mortality rates of diseases, as well as the associated social and economic costs.

Prevention and control of diseases are important because they can:

1. Prevent the spread of infectious diseases from one person to another or from one population to another.
2. Reduce the severity and duration of illness, thus improving the quality of life of individuals and communities.
3. Improve the overall health status of populations, leading to better productivity and economic development.
4. Reduce the burden on the healthcare system by decreasing the number of hospitalizations, emergency department visits, and medical expenses.
5. Strengthen public health systems and increase their capacity to respond to disease outbreaks and emergencies.

Prevention and control of disease requires a comprehensive approach that involves various stakeholders, including healthcare providers, policymakers, community leaders, and individuals themselves. It involves implementing effective interventions such as vaccination, health education, behavior change, environmental modifications, and early diagnosis and treatment.

II. Principles of Disease Prevention and Control

Prevention and control of diseases are fundamental aspects of public health that aim to reduce the burden of illnesses and promote health and well-being in populations. The concept of disease prevention and control involves a range of strategies and interventions designed to mitigate the spread of diseases, reduce their incidence, and manage their impact on individuals, communities, and societies.

Prevention and control of diseases can be broadly categorized into primary, secondary, and tertiary prevention strategies.

A. Primary prevention

Primary prevention refers to actions taken to prevent the onset of a disease before it occurs. It aims to reduce the incidence of a disease in the population by eliminating or reducing risk factors. Examples of primary prevention include health promotion campaigns to encourage healthy behaviors, vaccination programs, and environmental measures such as improving sanitation and hygiene.

B. Secondary prevention

Secondary prevention aims to identify and treat a disease in its early stages to prevent it from progressing and causing complications. It includes screening programs to detect diseases early, such as breast cancer screening or cervical cancer screening, and interventions to manage the disease and prevent its progression.

C. Tertiary prevention

Tertiary prevention focuses on the management and rehabilitation of individuals who have an existing disease or disability to prevent further complications and reduce the impact of the disease on their quality of life. Examples of tertiary prevention include rehabilitation programs for stroke survivors, diabetes management programs, and palliative care for individuals with terminal illnesses.

D. Active and passive immunization

Immunization is a crucial component of disease prevention and control. It involves the administration of a vaccine to stimulate the immune system and develop immunity against a particular infectious agent. Active immunization involves administering a vaccine containing a weakened or dead pathogen, while passive immunization involves the administration of pre-formed antibodies. Examples of active immunization include vaccination programs for diseases such as measles, mumps, and rubella, while passive immunization is used for diseases such as rabies or tetanus.

E. Control measures for infectious diseases

Control measures for infectious diseases aim to prevent or reduce the spread of the disease within the population. These measures may include isolation or quarantine of infected individuals, treatment of infected individuals, contact tracing to identify individuals who may have been exposed to the disease, and environmental measures such as improving sanitation and hygiene.

F. Risk assessment and management

Risk assessment and management involve identifying potential hazards and taking steps to reduce or eliminate the risk of exposure. This may involve measures such as hazard identification, risk analysis, risk evaluation, and risk treatment. Risk assessment and management are used to prevent or control both infectious and non-infectious diseases, such as occupational hazards, environmental pollutants, and chemical exposure.

Effective disease prevention and control strategies also require addressing social determinants of health, such as poverty, education, and social inequality, which can impact the incidence and severity of diseases. Additionally, public health education and awareness campaigns, screening and early detection programs, environmental health measures, and public policy and regulations are critical components of disease prevention and control efforts.

Understanding the concept of prevention and control of diseases is essential for promoting the health and well-being of individuals and communities, and for reducing the burden of diseases on society.

III.Strategies for Disease Prevention and Control

A. Public health education and awareness

Public health education and awareness are critical strategies for disease prevention and control. This involves informing individuals and communities about the risks associated with certain behaviors, such as smoking or unprotected sex, and providing information about the steps that can be taken to prevent diseases. This can be done through public health campaigns, educational programs, and the dissemination of information through various media channels.

B. Screening and early detection

Screening and early detection programs are essential for detecting diseases before they progress to a more advanced stage. This includes routine screenings for conditions such as cancer, diabetes, and high blood pressure. Early detection can lead to better treatment outcomes and reduce the overall burden of disease.

C. Vaccination and immunization programs

Vaccination and immunization programs are effective strategies for preventing the spread of infectious diseases. These programs involve the administration of vaccines to individuals to help them develop immunity to specific diseases. Vaccination programs have been successful in eradicating diseases such as smallpox and reducing the incidence of diseases such as measles, mumps, and rubella.

D. Treatment and management of diseases

Treatment and management of diseases are essential components of disease prevention and control. This involves providing appropriate medical care to individuals who have been diagnosed with a disease, as well as managing their symptoms and complications. Effective treatment and management can help to reduce the burden of disease on individuals and the community.

E. Environmental health measures

Environmental health measures involve ensuring that the physical environment is safe and healthy. This includes measures such as providing clean drinking water, improving sanitation, and reducing exposure to environmental toxins. These measures can help to prevent the spread of diseases and improve overall health outcomes.

F. Public policy and regulations

Public policy and regulations are critical for disease prevention and control. This includes policies related to food safety, workplace safety, and environmental health. Regulations can help to ensure that individuals and organizations are following established guidelines to prevent the spread of disease and promote good health outcomes.

IV. Social Causes of Diseases

A. Definition of social causes of diseases

Social causes of diseases refer to the societal and environmental factors that contribute to the development and spread of diseases. These factors are shaped by social, economic, political, and environmental conditions that influence the health status of individuals and populations.

B. Examples of social causes of diseases

There are several examples of social causes of diseases, including:

Poverty and inequality: Poverty and social inequality are associated with an increased risk of several diseases, including tuberculosis, HIV/AIDS, malaria, and malnutrition. Low-income individuals and communities often lack access to proper nutrition, healthcare, and safe living conditions.

Environmental factors: Environmental factors such as pollution, poor sanitation, and lack of access to clean water can contribute to the spread of diseases such as cholera, typhoid, and hepatitis A.

Lifestyle choices: Lifestyle choices such as smoking, excessive alcohol consumption, and drug abuse increase the risk of several chronic diseases such as heart disease, cancer, and respiratory diseases.

Occupational hazards: Exposure to occupational hazards such as asbestos, radiation, and chemicals can lead to the development of several diseases such as lung cancer, mesothelioma, and leukemia.

Social determinants of health: Social determinants of health such as education, income, and employment status have a significant impact on the health status of individuals and communities.

C. Impact of social causes of diseases on public health

Social causes of diseases have a significant impact on public health. They contribute to health inequalities and disparities, which are reflected in higher rates of illness and premature death among disadvantaged communities. Addressing social causes of diseases is essential to improving the health and well-being of individuals and communities. It requires a comprehensive and coordinated approach that involves multiple sectors, including healthcare, education, housing, and public policy.

V. Social problems of the sick

A. Definition of social problems of the sick

Social problems of the sick refer to the difficulties, challenges, and negative consequences experienced by individuals or groups who are suffering from a particular illness or disease. These social problems are often the result of social, economic, or cultural factors that affect the individual's ability to cope with their illness and access necessary resources.

B. Examples of social problems of the sick

Examples of social problems of the sick include stigma and discrimination, social isolation, financial burdens, loss of employment or income, disruptions in family and social relationships, and access to healthcare services.

Stigma and discrimination towards those who are suffering from a disease or illness can lead to social exclusion, bullying, and harassment, causing the person to feel isolated and unsupported. Financial burdens can arise from the cost of medical treatment, transportation to appointments, and medications, which can result in debt and poverty. Loss of employment or income can lead to further economic instability and worsen the financial burden. Disruptions in family and social relationships can occur due to the person's illness, which can cause stress, anxiety, and depression.

C. Impact of social problems of the sick on public health

Social problems of the sick can have a significant impact on public health. The negative consequences of these social problems can affect the individual's overall well-being and quality of life, leading to poorer health outcomes, increased healthcare utilization, and decreased life expectancy. The social and economic burden of these problems can also affect the broader community, leading to decreased productivity and increased healthcare costs. Therefore, addressing social problems of the sick is essential for promoting public health and improving the overall well-being of individuals and communities.

II

Social and Health Education

I. Introduction

A. Importance of food and nutrition for health

Good nutrition and healthy eating habits are essential for maintaining good health and preventing chronic diseases such as obesity, type 2 diabetes, hypertension, heart disease, and certain cancers. Adequate nutrition helps to maintain a healthy body weight, supports the immune system, and promotes the growth and repair of body tissues. In addition, good nutrition is essential for optimal cognitive and physical development, particularly in children.

B. Definition of Balanced Diet

A balanced diet is one that contains all the essential nutrients in the right proportions to promote good health. The essential nutrients include carbohydrates, proteins, fats, vitamins, minerals, and water. Each nutrient plays a critical role in the body, and a deficiency in any one of them can lead to various health problems.

A balanced diet should provide the appropriate amounts of nutrients needed to meet the body's energy requirements and support growth and development. The exact proportions of nutrients that make up a balanced diet depend on a person's age, gender, physical activity level, and other factors.

A balanced diet should include a variety of foods from all the major food groups, including fruits and vegetables, whole grains, lean proteins, and healthy fats. The recommended daily intake of each nutrient varies depending on age, gender, and other factors, but a balanced diet should generally provide a sufficient amount of each nutrient to meet the body's needs.

In addition to a balanced diet, other healthy lifestyle behaviors can promote good nutrition and overall health, such as limiting intake of processed and sugary foods, avoiding excessive alcohol consumption, staying hydrated, and engaging in regular physical activity.

II. Nutritional Deficiencies

A. Definition and types of nutritional deficiencies

Nutritional deficiencies refer to the inadequate intake or absorption of nutrients required for proper functioning and growth of the body. There are different types of nutritional deficiencies, including:

Macronutrient deficiencies: These are deficiencies of the three main macronutrients required by the body - carbohydrates, proteins, and fats. Deficiencies in these nutrients can lead to various health problems, including malnutrition.

Micronutrient deficiencies: These are deficiencies of essential vitamins and minerals required by the body in small quantities. Micronutrient deficiencies can lead to specific health problems such as anemia, goiter, and night blindness.

B. Causes of nutritional deficiencies

Nutritional deficiencies can be caused by various factors, including:

Poor dietary intake: A diet lacking in a variety of nutrients can lead to nutritional deficiencies.

Malabsorption: Conditions that affect the absorption of nutrients in the body, such as celiac disease, can lead to nutritional deficiencies.

Increased nutrient needs: Certain conditions, such as pregnancy, lactation, and growth spurts, increase the body's nutrient needs, which can result in deficiencies if not met.

Medical procedures: Certain medical procedures, such as weight loss surgery, can result in nutrient deficiencies.

C. Symptoms and effects of nutritional deficiencies

Nutritional deficiencies can result in a range of symptoms and health effects, depending on the type and severity of the deficiency. Some common symptoms and effects of nutritional deficiencies include:

1. Fatigue and weakness
2. Anemia
3. Stunted growth
4. Cognitive impairment
5. Bone disorders
6. Skin disorders
7. Immune system dysfunction
8. Increased risk of infections
9. Delayed wound healing
10. Increased risk of chronic diseases, such as cardiovascular disease and cancer.

It is important to identify and address nutritional deficiencies early to prevent long-term health problems.

A. Common vitamin deficiencies:

There are several types of vitamins that the human body requires for proper functioning, and deficiencies in any of these vitamins can have adverse health effects. The most common types of vitamin deficiencies are:

Vitamin D deficiency: Vitamin D is essential for maintaining healthy bones and teeth, and deficiency can lead to conditions such as rickets in children and osteomalacia in adults.

Vitamin B12 deficiency: Vitamin B12 is important for proper red blood cell formation, nerve function, and DNA synthesis. Deficiency can cause anemia and nerve damage.

Vitamin C deficiency: Vitamin C is crucial for maintaining a healthy immune system and skin, and deficiency can lead to scurvy, a condition characterized by weakness, fatigue, and bleeding gums.

Vitamin A deficiency: Vitamin A is important for vision, skin health, and immune function. Deficiency can lead to vision problems, skin disorders, and an increased risk of infections.

B. Symptoms and effects of vitamin deficiencies:

The symptoms and effects of vitamin deficiencies can vary depending on the specific vitamin and the severity of the deficiency. Some common symptoms and effects of vitamin deficiencies include:

- Weakness, fatigue, and lethargy
- Anemia
- Nerve damage
- Vision problems
- Skin disorders
- Increased risk of infections
- Delayed growth and development in children

C. Sources of vitamins:

Vitamins can be obtained from a variety of food sources, including fruits, vegetables, whole grains, and animal products. Some common sources of vitamins include:

- Vitamin D: Fatty fish, egg yolks, and fortified dairy products
- Vitamin B12: Meat, fish, dairy products, and fortified cereals

- Vitamin C: Citrus fruits, tomatoes, and broccoli
- Vitamin A: Leafy greens, carrots, sweet potatoes, and liver

It is important to maintain a balanced and varied diet to ensure adequate intake of all essential vitamins. In some cases, supplements may be recommended to address specific deficiencies.

IV. Malnutrition

A. Definition and types of malnutrition

Malnutrition is a condition that results from an inadequate or excessive intake of nutrients. There are two main types of malnutrition: undernutrition and overnutrition. Undernutrition occurs when there is a deficiency of essential nutrients, such as protein, vitamins, and minerals, in the body. This can lead to stunting, wasting, and other health problems. Overnutrition, on the other hand, occurs when there is an excess intake of nutrients, particularly calories, leading to overweight or obesity.

B. Causes and risk factors for malnutrition

Malnutrition can be caused by various factors, including poverty, limited access to food, lack of education on proper nutrition, and certain medical conditions that affect the absorption and utilization of nutrients. In underdeveloped countries, malnutrition is often associated with poverty, lack of access to clean water, and inadequate sanitation, which contribute to the spread of infectious diseases that can further worsen malnutrition.

C. Prevention and management of malnutrition

Prevention and management of malnutrition require a comprehensive approach that includes education on proper nutrition, access to healthy and affordable food, and medical interventions when necessary. In underdeveloped countries, improving access to clean water and sanitation facilities can also help prevent malnutrition. Strategies to address overnutrition include reducing the intake of calorie-dense foods, increasing physical activity, and behavior change interventions. In cases of severe malnutrition, medical interventions such as therapeutic feeding and nutritional supplements may be necessary.

V. Food and Health

A. The relationship between food and health: The food we consume plays an essential role in maintaining our overall health and well-being. A balanced and nutritious diet can help prevent chronic diseases such as obesity, diabetes, and heart disease. On the other hand, poor dietary habits, such as consuming foods that are high in saturated and trans fats, sodium, and added sugars, can increase the risk of these diseases.

B. Dietary guidelines for health promotion and disease prevention: Dietary guidelines are recommendations that provide information on what and how much to eat to maintain good health and prevent chronic diseases. These guidelines are typically developed by government agencies and health organizations based on scientific research. Examples of such guidelines include the Dietary Guidelines for Americans, the Mediterranean Diet, and the DASH (Dietary Approaches to Stop Hypertension) diet.

C. Food safety and hygiene: Ensuring that the food we eat is safe and free from harmful contaminants is an essential aspect of maintaining good health. Food safety practices include proper food handling, storage, and preparation to prevent contamination from bacteria, viruses, and other harmful pathogens. Food hygiene practices, such as washing hands before handling food and ensuring that kitchen utensils are clean, can also help prevent the spread of foodborne illnesses.

VI. Social and Health Education

A. The role of social and health education in promoting healthy eating

Social and health education plays a crucial role in promoting healthy eating habits by providing individuals with the necessary knowledge and skills to make informed decisions about their diet. It enables individuals to understand the importance of a balanced diet and the role of various nutrients in maintaining good health. Social and health education can also help individuals to understand the impact of their food choices on their overall health and well-being.

B. Strategies for promoting healthy eating habits

There are various strategies that can be employed to promote healthy eating habits. Some of these strategies include:

Nutrition education: This involves providing individuals with information about the importance of a balanced diet, the role of various nutrients in the body, and the impact of unhealthy food choices on health.

Food labeling: Providing clear and accurate information about the nutritional content of food products can help individuals make informed decisions about their food choices.

Food policies: Governments can introduce policies that promote the availability and affordability of healthy foods, such as subsidies for fruits and vegetables.

Community interventions: Programs that encourage healthy eating habits, such as cooking classes and community gardens, can also be effective in promoting healthy eating habits.

C. Challenges and barriers to healthy eating and nutrition education

There are several challenges and barriers to promoting healthy eating habits and nutrition education. Some of these challenges include:

Access to healthy foods: In some communities, healthy foods may not be readily available or may be too expensive, making it difficult for individuals to make healthy food choices.

Food marketing: The food industry often promotes unhealthy foods through advertising and marketing, making it difficult for individuals to make healthy food choices.

Cultural and social norms: Cultural and social norms may also influence food choices, making it difficult to promote healthy eating habits.

Lack of nutrition education: Many individuals lack basic knowledge about nutrition and healthy eating, making it difficult for them to make informed decisions about their diet.

Summary of key points

- Food and nutrition are important for good health.
- A balanced diet is one that contains all the necessary nutrients in the right amounts.
- Nutritional deficiencies can occur when the body does not receive enough of a particular nutrient, leading to various symptoms and health effects.
- Common vitamin deficiencies include deficiencies in vitamins A, C, and D, which can cause a range of health problems.
- Malnutrition is a condition that can result from a lack of proper nutrition, and can be caused by factors such as poverty, poor diet, and certain diseases.
- Prevention and management of malnutrition involves addressing underlying causes and ensuring adequate intake of essential nutrients.
- The relationship between food and health is important, and dietary guidelines can help promote healthy eating habits for disease prevention.
- Food safety and hygiene are also important for preventing foodborne illnesses.
- Social and health education can play an important role in promoting healthy eating habits and addressing barriers and challenges to nutrition education.

III

Sociology and Health

I. Introduction

A. Definition of Sociology and Health:

Sociology is the scientific study of human society and social behavior. It involves understanding how people interact with one another, how societies are organized and structured, and how social institutions function. Health, on the other hand, refers to the state of physical, mental, and social well-being.

Sociology and health are closely related because health is influenced by various social factors such as culture, social class, gender, race, and ethnicity. The study of sociology helps to understand how these factors affect health and disease.

B. Importance of Studying the Socio-Cultural Factors Related to Health and Disease:

The socio-cultural factors related to health and disease have a significant impact on the health outcomes of individuals and communities. These factors can influence health in various ways, including access to healthcare, health behaviors, and exposure to environmental risks.

Studying these factors can help identify the root causes of health disparities and inequalities, and inform the development of effective public health interventions. It can also help healthcare providers understand the social context of their patients and provide culturally sensitive care.

For example, understanding the cultural beliefs and practices of a community can help healthcare providers to design interventions that are culturally appropriate and acceptable to that community. Similarly, understanding the impact of poverty on health can inform the development of policies and programs to address this issue.

Studying the socio-cultural factors related to health and disease is essential for promoting health equity and improving health outcomes for all individuals and communities.

II. Socio-cultural Factors Related to Health and Disease

A. Definition of socio-cultural factors

Socio-cultural factors are the social, cultural, economic, and environmental conditions that affect the health and well-being of individuals and communities. These factors encompass a wide range of social and cultural dimensions, such as beliefs, values, norms, traditions, customs, social status, education, employment, income, housing, and access to healthcare.

B. Types of socio-cultural factors affecting health and disease

Socio-cultural factors can be broadly categorized into two types: structural factors and cultural factors. Structural factors are the external and objective conditions that affect health and disease, such as socioeconomic status, education, employment, housing, and access to healthcare. Cultural factors, on the other hand, are the internal and subjective conditions that shape health beliefs, attitudes, and behaviors, such as beliefs, values, norms, traditions, customs, and social networks.

C. Examples of socio-cultural factors affecting health and disease

Some examples of socio-cultural factors that affect health and disease include:

Socioeconomic status: People with lower socioeconomic status are more likely to experience poorer health outcomes due to limited access to healthcare, poorer living conditions, and higher levels of stress and trauma.

Education: Low levels of education have been linked to higher rates of chronic disease, lower life expectancy, and poorer mental health outcomes.

Housing: Poor housing conditions, such as overcrowding, lack of ventilation, and exposure to environmental toxins, can lead to respiratory diseases, asthma, and other health problems.

Cultural beliefs and practices: Certain cultural beliefs and practices may influence health behaviors and outcomes, such as the use of traditional medicine, dietary practices, and beliefs about mental illness.

Discrimination and social exclusion: Discrimination and social exclusion based on race, ethnicity, gender, sexual orientation, or disability can have a negative impact on mental and physical health, leading to stress, anxiety, and depression.

Social support networks: Strong social support networks have been linked to better mental and physical health outcomes, while social isolation and loneliness have been associated with higher rates of chronic disease and mortality.

III. Impact of Urbanization on Health and Disease

A. Definition of Urbanization

Urbanization is the process of increasing the proportion of people living in urban areas. It involves the growth of cities and towns as people move from rural to urban areas in search of better opportunities and a higher standard of living.

B. Health Issues Related to Urbanization

Urbanization has both positive and negative effects on health. While it offers better access to health care facilities and services, it also exposes people to various health risks. Some of the common health issues related to urbanization are:

Environmental Pollution:

Urban areas are known for their high levels of pollution, which can lead to various health problems such as respiratory diseases, cancer, and heart disease.

Infectious Diseases:

Urbanization can also contribute to the spread of infectious diseases such as tuberculosis, HIV/AIDS, and COVID-19, due to the high population density and poor sanitation.

Lifestyle-related Diseases: Urbanization can also lead to lifestyle-related diseases such as obesity, diabetes, and hypertension due to changes in diet and physical activity levels.

C. Factors Contributing to Health Problems in Urban Areas

Several factors contribute to health problems in urban areas, including:

Poor Housing Conditions: Many people living in urban areas live in overcrowded and poorly constructed housing, which can lead to poor health outcomes.

Lack of Access to Clean Water and Sanitation: Urban areas are often characterized by inadequate water and sanitation facilities, which can lead to the spread of infectious diseases.

Transportation: Transportation-related pollution can contribute to respiratory diseases and other health problems.

Economic Inequality: Urban areas often have high levels of economic inequality, which can result in poorer health outcomes for those living in poverty.

Social Isolation: Despite the high population density in urban areas, many people report feeling socially isolated, which can negatively impact their mental health.

IV. Poverty and Health

A. Definition of Poverty:

Poverty can be defined as the state of being extremely poor, lacking the resources to meet basic needs such as food, shelter, and clothing. Poverty is a complex social phenomenon that affects not only income and material resources but also health and social wellbeing.

B. Health Issues Related to Poverty:

Poverty is closely linked to poor health outcomes. Individuals living in poverty are more likely to experience a range of health issues, including:

Malnutrition: Individuals living in poverty may not have access to a balanced diet, leading to malnutrition and associated health problems.

Infectious Diseases: Poor living conditions and lack of access to healthcare services increase the risk of infectious diseases, such as tuberculosis, malaria, and HIV/AIDS.

Chronic Diseases: Poverty is also associated with an increased risk of chronic diseases such as diabetes, hypertension, and cardiovascular disease.

Mental Health: Living in poverty can also have a significant impact on mental health, with higher rates of depression, anxiety, and stress.

C. Factors Contributing to Health Problems in Impoverished Areas:

Several factors contribute to health problems in impoverished areas. These include:

Lack of Access to Healthcare: Individuals living in poverty may have limited access to healthcare services, making it difficult to address health issues.

Poor Living Conditions: Poverty is often associated with poor living conditions, such as overcrowding, lack of clean water, and inadequate sanitation, which increase the risk of infectious diseases.

Environmental Factors: Pollution, exposure to toxins, and other environmental factors may be more prevalent in impoverished areas, increasing the risk of health problems.

Limited Education: Low levels of education are associated with poorer health outcomes, and individuals living in poverty may have limited access to education and health information.

Overall, poverty is a significant social determinant of health, and addressing poverty is essential to improving health outcomes and reducing health disparities.V. Strategies to Address Socio-cultural Factors Affecting Health and DiseaseV. Strategies to Address Socio-cultural Factors Affecting Health and Disease

V. Strategies to Address Socio-cultural Factors Affecting Health and Disease

A. Education and awareness campaigns: One of the most effective ways to address socio-cultural factors affecting health and disease is through education and awareness campaigns. These campaigns aim to educate individuals and communities about the importance of healthy behaviors, as well as the risks associated with unhealthy behaviors. Such campaigns can be conducted through various means, such as public service announcements, social media, educational programs, and community events.

B. Community-based interventions: Another effective strategy is community-based interventions that involve working with local communities to develop and implement programs that address the underlying socio-cultural factors affecting health and disease. Community-based interventions may include initiatives such as community health fairs, health education classes, support groups, and outreach programs.

C. Public policy and regulations: Public policy and regulations play a crucial role in addressing socio-cultural factors affecting health and disease. Governments can implement policies and regulations that promote healthy behaviors, such as food labeling laws, restrictions on tobacco and alcohol advertising, and laws requiring workplace safety standards. Additionally, policies can address social and economic determinants of health, such as poverty, housing, and education.

A comprehensive approach that includes education and awareness campaigns, community-based interventions, and public policy and regulations is necessary to address the complex socio-cultural factors that contribute to health and disease.

VI. Challenges in Addressing Socio-cultural Factors Affecting Health and Disease

A. Limited Resources: One of the major challenges in addressing socio-cultural factors affecting health and disease is the limited resources available for intervention programs. This can be due to a lack of funding, manpower, or infrastructure. Limited resources may prevent effective implementation of interventions, resulting in inadequate coverage and effectiveness of health programs.

B. Social and Cultural Barriers: Social and cultural beliefs and practices can pose challenges to addressing socio-cultural factors affecting health and disease. For example, cultural beliefs and practices may influence dietary habits and health behaviors. Some communities may resist interventions that conflict with their cultural beliefs or values. Similarly, language barriers and low health literacy can make it difficult to effectively communicate health information and interventions to certain populations.

C. Political and Economic Factors: Political and economic factors can also pose challenges to addressing socio-cultural factors affecting health and disease. This may include issues such as corruption, limited access to resources, and political instability. Additionally, economic factors such as poverty and income inequality may impact health outcomes by limiting access to healthcare and healthy foods. Political and economic factors may also influence the distribution of resources, including healthcare facilities and health personnel, which can affect the quality and accessibility of healthcare services.

IV

Hygiene and Health

I. Introduction

A. Definition of hygiene and health

Hygiene can be defined as the practice of maintaining cleanliness and preventing the spread of diseases. It involves a range of activities such as handwashing, bathing, and keeping the environment clean. Hygiene is an important aspect of public health and plays a crucial role in preventing the transmission of infectious diseases.

Health, on the other hand, can be defined as a state of physical, mental, and social well-being. Personal hygiene practices are essential for maintaining good health and preventing the spread of infectious diseases.

B. Importance of personal hygiene for health

Personal hygiene practices are essential for maintaining good health and preventing the spread of infectious diseases. The human body is home to millions of microorganisms, including bacteria and viruses. While many of these microorganisms are harmless or even beneficial, others can cause infections and diseases.

Proper personal hygiene practices can help to reduce the risk of infections and diseases by preventing the spread of harmful microorganisms. For example, washing hands regularly with soap and water can help to prevent the spread of diseases such as influenza, diarrhea, and hepatitis A. Similarly, keeping the environment clean and maintaining good personal hygiene can help to prevent the spread of infections such as ringworm, scabies, and lice.

In addition to preventing the spread of diseases, personal hygiene practices can also have a positive impact on mental health. Good personal hygiene practices can help to boost self-esteem and confidence, leading to improved mental well-being.

II. Personal Hygiene and Health Care

A. Definition and importance of personal hygiene

Personal hygiene refers to the practices and habits that individuals engage in to maintain their physical cleanliness and well-being. Good personal hygiene involves taking care of various aspects of one's body, including skin, hair, teeth, nails, and clothing. It is an essential aspect of overall health and well-being as it helps prevent the spread of infections and illnesses, maintain healthy skin and hair, and promote a positive self-image.

The importance of personal hygiene cannot be overstated, as it plays a critical role in preventing the spread of infectious diseases. Proper hand hygiene, for example, is one of the most effective ways to prevent the spread of communicable diseases such as influenza, the common cold, and foodborne illnesses. Similarly, maintaining good oral hygiene can help prevent tooth decay, gum disease, and bad breath. Good personal hygiene also promotes a positive self-image, which can improve mental health and well-being.

B. Practices for maintaining personal hygiene

There are several practices that can help individuals maintain good personal hygiene. These include:

Hand hygiene: washing hands with soap and water before and after eating, after using the toilet, after handling pets, and after being in public places.

Oral hygiene: brushing teeth twice a day with fluoride toothpaste, flossing daily, and using mouthwash.

Bathing and showering: bathing or showering daily with soap and water.

Hair hygiene: washing hair regularly with shampoo.

Nail hygiene: keeping nails clean and trimmed.

Clothing hygiene: wearing clean clothes and changing clothes daily.

Environmental hygiene: keeping the surroundings clean and free from dust, dirt, and other pollutants.

Food hygiene: following proper food handling and storage practices to prevent foodborne illnesses.

Sexual hygiene: practicing safe sex and getting regular sexual health check-ups.

By following these practices, individuals can maintain good personal hygiene and prevent the spread of diseases.

C. Benefits of good personal hygiene

Good personal hygiene has several benefits, including:

Prevention of illness: Good personal hygiene practices can help prevent the spread of illnesses and infections, such as the common cold, influenza, and foodborne illnesses.

Improved physical appearance: Maintaining good personal hygiene can help individuals look and feel better. It can also help prevent body odor and improve overall skin health.

Increased self-confidence: Good personal hygiene can boost self-esteem and confidence, particularly in social situations.

Better dental health: Regular brushing, flossing, and dental check-ups can help prevent tooth decay, gum disease, and bad breath.

Improved mental health: Good personal hygiene can promote mental well-being by reducing anxiety, stress, and depression.

Greater respect from others: Good personal hygiene is often associated with professionalism, social grace, and respect for oneself and others.

D. Health problems caused by poor personal hygiene:

Poor personal hygiene can lead to a variety of health problems, ranging from minor skin infections to serious and potentially life-threatening diseases. Some of the common health problems associated with poor personal hygiene are:

Skin infections: When the skin is not kept clean and dry, it can become a breeding ground for bacteria and fungi, leading to various skin infections such as acne, boils, and fungal infections like ringworm and athlete's foot.

Oral health problems: Poor oral hygiene can lead to cavities, gum disease, bad breath, and even tooth loss. Failing to brush and floss regularly can result in a buildup of plaque and bacteria in the mouth, which can cause inflammation and infection.

Gastrointestinal infections: Poor personal hygiene, such as not washing hands after using the bathroom or before handling food, can lead to gastrointestinal infections such as diarrhea, vomiting, and food poisoning.

Respiratory infections: Poor hygiene practices, such as not covering the mouth and nose when coughing or sneezing, can lead to the spread of respiratory infections like the common cold and influenza.

Sexually transmitted infections: Poor personal hygiene, particularly in the genital area, can increase the risk of sexually transmitted infections (STIs) such as chlamydia, gonorrhea, and herpes.

It is important to note that good personal hygiene practices not only prevent these health problems but also contribute to overall physical and mental well-being.

III. Avoidable Habits

A. Definition of Avoidable Habits

Avoidable habits are behaviors or actions that can be modified or eliminated to reduce the risk of negative health outcomes.

B. Types of Avoidable Habits

Affecting Health There are several types of avoidable habits that can affect health, including:

Poor diet: Consuming a diet high in processed foods, sugar, and saturated fats can lead to obesity, type 2 diabetes, and heart disease.

Lack of physical activity: Sedentary lifestyles and a lack of exercise can contribute to poor cardiovascular health, obesity, and chronic disease.

Tobacco use: Smoking cigarettes or using other tobacco products can increase the risk of lung cancer, heart disease, stroke, and other health problems.

Excessive alcohol consumption: Heavy drinking can lead to liver disease, high blood pressure, and increased risk of certain cancers.

Poor sleep habits: Insufficient sleep or poor sleep quality can lead to an increased risk of obesity, diabetes, cardiovascular disease, and mental health issues.

C. Examples of Avoidable Habits

Affecting Health Some specific examples of avoidable habits that can negatively impact health include:

1. Consuming a diet high in sugar and processed foods, while low in fruits, vegetables, and whole grains.
2. Spending a significant amount of time sitting or engaging in sedentary activities, such as watching television or using a computer.
3. Smoking cigarettes or using other tobacco products.
4. Binge drinking or drinking heavily on a regular basis.
5. Engaging in risky sexual behaviors, such as unprotected sex or having multiple partners.
6. By making positive changes and adopting healthy habits, individuals can improve their overall health and reduce the risk of negative health outcomes associated with avoidable habits.

IV. Strategies to Promote Good Hygiene and Health

A. Education and awareness campaigns

Education and awareness campaigns are important strategies to promote good hygiene and health. These campaigns can be conducted through various mediums such as television, radio, social media, and educational materials like brochures and posters. They can be targeted towards specific populations like school children, health workers, or people in high-risk environments. The campaigns can focus on specific hygiene practices like handwashing, dental hygiene, and proper waste disposal, and provide information on the benefits of these practices. Education and awareness campaigns can also highlight the consequences of poor hygiene practices and encourage people to adopt healthy behaviors.

B. Promotion of healthy behaviors and practices

Promoting healthy behaviors and practices is another strategy to promote good hygiene and health. This can be achieved through community-based interventions like health education classes, workshops, and support groups. These interventions can provide practical guidance and support to people on how to adopt healthy behaviors like regular exercise, healthy eating habits, and proper sleep hygiene. They can also provide information on how to avoid risk factors like smoking, alcohol, and drug abuse.

C. Availability of resources and facilities

The availability of resources and facilities is another important strategy to promote good hygiene and health. Governments and other organizations can invest in the provision of clean water and sanitation facilities, adequate healthcare facilities, and appropriate waste management systems. Availability of resources and facilities will help people to access basic hygiene and healthcare services, which will reduce the risk of infection and disease transmission. Additionally, providing adequate hygiene supplies like soap, sanitizers, and disinfectants in public places like schools, hospitals, and workplaces can also promote good hygiene practices.

Promoting good hygiene and health requires a multi-faceted approach that includes education and awareness campaigns, promotion of healthy behaviors and practices, and the availability of resources and facilities. By adopting these strategies, individuals, communities, and governments can work together to promote and maintain good hygiene and health practices, which can reduce the risk of illness and improve overall well-being.

V. Challenges in Promoting Good Hygiene and Health

A. Cultural and social barriers

Promoting good hygiene and health can be challenging due to cultural and social barriers. Certain cultures may not prioritize personal hygiene practices, or may have different standards for what is considered clean. Additionally, social norms may discourage certain behaviors such as hand-washing or the use of condoms. It is important to consider cultural and social factors when designing hygiene and health promotion campaigns in order to effectively reach and engage the target population.

B. Limited resources and access to facilities

Another challenge to promoting good hygiene and health is limited resources and access to facilities. This is particularly true in low-income or developing areas where basic resources such as clean water, soap, and sanitary toilets may be scarce. Lack of access to health facilities and trained healthcare professionals can also limit the ability to receive proper medical care and advice. Governments and aid organizations may need to invest in infrastructure and resources to improve access to basic hygiene and health services.

C. Resistance to change and lack of motivation

Promoting good hygiene and health can be challenging due to resistance to change and lack of motivation. Even when education and awareness campaigns are effective, some individuals may not be motivated to adopt new behaviors or may have difficulty breaking old habits. Resistance to change can also be influenced by cultural and social factors. Additionally, some individuals may not prioritize personal hygiene and health due to competing demands such as work or caring for family members. Strategies to promote good hygiene and health should take into account these individual factors and work to create a supportive environment that encourages and motivates individuals to make positive changes.

V
Preventive Medicine

Cholera

I. Introduction

A. Definition of Cholera

Cholera is an acute diarrheal illness caused by the bacterium Vibrio cholerae. The disease is characterized by sudden onset of watery diarrhea, which can rapidly lead to dehydration and, in severe cases, death.

B. Historical Background of Cholera

Cholera has been known to humanity for centuries. The earliest recorded pandemics occurred in India, where the disease is believed to have originated. Cholera has since spread to different parts of the world, causing numerous outbreaks and epidemics.

The first pandemic occurred in 1817, and subsequent pandemics occurred in 1829, 1852, and 1863. These pandemics spread to Europe, Africa, Asia, and the Americas. The fifth pandemic, which began in 1881, was the most severe, and it lasted for over 20 years.

C. Major Cholera Outbreaks

Cholera has caused several major outbreaks in the 20th and 21st centuries. The most recent pandemic, the seventh pandemic, began in Indonesia in 1961 and spread to other parts of Asia, Africa, and Latin America. Since then, cholera has continued to cause outbreaks and epidemics in many countries, particularly in areas with poor sanitation and hygiene.

In recent years, large cholera outbreaks have occurred in Yemen, Haiti, and Zimbabwe, causing significant morbidity and mortality. The ongoing COVID-19 pandemic has also created challenges for the management and control of cholera outbreaks, as resources and attention are diverted to managing the pandemic.

II. Epidemiology

A. Global Distribution of Cholera

Cholera is endemic in many parts of the world, particularly in developing countries with poor sanitation and hygiene. The World Health Organization (WHO) estimates that there are between 1.3 and 4 million cases of cholera every year, and 21,000 to 143,000 deaths due to the disease.

Cholera is most common in parts of Africa, South Asia, and Southeast Asia. In recent years, there have been large cholera outbreaks in Yemen, Haiti, and Zimbabwe.

B. Demographics of Infected Populations

Cholera affects people of all ages, but children under the age of 5 and adults over the age of 50 are at higher risk of developing severe disease. Pregnant women and people with underlying medical conditions, such as malnutrition and immunodeficiency, are also at increased risk.

C. Risk Factors for Contracting Cholera

Cholera is primarily transmitted through contaminated water and food. In areas with poor sanitation and hygiene, the risk of transmission is higher. Other risk factors for contracting cholera include:

1. Drinking untreated water from lakes, rivers, or wells
2. Eating raw or undercooked seafood from contaminated waters
3. Poor hand hygiene
4. Living in overcrowded and unsanitary conditions
5. Traveling to areas with known cholera outbreaks

Understanding these risk factors can help individuals and public health authorities implement measures to prevent and control cholera outbreaks.

III. Pathophysiology

A. Structure of the Cholera Bacterium

Cholera is caused by the bacterium Vibrio cholerae, which is a curved, gram-negative rod-shaped bacterium. The bacterium has two major serogroups, O1 and O139, which are responsible for epidemic cholera. The bacterium produces a toxin known as cholera toxin, which is responsible for the symptoms of the disease.

B. Mechanisms of Bacterial Infection in the Human Body

Cholera is primarily transmitted through the consumption of contaminated water or food. Once ingested, the bacteria pass through the stomach and into the small intestine, where they colonize and produce cholera toxin. The toxin causes the cells in the intestinal lining to secrete large amounts of fluid, leading to profuse watery diarrhea, vomiting, and dehydration.

C. Immune Response to Cholera Infection

The immune response to cholera infection is primarily mediated by the production of antibodies against the cholera toxin. These antibodies can neutralize the toxin and prevent its harmful effects. However, immunity to cholera is short-lived, and individuals can be reinfected with the bacterium.

Understanding the mechanisms of cholera infection and the immune response to the bacterium can help in the development of effective prevention and treatment strategies.

Clinical Presentation

A. Incubation Period

The incubation period for cholera ranges from a few hours to five days, with the average being 2-3 days.

B. Symptoms of Cholera Infection

The symptoms of cholera can range from mild to severe, and include:

- Profuse, watery diarrhea
- Vomiting
- Dehydration
- Muscle cramps
- Rapid heart rate
- Low blood pressure

- Sunken eyes
- Dry mouth and throat
- Fatigue
- Confusion

C. Complications of Cholera Infection

Complications of cholera infection can include:

- Severe dehydration, which can lead to shock and organ failure
- Electrolyte imbalances, such as low potassium levels
- Kidney failure
- Coma
- Death

Prompt treatment and rehydration can reduce the risk of complications and improve outcomes for individuals with cholera infection.

V. Diagnosis

A. Diagnostic Tests for Cholera Infection

The following diagnostic tests can be used to diagnose cholera infection:

Stool culture: A sample of stool is taken and tested in a laboratory to detect the presence of Vibrio cholerae bacteria.

Rapid diagnostic tests: These tests use a strip or card to detect the presence of cholera toxin in a stool sample.

Polymerase chain reaction (PCR) test: This test detects the genetic material of the Vibrio cholerae bacteria in a stool sample.

B. Role of Laboratory Confirmation

Laboratory confirmation is important for the accurate diagnosis of cholera infection and to identify the specific strain of Vibrio cholerae that is causing the outbreak. This information is important for the development of appropriate public health measures, such as identifying the source of the outbreak and implementing control measures to prevent further spread. In addition, laboratory confirmation can help to differentiate cholera from other causes of diarrhea and guide appropriate treatment.

VI. Prevention and Control

A. Infection Control Measures

Isolation of infected individuals: Infected individuals should be isolated to prevent the spread of the disease.

Quarantine of contacts: Contacts of infected individuals should be monitored and quarantined if necessary to prevent the spread of the disease.

Safe handling of food and water: Food and water should be prepared and stored in a hygienic manner to prevent contamination with Vibrio cholerae bacteria.

Disinfection of contaminated surfaces: Surfaces that may be contaminated with Vibrio cholerae bacteria should be disinfected with a suitable disinfectant.

B. Personal Hygiene and Sanitation

Hand washing: Regular hand washing with soap and water or with an alcohol-based hand sanitizer can help to prevent the spread of the disease.

Sanitation: Improving sanitation, such as access to clean water and proper disposal of human waste, can help to prevent the spread of cholera.

C. Vaccination

Oral cholera vaccine: The oral cholera vaccine is a safe and effective way to prevent cholera infection. It is recommended for individuals who live in areas with a high risk of cholera or who are traveling to areas with a cholera outbreak.

D. Public Health Response to Cholera Outbreaks

Rapid response: Prompt identification and response to cholera outbreaks is important to prevent the spread of the disease.

Contact tracing: Contacts of infected individuals should be identified and monitored to prevent further spread of the disease.

Health education: Public health messages should be disseminated to increase awareness of cholera and to promote hygiene and sanitation practices.

VII. Treatment

A. Fluid replacement therapy

One of the most important components of treating cholera is prompt and effective rehydration. This can be achieved through oral or intravenous fluid replacement therapy. Oral rehydration therapy (ORT) is the preferred method for mild to moderate dehydration, while intravenous fluid replacement therapy is indicated for severe dehydration. The goal of fluid replacement therapy is to replace the fluids and electrolytes that are lost due to vomiting and diarrhea, and to prevent dehydration and electrolyte imbalances.

B. Antibiotic therapy

Antibiotics are an effective treatment for cholera, and they can significantly reduce the duration and severity of the illness. Antibiotics are typically given in conjunction with fluid replacement therapy, and are recommended for all patients with severe cholera or those at high risk of severe illness, such as young children or the elderly. The most commonly used antibiotics for cholera treatment include tetracycline, doxycycline, azithromycin, and ciprofloxacin.

C. Zinc supplements

Zinc supplements are recommended for the treatment of cholera in children under the age of five. Zinc has been shown to reduce the severity and duration of diarrhea in young children, and can also improve the immune response to cholera infection.

D. Oral rehydration salts

Oral rehydration salts (ORS) are a combination of glucose and electrolytes that are dissolved in water and taken orally. They are a safe and effective method for treating dehydration caused by cholera and other diarrheal illnesses. ORS works by replacing the fluids and electrolytes that are lost due to vomiting and diarrhea, and can prevent the need for intravenous fluid replacement therapy. ORS is widely available and can be administered at home, making it a cost-effective and practical option for treating cholera in resource-limited settings.

Severe Acute Respiratory Syndrome (SARS)

I. Introduction

Severe Acute Respiratory Syndrome (SARS) is a highly contagious viral respiratory illness caused by the SARS coronavirus (SARS-CoV). The virus was first identified in 2003 during a global outbreak that started in China and spread to several other countries. SARS-CoV is a member of the Coronaviridae family, which also includes other human and animal coronaviruses.

The first cases of SARS were reported in the Guangdong province of China in November 2002, and the virus quickly spread to other regions of the country. The outbreak was initially concealed by Chinese officials, which led to delays in identifying and containing the virus. The outbreak eventually spread to other countries, including Hong Kong, Taiwan, Canada, and Singapore, and resulted in over 8,000 confirmed cases and 774 deaths worldwide.

The transmission of SARS-CoV occurs primarily through respiratory droplets generated by coughing or sneezing, as well as through close contact with infected individuals or contaminated surfaces. The virus can also be transmitted through the fecal-oral route or by direct contact with bodily fluids.

The SARS outbreak of 2003 had significant global public health and economic consequences. The rapid spread of the virus led to widespread panic and disruption of international travel and trade. In response, international organizations such as the World Health Organization (WHO) worked to coordinate global efforts to contain the virus and prevent further spread.

Understanding the history and transmission of SARS-CoV is essential for public health officials and healthcare workers in managing suspected cases and preventing the spread of the virus. As such, this lecture will provide an in-depth overview of the historical background and transmission of SARS, as well as its epidemiology, pathophysiology, clinical presentation, diagnosis, prevention and control measures, and treatment options.

II. Epidemiology

Severe Acute Respiratory Syndrome (SARS) is a highly infectious viral respiratory illness caused by the SARS coronavirus (SARS-CoV). The following subsections provide an overview of the global distribution of SARS, the demographics of infected populations, and the risk factors associated with contracting SARS.

A. Global distribution of SARS

- SARS was first identified in China in November 2002, and the initial outbreak quickly spread to other regions of the country.
- The outbreak eventually spread to other countries, including Hong Kong, Taiwan, Canada, and Singapore.

- The global outbreak resulted in over 8,000 confirmed cases and 774 deaths.

B. Demographics of infected populations

- SARS affects individuals of all ages, but the elderly and individuals with underlying medical conditions are at increased risk for severe illness and death.
- Healthcare workers are also at increased risk of contracting SARS due to their frequent exposure to infected individuals.
- Males and females are equally affected by SARS.

C. Risk factors for contracting SARS

- Close contact with infected individuals or contaminated surfaces is the primary mode of transmission for SARS-CoV.
- Healthcare workers who care for infected individuals are at increased risk of contracting the virus.
- Travel to areas with active SARS outbreaks is also a risk factor for contracting SARS.

Understanding the epidemiology of SARS is critical for developing effective public health interventions and strategies to prevent the spread of the virus. Healthcare professionals and public health officials must be knowledgeable about the risk factors associated with SARS to prevent further transmission of the virus.

III. Pathophysiology

Severe Acute Respiratory Syndrome (SARS) is caused by a coronavirus known as SARS-CoV. This section provides an overview of the structure of the virus, mechanisms of viral entry into host cells, and the immune response to SARS-CoV infection.

A. Structure of the SARS virus

SARS-CoV is an enveloped, positive-sense, single-stranded RNA virus.

The virus has a crown-like appearance due to the presence of spike proteins on its surface.

The viral genome encodes several structural and non-structural proteins necessary for viral replication.

B. Mechanisms of viral entry into host cells

SARS-CoV enters host cells through the binding of its spike proteins to angiotensin-converting enzyme 2 (ACE2) receptors on the surface of human cells.

After binding to ACE2, the virus is internalized through receptor-mediated endocytosis and undergoes fusion with the host cell membrane.

The virus then releases its RNA genome into the host cell, where it replicates and produces new virions.

C. Immune response to SARS virus infection

The immune response to SARS-CoV infection is complex and involves both innate and adaptive immune responses.

The innate immune response is the first line of defense against the virus and includes the production of type I interferons, pro-inflammatory cytokines, and chemokines.

The adaptive immune response is activated later and involves the production of virus-specific antibodies and T cells.

IV. Clinical Presentation

A. Incubation period

The incubation period for SARS-CoV ranges from 2 to 10 days, with an average of 4 to 6 days.

During this time, individuals may not experience any symptoms but are still capable of transmitting the virus to others.

B. Symptoms of SARS virus infection

The symptoms of SARS are similar to those of other respiratory illnesses, including fever, cough, and shortness of breath.

Other symptoms may include headache, body aches, and diarrhea.

In severe cases, SARS can lead to respiratory failure, requiring mechanical ventilation and possibly resulting in death.

C. Complications of SARS virus infection

SARS can lead to a severe form of pneumonia, which can cause lung damage and respiratory failure.

Other complications may include kidney failure, liver failure, and cardiac dysfunction.

Long-term complications of SARS are still being studied, but some individuals may experience ongoing respiratory issues or post-traumatic stress disorder.

V. Diagnosis

This section will cover the diagnostic tests for SARS virus infection and the role of laboratory confirmation.

A. Diagnostic tests for SARS virus infection

Polymerase chain reaction (PCR) testing is the gold standard for diagnosing SARS-CoV infection.

PCR testing involves detecting the viral RNA in respiratory specimens such as sputum, nasopharyngeal swabs, or bronchoalveolar lavage fluid.

Other diagnostic tests may include serological testing to detect antibodies against SARS-CoV.

B. Role of laboratory confirmation

Laboratory confirmation is essential for the diagnosis of SARS-CoV infection and for tracking the spread of the virus.

PCR testing can identify infected individuals even before they become symptomatic, allowing for early detection and isolation to prevent further transmission.

Serological testing can be useful in identifying individuals who have been previously infected and have developed antibodies against the virus.

Diagnostic testing for SARS-CoV is critical in controlling the spread of the virus. Public health measures such as contact tracing and quarantine can be initiated once an individual tests positive for SARS-CoV, and laboratory confirmation can provide valuable information for understanding the epidemiology of the disease.

VI. Prevention and Control

A. Infection control measures

- Hand hygiene is essential in preventing the spread of SARS-CoV, as the virus can survive on surfaces for several hours.
- Isolation precautions should be implemented for individuals suspected or confirmed to have SARS-CoV infection.
- Environmental cleaning and disinfection of high-touch surfaces should be performed regularly.

B. Personal protective equipment

Healthcare workers who care for individuals with suspected or confirmed SARS-CoV infection should wear appropriate personal protective equipment (PPE).

PPE for SARS-CoV may include N95 respirators, gloves, gowns, and eye protection.

Proper use of PPE and appropriate doffing procedures are essential in preventing transmission of SARS-CoV.

C. Public health response to SARS virus outbreaks

SARS-CoV outbreaks require a coordinated public health response, including case identification and contact tracing.

Isolation measures may be implemented to prevent further spread of the virus.

Public health messaging should emphasize the importance of hand hygiene, social distancing, and other infection control measures.

Prevention and control of SARS-CoV requires a multi-faceted approach. Early detection and isolation of infected individuals, proper use of PPE, and implementation of infection control measures can help prevent the spread of the virus. Public health responses should be timely and coordinated to limit the impact of SARS-CoV outbreaks.

VII. Treatment

A. Antiviral therapy

Antiviral medications have been used to treat SARS-CoV infection.

Ribavirin, a broad-spectrum antiviral medication, has been used in the treatment of SARS-CoV infection.

Other antiviral medications, such as lopinavir/ritonavir, have been investigated for their potential use in the treatment of SARS-CoV.

B. Supportive care

Supportive care is an important aspect of the management of SARS-CoV infection.

Oxygen therapy and mechanical ventilation may be necessary in severe cases.

Other supportive measures may include fluid and electrolyte management, nutritional support, and treatment of secondary infections.

C. Experimental treatments

In addition to antiviral medications, other experimental treatments have been investigated for their potential use in the treatment of SARS-CoV.

Convalescent plasma therapy, in which plasma from individuals who have recovered from SARS-CoV infection is administered to infected individuals, has been investigated.

Other experimental treatments, such as monoclonal antibodies and interferon therapy, have also been studied.

The treatment of SARS-CoV infection is largely supportive, with antiviral medications used in some cases. Supportive care measures, such as oxygen therapy and fluid management, are important in managing severe cases. Experimental treatments are also being investigated for their potential use in the treatment of SARS-CoV infection.

Ebola virus

Introduction:

Ebola virus is a highly infectious and often fatal virus that belongs to the family Filoviridae. The virus was first identified in 1976, when simultaneous outbreaks occurred in Sudan and the Democratic Republic of Congo (formerly known as Zaire). The virus was named after the Ebola River, located near the site of the first identified outbreak in Sudan.

Ebola virus is transmitted through direct contact with bodily fluids of infected individuals or through contact with contaminated surfaces or materials. The virus can also be transmitted through contact with infected animals, such as fruit bats and primates. The virus has the ability to cause severe and often fatal disease in humans, with a case fatality rate ranging from 50% to 90%.

Since the initial outbreaks in 1976, there have been sporadic outbreaks of Ebola virus in Central Africa. However, the largest and deadliest outbreak occurred in West Africa from 2014 to 2016, with a total of 28,616 reported cases and 11,310 deaths. The outbreak was declared a public health emergency of international concern by the World Health Organization (WHO) and prompted a global response to control the spread of the virus.

II. Epidemiology

Ebola virus is primarily found in Central and West Africa, particularly in areas surrounding tropical rainforests. The virus has been identified in a number of African countries, including the Democratic Republic of Congo, Sudan, Gabon, Uganda, Guinea, Sierra Leone, and Liberia. The virus is believed to be endemic in these regions, with sporadic outbreaks occurring every few years.

The demographics of those infected with Ebola virus vary depending on the outbreak. However, the majority of cases have occurred in rural areas with limited access to healthcare facilities. During the 2014-2016 outbreak in West Africa, for example, the highest number of cases occurred among healthcare workers and those caring for sick family members at home. Women were also disproportionately affected, as they often assume caregiving roles in African societies.

Several risk factors have been identified for contracting Ebola virus. Direct contact with bodily fluids of infected individuals is the primary mode of transmission, with healthcare workers and family members of infected individuals being at the highest risk. Other risk factors include contact with infected animals or their bodily fluids, as well as contact with contaminated surfaces or materials. Additionally, traditional burial practices that involve close contact with the deceased have been identified as a risk factor for Ebola virus transmission.

III. Pathophysiology

Ebola virus is a highly infectious, single-stranded RNA virus that belongs to the family Filoviridae. The virus is characterized by its filamentous shape and its surface glycoprotein spikes that resemble a shepherd's crook. These spikes enable the virus to attach to host cells and initiate the process of viral entry.

The viral entry into host cells occurs through a series of complex mechanisms that involve the binding of the viral glycoprotein to specific host cell receptors, followed by the fusion of the viral and host cell membranes. Once inside the host cell, the virus begins to replicate and produce new viral particles, which then infect neighboring cells.

The immune response to Ebola virus infection is a critical component of the pathophysiology of the disease. Following infection, the innate immune system is activated, leading to the production of cytokines and chemokines, such as interleukin-6 (IL-6) and interferon-alpha (IFN-α), which are important for mounting an effective immune response against the virus.

In addition to the innate immune response, adaptive immunity also plays a role in the pathophysiology of Ebola virus infection. Following infection, B cells produce antibodies that target the virus, while T cells are activated to destroy infected cells. This immune response is crucial for clearing the virus from the body and preventing the development of severe disease.

However, in some cases, the immune response to Ebola virus infection can be dysregulated, leading to an excessive production of cytokines and chemokines, known as a cytokine storm. This cytokine storm can lead to widespread tissue damage and multi-organ failure, which is a hallmark of severe Ebola virus disease.

IV. Clinical Presentation

The clinical presentation of Ebola virus infection can vary depending on the stage of the disease. The incubation period for Ebola virus is typically 2-21 days, with symptoms developing gradually over the course of several days. However, in rare cases, the incubation period can be up to 42 days.

Early symptoms of Ebola virus infection are nonspecific and can be similar to those of other infectious diseases, including fever, fatigue, muscle pain, and headache. As the disease progresses, patients may experience vomiting, diarrhea, and abdominal pain. In some cases, patients may develop a rash, hiccups, or conjunctivitis.

In severe cases of Ebola virus infection, patients may develop hemorrhagic fever, which is characterized by internal and external bleeding. Hemorrhagic fever is not a universal symptom of Ebola virus infection and only occurs in a minority of cases. Other complications of Ebola virus infection can include respiratory failure, shock, and organ failure.

It is important to note that early diagnosis and clinical suspicion are critical for effective management of Ebola virus infection. Given the nonspecific nature of early symptoms and the potential for rapid disease progression, healthcare workers should be vigilant for any signs of illness in patients who may have been exposed to the virus.

Patients with suspected Ebola virus infection should be promptly isolated and undergo laboratory testing to confirm the diagnosis. Given the high mortality rate associated with Ebola virus infection, early diagnosis and management are critical for improving patient outcomes.

V. Diagnosis

The diagnosis of Ebola virus infection requires laboratory confirmation. Clinical suspicion of Ebola virus infection is based on a patient's symptoms and history of potential exposure to the virus. However, given the nonspecific nature of early symptoms and the potential for rapid disease progression, laboratory testing is necessary to confirm the diagnosis.

Several diagnostic tests are available for Ebola virus infection, including polymerase chain reaction (PCR) assays, antigen detection tests, and antibody-based tests. PCR assays detect viral RNA in patient samples, while antigen detection tests detect viral proteins. Antibody-based tests detect the presence of antibodies produced by the immune system in response to the virus.

Laboratory confirmation of Ebola virus infection is critical for several reasons. First, it allows for appropriate management of infected patients, including isolation and infection control measures. Second, it enables public health officials to track and respond to outbreaks of the virus, including identifying contacts of infected individuals who may be at risk for developing the disease.

It is important to note that laboratory confirmation of Ebola virus infection can be challenging, particularly in resource-limited settings. PCR assays, in particular, require specialized equipment and expertise to perform and interpret the results. As such, laboratory testing for Ebola virus infection should be conducted in certified laboratories with appropriate biosafety measures and trained personnel.

Sure, here's an expanded version of the Prevention and Control section with additional information in an academic tone:

VI. Prevention and Control

Preventing and controlling the spread of Ebola virus infection requires a multi-faceted approach that includes infection control measures, personal protective equipment, and public health response to outbreaks.

Infection control measures are critical for preventing transmission of the virus in healthcare settings. These measures include standard precautions, such as hand hygiene, personal protective equipment (PPE), and environmental cleaning and disinfection. In addition, transmission-based precautions, including contact and droplet precautions, should be implemented for suspected or confirmed cases of Ebola virus infection.

Personal protective equipment is an essential component of infection control measures and includes items such as gloves, gowns, masks, and eye protection. Proper use of PPE can significantly reduce the risk of healthcare worker infection, as well as prevent transmission of the virus to other patients and visitors.

Public health response to Ebola virus outbreaks is also critical for preventing and controlling the spread of the virus. This response includes identifying and isolating cases, tracing and monitoring contacts of infected individuals, and implementing social distancing measures to prevent the spread of the virus in the community.

In addition, effective communication and engagement with affected communities is critical for building trust and promoting compliance with infection control measures and public health interventions.

In recent years, several experimental vaccines and treatments for Ebola virus infection have been developed and tested, with promising results. These include the rVSV-ZEBOV vaccine, which was found to be highly effective in preventing Ebola virus infection in a large-scale clinical trial conducted during the 2014-2016 West Africa outbreak.

Influenza

I. Introduction

A. Definition of influenza: Influenza, commonly known as the flu, is a highly contagious respiratory illness caused by influenza viruses. The illness is characterized by sudden onset of fever, cough, sore throat, headache, muscle aches, and fatigue. Influenza viruses can infect humans, birds, and other animals, and are categorized into three types: A, B, and C. Influenza type A viruses are further classified into subtypes based on their surface antigens, hemagglutinin (H) and neuraminidase (N). Influenza viruses have the ability to mutate and undergo genetic reassortment, resulting in the emergence of new strains that can cause pandemics.

B. Historical background of influenza: Influenza has been recognized as a disease for over 2,000 years. Major influenza pandemics have occurred throughout history, causing significant morbidity and mortality. The most well-known pandemic occurred in 1918, known as the Spanish flu, which caused an estimated 50 million deaths worldwide. Other pandemics include the Asian flu in 1957 and the Hong Kong flu in 1968. Influenza continues to be a major global health threat, with seasonal epidemics occurring every year.

C. Major influenza pandemics: In addition to the pandemics mentioned above, other significant influenza pandemics include the 1889-1890 Russian flu pandemic, the 1957-1958 Asian flu pandemic, the 1968-1969 Hong Kong flu pandemic, and the 2009 H1N1 pandemic. The 2009 H1N1 pandemic, also known as swine flu, was caused by a novel influenza A virus that emerged in Mexico and quickly spread worldwide, leading to an estimated 284,000 deaths.

II. Epidemiology

Influenza is a contagious respiratory illness caused by influenza viruses. Influenza is a global health concern and affects millions of people every year. Influenza viruses are classified into types A, B, and C. Influenza A viruses are further classified into subtypes based on the two surface glycoproteins, hemagglutinin (HA) and neuraminidase (NA). Influenza viruses are known for their ability to mutate frequently and generate new strains, which can cause periodic outbreaks or pandemics.

Influenza has a global distribution and affects people of all ages. However, some age groups are more susceptible to severe illness and complications from influenza infection, including young children, pregnant women, older adults, and people with underlying medical conditions. Influenza typically spreads through respiratory droplets produced when an infected person coughs or sneezes.

The risk factors for contracting influenza include close contact with infected individuals, living in crowded or institutional settings, poor hand hygiene, and not getting vaccinated. The risk of contracting influenza can also vary depending on the strain of the virus circulating in a particular region.

Influenza has a seasonal pattern and tends to be more prevalent during the winter months in temperate regions. In tropical regions, influenza activity can occur throughout the year. Influenza can cause periodic outbreaks and pandemics. Major influenza pandemics in history include the Spanish flu (1918-1919), the Asian flu (1957-1958), the Hong Kong flu (1968-1969), and the H1N1 pandemic (2009-2010).

III. Pathophysiology

A. Structure of the influenza virus

Influenza viruses are classified into three types: A, B, and C, based on the nucleoprotein and matrix protein. The A and B types cause seasonal epidemics, while the C type is generally milder and causes sporadic cases of infection. The influenza virus is an enveloped virus with a negative-sense single-stranded RNA genome. The genome is segmented, meaning that it is made up of eight separate RNA molecules that code for 10 different viral proteins. The two surface proteins on the virus, hemagglutinin (HA) and neuraminidase (NA), are important in the pathogenesis of influenza.

B. Mechanisms of viral entry into host cells

The influenza virus enters host cells by binding to sialic acid receptors on the surface of respiratory epithelial cells. The HA protein on the virus binds to these receptors, allowing the virus to enter the cell via receptor-mediated endocytosis. Once inside the cell, the virus replicates its RNA genome and produces viral proteins. The newly formed virus particles are then released from the cell surface by the action of the NA protein, which cleaves the sialic acid receptors, allowing the newly formed virus particles to spread and infect neighboring cells.

C. Immune response to influenza virus infection

The immune response to influenza virus infection involves both innate and adaptive immune mechanisms. The innate immune system responds rapidly to infection and includes natural killer cells, macrophages, and dendritic cells. These cells recognize and respond to viral proteins, producing cytokines and chemokines that recruit and activate other immune cells.

The adaptive immune system, which includes B and T cells, also responds to the virus. B cells produce antibodies that can neutralize the virus, while T cells can recognize and kill infected cells. The adaptive immune response is critical for controlling the infection and providing protection against future infections with the same virus. However, the influenza virus can mutate rapidly, resulting in antigenic drift and antigenic shift, which can evade the immune response and lead to recurrent epidemics and pandemics.

IV. Clinical Presentation

A. Incubation period:

The incubation period of influenza is typically 1-4 days, with an average of 2 days. During this time, individuals may be asymptomatic but still contagious.

B. Symptoms of influenza infection:

The symptoms of influenza infection can range from mild to severe and can include fever, cough, sore throat, fatigue, muscle aches, and headache. In some cases, individuals may also experience vomiting and diarrhea. The severity and duration of symptoms can vary depending on the age and health status of the individual, as well as the strain of the virus.

C. Complications of influenza infection:

Influenza can lead to a range of complications, particularly in high-risk individuals such as young children, older adults, and individuals with weakened immune systems. Common complications include pneumonia, bronchitis, sinus infections, and ear infections. In severe cases, influenza can also lead to respiratory failure, sepsis, and death. Additionally, individuals with underlying health conditions such as heart disease, diabetes, or asthma may be at increased risk for serious complications from influenza.

V. Diagnosis

Influenza infection can be diagnosed through several methods, including clinical diagnosis, rapid diagnostic tests, and laboratory confirmation. Clinical diagnosis is based on the presence of symptoms such as fever, cough, and body aches, and the timing of symptom onset during influenza season. However, clinical diagnosis alone is not sufficient to differentiate between influenza and other respiratory infections, and laboratory confirmation is often required.

Rapid diagnostic tests, such as rapid influenza diagnostic tests (RIDTs), can provide results within 15-30 minutes and are often used in clinical settings. RIDTs detect influenza viral antigens in respiratory specimens, such as nasal or throat swabs, but have lower sensitivity and specificity compared to laboratory tests.

Laboratory confirmation of influenza infection involves the detection of viral nucleic acid in respiratory specimens using polymerase chain reaction (PCR) tests or viral culture. PCR tests are highly sensitive and specific, and can distinguish between influenza A and B viruses, as well as detect genetic changes in the virus that may affect its ability to cause disease or respond to antiviral treatment. Viral culture involves growing influenza virus in specialized laboratory conditions, and is typically used for surveillance purposes rather than individual patient diagnosis due to its longer turnaround time.

VI. Prevention and Control

A. Infection control measures:

Infection control measures are essential in preventing the spread of influenza. This includes implementing respiratory hygiene and cough etiquette, including covering coughs and sneezes with tissues or the elbow, disposing of tissues properly, and hand hygiene. Hand hygiene is especially important, and individuals should be encouraged to wash their hands frequently with soap and water or to use alcohol-based hand sanitizers. Healthcare facilities should also have infection control protocols in place to prevent transmission of influenza within the facility.

B. Vaccination: Vaccination is a key strategy in preventing and controlling influenza. The seasonal influenza vaccine is typically recommended for all individuals over the age of 6 months. The vaccine is formulated each year to protect against the most prevalent strains of the virus. Vaccination is particularly important for high-risk individuals, including the elderly, young children, pregnant women, and individuals with certain underlying health conditions.

C. Antiviral therapy: Antiviral medications are available for the treatment and prevention of influenza. These medications are most effective when administered early in the course of illness, within 48 hours of symptom onset. Antivirals can be used to treat individuals with confirmed or suspected influenza and to prevent influenza in individuals who have been exposed to the virus. Antivirals are particularly important for individuals at high risk of complications from influenza.

D. Public health response to influenza outbreaks: Public health officials play a critical role in responding to influenza outbreaks. This includes monitoring the spread of the virus, conducting surveillance to identify new strains or changes in the virus, and coordinating vaccination campaigns. Public health officials may also recommend school closures or other social distancing measures to slow the spread of the virus during outbreaks. In addition, public health officials may work with healthcare providers and facilities to implement infection control measures and provide guidance on antiviral treatment and prophylaxis.

VII. Treatment

A. Antiviral therapy: Antiviral medications are available for the treatment of influenza infections. These medications work by blocking the replication of the influenza virus, thereby reducing the severity and duration of symptoms. The most commonly used antiviral medications for influenza include oseltamivir, zanamivir, and peramivir. These medications are most effective when taken within 48 hours of the onset of symptoms, so it is important to seek medical care as soon as possible if you suspect you have influenza.

B. Supportive care: Supportive care is an important part of treating influenza infections. This may include measures such as rest, hydration, and over-the-counter medications to manage symptoms such as fever and cough. In severe cases, hospitalization may be necessary to provide more intensive supportive care, such as oxygen therapy or mechanical ventilation.

C. Experimental treatments: There are ongoing efforts to develop new treatments for influenza, including vaccines that provide broader protection against different strains of the virus, and medications that can target the virus more specifically. Some experimental treatments currently being investigated include monoclonal antibodies, which are laboratory-produced proteins that can target specific parts of the influenza virus, and gene therapy, which involves modifying the genes of host cells to make them more resistant to viral infections. While these treatments are not yet widely available, they represent promising avenues for future influenza research and treatment.

VIII. Influenza Vaccination

A. Types of influenza vaccines: Influenza vaccines are available in different forms, including inactivated influenza vaccine (IIV), live attenuated influenza vaccine (LAIV), and recombinant influenza vaccine (RIV). The inactivated influenza vaccine is made from a killed virus and is approved for use in people aged 6 months and older, while the live attenuated influenza vaccine contains a weakened virus and is approved for use in healthy individuals aged 2-49 years who are not pregnant. The recombinant influenza vaccine is produced using a genetic sequence of the virus rather than growing the virus, and is approved for use in individuals aged 18 years and older.

B. Who should receive influenza vaccine: The Centers for Disease Control and Prevention (CDC) recommends that everyone aged 6 months and older receive an annual influenza vaccine, with few exceptions. This includes pregnant women, young children, older adults, and individuals with certain underlying health conditions that put them at increased risk of complications from influenza.

C. Benefits and risks of influenza vaccination: Influenza vaccination is highly effective in preventing influenza infection and associated complications. It can also reduce the severity of illness in individuals who do get infected. However, like all vaccines, influenza vaccination may have some risks, such as mild side effects like soreness or redness at the injection site, and in rare cases, more serious side effects such as allergic reactions. Overall, the benefits of influenza vaccination far outweigh the risks. It is important for individuals to discuss any concerns they may have with their healthcare provider.

Acute respiratory infection

I. Introduction

A. Definition of acute respiratory infection

Acute respiratory infections (ARIs) are a group of infections that affect the respiratory system, including the lungs, throat, and nose. ARIs can be caused by a variety of pathogens, such as bacteria, viruses, and fungi. The symptoms of ARIs vary depending on the specific type of infection and can range from mild to severe. ARIs can be contagious and are a significant cause of morbidity and mortality worldwide.

B. Importance of acute respiratory infection in public health

ARIs are one of the most common reasons for seeking medical care and hospitalization globally. According to the World Health Organization (WHO), acute respiratory infections are responsible for approximately 3.5 million deaths per year, with the majority occurring in low- and middle-income countries. ARIs can have a significant impact on public health, as they can result in substantial economic and social costs, including loss of productivity, increased healthcare costs, and decreased quality of life.

C. Impact of acute respiratory infection on global health

The impact of ARIs on global health can be significant. In addition to causing a high number of deaths each year, ARIs can lead to long-term complications such as chronic obstructive pulmonary disease (COPD), asthma, and bronchiolitis. ARIs can also lead to severe respiratory distress syndrome (ARDS) and sepsis, which can be life-threatening. ARIs can have a disproportionate impact on vulnerable populations, including young children, elderly individuals, and those with underlying medical conditions.

II. Epidemiology

Acute respiratory infections (ARIs) are among the leading causes of morbidity and mortality worldwide, particularly in low- and middle-income countries. ARIs can affect individuals of all ages, but young children, elderly individuals, and those with underlying health conditions are at a higher risk of developing severe disease.

A. Global distribution of acute respiratory infection

ARIs are widespread globally, with the highest burden in low- and middle-income countries. According to the World Health Organization (WHO), ARIs account for approximately 3.2 million deaths each year, with more than 90% of these deaths occurring in developing countries.

B. Demographics of infected populations

Children under the age of five are at the greatest risk of developing ARIs. Infants, in particular, are at high risk of developing severe disease, which can lead to hospitalization and death. The elderly population is also at increased risk of severe illness and death from ARIs, as are individuals with underlying medical conditions such as chronic respiratory disease, cardiovascular disease, and diabetes.

C. Risk factors for contracting acute respiratory infection

The risk of contracting ARIs is highest in crowded or institutional settings such as schools, daycares, nursing homes, and prisons. Other factors that increase the risk of ARIs include poor nutrition, exposure to indoor air pollution, and tobacco smoking. Additionally, individuals who are immunocompromised, such as those living with HIV or undergoing cancer treatment, are also at increased risk of developing ARIs.

III. Pathophysiology

A. Anatomy and physiology of the respiratory system

The respiratory system is responsible for gas exchange between the body and the environment. It is composed of several organs, including the nose, mouth, pharynx, larynx, trachea, bronchi, bronchioles, and lungs. The nose and mouth warm, moisten, and filter air as it enters the respiratory system. The air then travels through the pharynx, larynx, and trachea, where it is further filtered and humidified. The trachea branches into two main bronchi, which divide into smaller bronchioles that eventually lead to the alveoli, where gas exchange occurs. The lungs are composed of millions of alveoli, which are tiny air sacs surrounded by capillaries. Oxygen from the air diffuses into the blood vessels surrounding the alveoli, while carbon dioxide from the blood diffuses into the alveoli to be expelled during exhalation.

B. Mechanisms of acute respiratory infection

Acute respiratory infections (ARIs) are caused by a wide range of viral and bacterial pathogens that can affect the upper and lower respiratory tract. The most common viral pathogens associated with ARIs include influenza, respiratory syncytial virus, rhinovirus, adenovirus, and coronavirus. The most common bacterial pathogens include Streptococcus pneumoniae, Haemophilus influenzae, and Moraxella catarrhalis. ARIs can be transmitted through direct contact with infected individuals, respiratory droplets, or contact with contaminated surfaces.

Upon infection, the pathogens invade the respiratory system and replicate within the respiratory epithelium, leading to inflammation and damage to the respiratory tissues. The immune response is activated to clear the infection and repair the damaged tissue. The immune response can lead to the production of mucus, which can obstruct the airways and further exacerbate symptoms.

C. Immune response to acute respiratory infection

The immune response to acute respiratory infections involves both innate and adaptive immune mechanisms. The innate immune response is the first line of defense against pathogens and is composed of various cells and molecules that recognize and eliminate the invading pathogen. These cells include macrophages, neutrophils, and natural killer cells. The adaptive immune response involves the activation of antigen-specific lymphocytes, including T cells and B cells, which can recognize and neutralize the pathogen.

During an acute respiratory infection, the immune response is initiated by the recognition of pathogen-associated molecular patterns by pattern recognition receptors on immune cells. This recognition leads to the production of cytokines and chemokines, which activate immune cells and recruit them to the site of infection. The activation of T cells and B cells leads to the production of antibodies and the clearance of the pathogen. The immune response can also lead to the production of memory cells, which can provide long-term protection against future infections. However, excessive or dysregulated immune responses can lead to tissue damage and exacerbation of symptoms.

IV. Clinical Presentation

A. Incubation period

The incubation period of acute respiratory infection can vary depending on the specific pathogen causing the infection. In general, the incubation period ranges from 1-7 days, with most cases presenting within 2-4 days after exposure to the pathogen.

B. Symptoms of acute respiratory infection

The symptoms of acute respiratory infection can vary depending on the specific pathogen causing the infection, but typically include:

- Cough
- Sore throat
- Runny or stuffy nose
- Fever
- Headache
- Muscle aches
- Fatigue
- Shortness of breath

In some cases, acute respiratory infection can lead to more severe symptoms, such as pneumonia, which can cause chest pain, cough with phlegm, and difficulty breathing.

C. Complications of acute respiratory infection

Complications of acute respiratory infection can vary depending on the specific pathogen causing the infection and the severity of the infection. Complications can include:

- Pneumonia
- Bronchitis
- Sinusitis
- Ear infections
- Dehydration
- Respiratory failure
- Sepsis
- Death

Individuals who are at a higher risk of developing complications from acute respiratory infection include young children, older adults, pregnant women, and individuals with underlying medical conditions such as asthma, chronic obstructive pulmonary disease

(COPD), and heart disease.

V. Diagnosis

A. Diagnostic tests for acute respiratory infection:

The diagnosis of acute respiratory infection (ARI) is typically based on clinical presentation, but laboratory testing can aid in confirming the diagnosis and identifying the causative agent. Diagnostic tests for ARI may include:

Physical examination: A physical examination is an important part of the diagnosis of ARI. It includes assessment of vital signs, respiratory rate, oxygen saturation, and auscultation of the chest for abnormal breath sounds.

Imaging studies: Imaging studies such as chest X-ray or computed tomography (CT) scan may be used to evaluate the lungs and identify abnormalities.

Laboratory tests: Laboratory tests may include blood tests, sputum culture, nasal swab or throat swab for viral culture, and antigen or antibody testing for specific respiratory viruses.

B. Role of laboratory confirmation:

Laboratory confirmation of ARI is important for identifying the causative agent, guiding treatment decisions, and informing public health measures. In some cases, laboratory testing may also be necessary to rule out other potential causes of respiratory symptoms. However, it is important to note that laboratory testing is not always necessary for the diagnosis and management of ARI, as it can be diagnosed based on clinical presentation alone. Additionally, laboratory testing may not always be readily available in resource-limited settings.

VI. Prevention and Control

Acute respiratory infections (ARIs) can be prevented and controlled through various measures. These measures include infection control measures, personal hygiene and sanitation, vaccination, and public health response to outbreaks of ARI.

A. Infection control measures

Infection control measures are aimed at preventing the spread of respiratory infections in healthcare settings, as well as in the community. These measures include:

Hand hygiene: Regular and thorough handwashing with soap and water, or alcohol-based hand rub, can help prevent the spread of respiratory infections.

Respiratory hygiene: Covering the mouth and nose with a tissue when coughing or sneezing, and disposing of used tissues properly, can help prevent the spread of respiratory infections.

Environmental hygiene: Regular cleaning and disinfection of surfaces and objects that are frequently touched, such as doorknobs, light switches, and countertops, can help prevent the spread of respiratory infections.

Personal protective equipment: Healthcare workers and others who may come into contact with respiratory infections may need to wear personal protective equipment, such as masks and gloves, to prevent the spread of infection.

B. Personal hygiene and sanitation

Personal hygiene and sanitation practices can help prevent the spread of respiratory infections. These practices include:

Regular handwashing: Regular and thorough handwashing with soap and water, or alcohol-based hand rub, can help prevent the spread of respiratory infections.

Avoiding close contact with sick individuals: Staying away from individuals who have respiratory infections, and avoiding close contact with them, can help prevent the spread of infection.

Covering the mouth and nose: Covering the mouth and nose with a tissue when coughing or sneezing, and disposing of used tissues properly, can help prevent the spread of respiratory infections.

Cleaning and disinfection: Regular cleaning and disinfection of surfaces and objects that are frequently touched, such as doorknobs, light switches, and countertops, can help prevent the spread of respiratory infections.

C. Vaccination

Vaccination is an effective way to prevent certain types of respiratory infections. Vaccines are available for influenza, pneumococcal disease, and other respiratory infections. It is recommended that individuals who are at high risk of developing severe respiratory infections, such as the elderly and those with chronic medical conditions, receive these vaccines.

D. Public health response to outbreaks of acute respiratory infection

Public health authorities play an important role in responding to outbreaks of respiratory infections. These responses may include:

Surveillance: Monitoring the incidence and spread of respiratory infections, and identifying outbreaks as they occur.

Contact tracing: Identifying individuals who may have been exposed to respiratory infections, and monitoring their health status.

Isolation and quarantine: Isolating individuals who are infected with respiratory infections, and quarantining individuals who may have been exposed to respiratory infections, can help prevent the spread of infection.

Mass vaccination campaigns: In response to outbreaks of respiratory infections, public health authorities may conduct mass vaccination campaigns to help prevent the spread of infection.

VII. Treatment

A. Supportive Care: Supportive care is the cornerstone of treatment for acute respiratory infection. This involves managing symptoms such as fever, cough, and congestion. Patients with acute respiratory infection may benefit from bed rest, plenty of fluids, and over-the-counter medications such as acetaminophen or ibuprofen to relieve pain and fever. For patients with severe respiratory distress, hospitalization and respiratory support may be necessary.

B. Antibiotic Therapy: Antibiotics are only effective against bacterial infections and are not recommended for the treatment of viral infections. If a bacterial infection is suspected or confirmed, antibiotics may be prescribed to treat the infection. It is important to note that overuse of antibiotics can lead to antibiotic resistance, which can make infections more difficult to treat in the future.

C. Antiviral Therapy: Antiviral therapy is recommended for the treatment of certain viral respiratory infections such as influenza. These medications work by inhibiting the replication of the virus and can shorten the duration and severity of symptoms. It is important to note that antiviral therapy is most effective when started early in the course of the illness.

D. Oxygen Therapy: Patients with severe respiratory distress may require oxygen therapy to maintain adequate oxygenation of the blood. Oxygen can be delivered through a variety of methods, including nasal cannula, face mask, or mechanical ventilation. It is important to closely monitor oxygen levels to ensure that the patient is receiving the appropriate amount of oxygen. In severe cases, extracorporeal membrane oxygenation (ECMO) may be necessary to support respiratory function.

VIII. Acute Respiratory Infection in Children

A. Importance of acute respiratory infection in children

Acute respiratory infection (ARI) is a significant cause of morbidity and mortality in children worldwide, particularly in low- and middle-income countries. It is estimated that ARI accounts for approximately 15% of all deaths in children under the age of five. Children are particularly susceptible to ARI due to their immature immune systems and frequent exposure to pathogens in their environments. ARI in children can lead to severe complications such as pneumonia, bronchiolitis, and asthma exacerbations.

B. Unique aspects of acute respiratory infection in children

The clinical presentation of ARI in children can be different from that in adults, with symptoms such as fever, cough, and congestion being more common. Young children may also experience difficulty breathing, rapid breathing, and wheezing.

Infants and young children are at increased risk of severe disease and complications from ARI due to their small airways, immature immune systems, and decreased ability to clear mucus from their airways.

C. Diagnosis and management of acute respiratory infection in children

Diagnosis of ARI in children is based on clinical presentation and may be confirmed through laboratory testing, particularly in severe cases or outbreaks. Management of ARI in children includes supportive care such as maintaining hydration, managing fever, and providing supplemental oxygen when necessary. Antibiotics may be prescribed in cases of bacterial infection, and antiviral medication may be used for certain viral infections. Prevention measures such as vaccination and hand hygiene are critical in reducing the incidence of ARI in children. In severe cases, hospitalization and intensive care may be necessary, particularly in young infants or those with underlying medical conditions.

IX. Acute Respiratory Infection in Elderly

A. Importance of acute respiratory infection in elderly

Acute respiratory infections (ARIs) are a major cause of morbidity and mortality among elderly individuals. The risk of developing severe complications from ARIs, such as pneumonia, is higher in the elderly population, especially those with underlying chronic medical conditions. ARIs can also exacerbate existing conditions, leading to hospitalization and increased healthcare costs.

B. Unique aspects of acute respiratory infection in elderly

The elderly population is more susceptible to ARIs due to age-related changes in the immune system and underlying medical conditions. These changes can result in a reduced ability to fight off infections, making them more vulnerable to severe outcomes. Additionally, older individuals may present with atypical symptoms, making diagnosis and management challenging.

C. Diagnosis and management of acute respiratory infection in elderly

Diagnosis of ARIs in the elderly is based on clinical presentation, laboratory tests, and imaging studies. Treatment is focused on managing symptoms and preventing complications. Antibiotic therapy is usually reserved for bacterial infections, as viral ARIs are self-limiting and typically do not require specific antiviral therapy. Elderly patients with severe symptoms or complications may require hospitalization and supportive care, including oxygen therapy and mechanical ventilation.

Prevention measures include vaccination against influenza and pneumococcal disease, as well as adherence to infection control practices such as hand hygiene and wearing masks during outbreaks. It is also important to manage underlying chronic medical conditions that can increase the risk of severe complications from ARIs.

X. Summary of key points:

Acute respiratory infections are a significant public health concern worldwide, affecting individuals of all ages and causing significant morbidity and mortality. The epidemiology of acute respiratory infection is complex, influenced by factors such as age, comorbidities, and socioeconomic status. The pathophysiology of acute respiratory infection involves a complex interplay between the host immune response and the infecting pathogen. Diagnosis of acute respiratory infection is primarily based on clinical features and may be supported by laboratory testing. Infection control measures, personal hygiene and sanitation, vaccination, and public health responses are critical in the prevention and control of acute respiratory infections. Treatment of acute respiratory infection is primarily supportive, with antibiotics and antiviral therapies used in cases of bacterial and viral infections, respectively. Oxygen therapy may also be necessary in severe cases. Unique aspects of acute respiratory infection in children and the elderly require tailored approaches to diagnosis and management.

Malaria

I. Introduction

A. Definition of malaria

Malaria is a life-threatening disease caused by Plasmodium parasites, which are transmitted to humans through the bites of infected female Anopheles mosquitoes. The disease is characterized by high fever, chills, flu-like symptoms, and can lead to severe complications or even death if left untreated.

B. Historical background of malaria

Malaria has been a major public health problem for thousands of years, with evidence of the disease found in ancient Egyptian and Chinese texts. The disease has affected humans throughout history, with notable outbreaks in Europe during the Middle Ages and in North America during the colonial period.

C. Importance of malaria in public health

Malaria remains a significant global health threat, with an estimated 229 million cases and 409,000 deaths reported in 2019 alone, according to the World Health Organization. The disease is most prevalent in sub-Saharan Africa, where children under the age of five are at the highest risk of infection and death. Malaria also has a significant economic impact, with billions of dollars lost annually due to treatment costs, lost productivity, and decreased tourism in affected regions. Despite advances in prevention and treatment, malaria continues to pose a significant public health challenge, especially in low- and middle-income countries.

II. Epidemiology

A. Global distribution of malaria:

Malaria is a global public health problem, with an estimated 229 million cases and 409,000 deaths reported worldwide in 2019. The majority of cases (94%) and deaths (96%) occur in sub-Saharan Africa, with children under five years of age being the most affected. Other regions with high malaria burden include Southeast Asia, the Eastern Mediterranean, and the Western Pacific. Malaria transmission is influenced by various factors such as climate, population density, and socio-economic status, among others.

B. Demographics of infected populations:

Malaria disproportionately affects children under the age of five years, pregnant women, and non-immune travelers to endemic areas. In 2019, an estimated 67% of all malaria deaths occurred in children under the age of five years. Pregnant women are also at higher risk of severe malaria, which can lead to adverse outcomes such as maternal anemia, fetal loss, and low birth weight. Non-immune travelers to endemic areas are also at risk of contracting malaria, and preventive measures such as chemoprophylaxis and insecticide-treated bed nets are recommended for their protection.

C. Risk factors for contracting malaria:

The risk of contracting malaria is influenced by various factors such as geographic location, seasonality, and individual behavior. Individuals living in endemic areas are at higher risk of contracting malaria due to increased exposure to infected mosquitoes. The risk is also higher during the rainy season when mosquito breeding is more prevalent. Other risk factors include lack of access to preventive measures such as insecticide-treated bed nets and antimalarial drugs, poor housing conditions, and outdoor activities during peak mosquito biting times. Factors such as age, genetic predisposition, and co-infection with other diseases can also influence the risk of contracting malaria.

III. Pathophysiology

A. Life cycle of the malaria parasite:

Malaria is caused by a group of parasitic protozoa of the Plasmodium genus, which are transmitted through the bites of infected female Anopheles mosquitoes. The life cycle of the malaria parasite involves two hosts - the human host and the mosquito vector. The parasite goes through several stages during its life cycle, including sporozoites, merozoites, gametocytes, and gametes.

B. Mechanisms of transmission of the malaria parasite:

Malaria is primarily transmitted through the bites of infected female Anopheles mosquitoes. When a mosquito bites a person infected with malaria, it ingests the malaria parasites along with the blood meal. Inside the mosquito's gut, the parasites multiply and develop into sporozoites. These sporozoites then travel to the mosquito's salivary glands, where they can be transmitted to another person when the mosquito takes its next blood meal.

C. Immune response to malaria infection:

The immune response to malaria infection is complex and involves both innate and adaptive immune responses. When the malaria parasites enter the human host, they are first recognized by the innate immune system, which includes cells such as macrophages and dendritic cells. These cells can recognize the parasites through specific receptors and activate an immune response.

The adaptive immune response is also activated during malaria infection. This involves the activation of specific immune cells such as T cells and B cells, which can recognize and eliminate the parasites. However, the malaria parasite has developed strategies to evade the immune system, such as antigenic variation, which allows it to change its surface proteins and avoid recognition by the immune system. As a result, the immune response to malaria infection is often not effective in eliminating the parasite completely, leading to persistent infections and repeated episodes of malaria.

IV. Clinical Presentation

A. Incubation period:

The incubation period of malaria refers to the time between when a person is infected with the malaria parasite and when they begin to experience symptoms. The incubation period can vary depending on several factors, including the species of malaria parasite, the person's immunity to malaria, and the dose of the parasite that was transmitted.

For most species of malaria, the incubation period ranges from 7 to 30 days. However, in some cases, the incubation period can be as short as 9 days or as long as several months. In general, the incubation period is shorter for infections with the P. falciparum species, which is the most deadly form of malaria, than for infections with other species.

During the incubation period, the malaria parasite multiplies in the liver before entering the bloodstream and infecting red blood cells. As the infection progresses, the person may begin to experience symptoms of malaria.

It's worth noting that some people may be infected with malaria but never develop symptoms. This is known as asymptomatic malaria and can occur in people with partial immunity to malaria or in those who have taken antimalarial medications as a preventative measure.

B. Symptoms of malaria infection :

Malaria infection can present with a wide range of symptoms, and the severity of symptoms can vary depending on the species of the parasite and the immunity of the infected individual. The incubation period, or the time from initial infection to onset of symptoms, can range from 7 days to several weeks.

The typical symptoms of malaria include fever, chills, headache, muscle aches, and fatigue. These symptoms are often cyclic, with fever and chills occurring in cycles that can last from a few hours to several days. In addition to these common symptoms, other signs and symptoms of malaria infection may include:

- Nausea and vomiting

- Diarrhea
- Cough
- Abdominal pain
- Anemia
- Jaundice
- Seizures
- Impaired consciousness
- Difficulty breathing

In severe cases, malaria infection can lead to complications such as cerebral malaria, which can cause brain damage, seizures, and coma. Other complications can include kidney failure, severe anemia, and respiratory distress.

It is important to note that the symptoms of malaria can mimic those of other common illnesses, such as the flu, and therefore a proper diagnosis requires laboratory confirmation of the infection.

C. Complications of Malaria Infection:

Malaria infection can cause a range of complications that can be life-threatening if not promptly diagnosed and treated. Some of the complications associated with malaria infection include:

Severe Anemia: Malaria infection can lead to the destruction of red blood cells, causing anemia. Severe anemia can lead to organ damage and even death, particularly in children under the age of five and pregnant women.

Cerebral Malaria: This is a severe form of malaria that affects the brain and can cause seizures, coma, and even death. It is more common in children and pregnant women.

Acute Respiratory Distress Syndrome (ARDS): ARDS is a severe lung condition that can develop as a result of severe malaria infection. It can lead to respiratory failure and even death.

Organ Failure: Malaria infection can cause damage to vital organs such as the liver, kidneys, and spleen, leading to organ failure.

Pregnancy Complications: Pregnant women infected with malaria are at increased risk of developing complications such as anemia, miscarriage, stillbirth, and low birth weight babies.

Hyperparasitemia: This is a severe form of malaria infection that is characterized by high levels of malaria parasites in the blood. It can lead to multiple organ failure and death if not promptly diagnosed and treated.

Post-Malaria Neurological Syndrome: This is a rare complication of malaria infection that can occur weeks or even months after recovery. It is characterized by symptoms such as headache, dizziness, and difficulty in movement.

The risk of developing complications is higher in individuals who have weakened immune systems, such as children under five, pregnant women, and individuals with HIV/AIDS. Prompt diagnosis and treatment are essential to prevent the development of severe malaria and its associated complications.

V. Diagnosis

A. Diagnostic tests for malaria infection:

Diagnosis of malaria infection involves a combination of clinical assessment and laboratory testing. The clinical diagnosis is often based on the presence of symptoms such as fever, headache, chills, and flu-like symptoms, especially in individuals with a history of travel to an endemic area. However, clinical diagnosis alone is not sufficient, as the symptoms of malaria are non-specific and can be caused by other infections as well.

Laboratory diagnosis of malaria involves the identification of the parasite or its antigens in the blood. Microscopic examination of stained blood films remains the gold standard for malaria diagnosis. This technique involves the examination of thin and thick blood films under a microscope, which allows the detection and identification of the malaria parasite.

Rapid diagnostic tests (RDTs) have also been developed to detect malaria antigens in the blood, providing a quick and reliable diagnosis of malaria infection in the field settings. These tests are based on the detection of specific malaria antigens, such as histidine-rich protein 2 (HRP-2) and Plasmodium lactate dehydrogenase (pLDH), which are released by the parasite.

Molecular methods such as polymerase chain reaction (PCR) can also be used for malaria diagnosis. PCR-based tests can detect very low levels of parasite DNA in the blood, making them highly sensitive and specific. However, these tests require specialized equipment and trained personnel, which limit their use in resource-limited settings.

In addition to laboratory testing, it is important to obtain a thorough travel history and to consider the possibility of other co-infections or medical conditions that may present with similar symptoms. Clinical suspicion should be maintained even if laboratory tests are negative, as low levels of parasitemia or antigenemia can occur in some cases.

B. Role of laboratory confirmation:

Laboratory confirmation of malaria infection is important for accurate diagnosis and appropriate treatment. Microscopic examination of blood smears remains the gold standard for malaria diagnosis, although newer diagnostic techniques such as rapid diagnostic tests (RDTs) and molecular assays are increasingly being used.

Microscopic examination involves staining thin and thick blood smears with Giemsa stain and examining them under a microscope for the presence of malaria parasites. This method can differentiate between the different species of malaria parasites and determine the parasitemia level, which is important for determining the severity of infection and guiding treatment.

RDTs are simple, rapid, and accurate diagnostic tests that detect specific malaria antigens in blood samples. They do not require specialized laboratory equipment or training, making them particularly useful in resource-limited settings where microscopy may not be available.

Molecular assays such as polymerase chain reaction (PCR) can detect very low levels of malaria parasites in blood samples and can also differentiate between species. They are particularly useful in detecting low-level and asymptomatic infections, and in monitoring treatment efficacy.

Laboratory confirmation of malaria infection is important not only for accurate diagnosis and treatment, but also for surveillance and monitoring of the disease burden in endemic areas, tracking of drug resistance, and evaluation of control and elimination programs.

VI. Prevention and Control

A. Vector control measures: Vector control is a key component of malaria prevention and control efforts. This involves measures to reduce the number of mosquitoes that transmit malaria, such as indoor residual spraying with insecticides and the use of insecticide-treated bed nets. These interventions have been shown to be effective in reducing malaria transmission and have been widely implemented in endemic regions.

B. Chemoprophylaxis: Chemoprophylaxis involves the use of antimalarial drugs to prevent malaria infection. This approach is particularly useful for individuals who are at high risk of infection, such as travelers to endemic regions and pregnant women. The choice of drug and dosage depends on the type of malaria parasite present in the area and the individual's health status.

C. Vaccination: Despite extensive research, there is currently no highly effective malaria vaccine. However, several vaccine candidates are in development and some have shown promising results in clinical trials. The most advanced candidate is the RTS,S/AS01 vaccine, which has been shown to provide partial protection against malaria in young children in clinical trials conducted in sub-Saharan Africa.

D. Public health response to outbreaks of malaria: In areas where malaria is endemic, public health authorities often implement surveillance systems to monitor the incidence and spread of the disease. Rapid diagnosis and treatment of malaria cases is critical to prevent outbreaks, and health education campaigns are often used to raise awareness about the disease and promote preventative measures. In addition, international organizations such as the World Health Organization (WHO) provide technical and financial assistance to countries with high malaria burdens to support prevention and control efforts.

VII. Treatment

A. Antimalarial drugs: There are several classes of drugs used for the treatment of malaria, including artemisinin-based combination therapies (ACTs), chloroquine, quinine, mefloquine, and atovaquone-proguanil. The choice of drug depends on several factors, including the species of malaria parasite, the severity of infection, the patient's age and weight, and any underlying medical conditions. Resistance to antimalarial drugs is a growing concern and efforts are ongoing to develop new drugs and drug combinations to combat this issue.

B. Supportive care: In addition to antimalarial drugs, supportive care is often needed to manage symptoms and complications of malaria infection. This may include measures to control fever and dehydration, as well as treatment of any secondary infections or complications such as anemia or cerebral malaria.

C. Experimental treatments: There are several experimental treatments for malaria currently under investigation, including new drugs and vaccine candidates. One promising area of research involves the use of genetically modified mosquitoes to reduce the spread of malaria. Other approaches include the use of monoclonal antibodies to target specific parts of the malaria parasite, and the development of new drugs that target unique features of the parasite's life cycle. Clinical trials are ongoing to test the safety and efficacy of these and other potential treatments.

VIII. Malaria in Specific Populations

A. Malaria in pregnant women: Pregnant women are at increased risk of severe malaria infection due to their reduced immunity. Malaria infection during pregnancy is associated with adverse outcomes such as maternal anemia, low birth weight, preterm delivery, and stillbirth. The risk of infection is also higher in pregnant women because of their increased contact with mosquitoes. Prevention and treatment of malaria in pregnant women is crucial in reducing the burden of malaria in endemic areas.

B. Malaria in children: Children under the age of 5 years are at a higher risk of severe malaria infection and death. They have a weaker immune system and lack previous exposure to the parasite. Malaria infection in children can lead to severe anemia, respiratory distress, cerebral malaria, and death. Prevention and early diagnosis and treatment of malaria in children are important in reducing the burden of malaria in endemic areas.

C. Malaria in travelers: Travelers to malaria-endemic areas are at risk of contracting malaria infection if they are not taking appropriate preventive measures. The risk of infection depends on the duration of travel, the time of year, and the level of malaria transmission in the destination. Travelers can prevent malaria infection by taking chemoprophylaxis, using insecticide-treated bed nets, and avoiding mosquito bites.

D. Malaria in non-endemic areas: Malaria is no longer endemic in many countries, but it can still occur in non-endemic areas as a result of imported cases. Imported malaria cases can occur in travelers returning from malaria-endemic areas or migrants from endemic areas. The timely diagnosis and treatment of imported cases are crucial in preventing local transmission of the disease. Healthcare providers in non-endemic areas need to be aware of the possibility of imported cases and should take appropriate measures to prevent the spread of the disease.

IX. Summary of keypoints:

Malaria remains a significant public health challenge, particularly in low- and middle-income countries. While progress has been made in reducing the global burden of malaria, there is still much work to be done. Future directions in research and management of malaria include the development of new drugs and vaccines, improved vector control measures, and the use of innovative strategies for disease surveillance and outbreak response.

One promising area of research is the development of a highly effective malaria vaccine. While progress has been made in this area, there are still many challenges to be overcome, including the complex biology of the malaria parasite and the variability of the disease in different populations. Additionally, the development of new drugs is needed to combat the emergence of drug-resistant strains of the malaria parasite.

In addition to these research efforts, the management of malaria also requires effective public health interventions. This includes improving access to diagnosis and treatment, expanding vector control measures, and strengthening health systems in areas where malaria is endemic. Additionally, efforts are needed to address the social and economic determinants of malaria, such as poverty, inequality, and inadequate housing and sanitation.

Chikungunya

I. Introduction

A. Definition of Chikungunya:

Chikungunya is a viral disease caused by the Chikungunya virus, an RNA virus in the alphavirus genus of the family Togaviridae. The disease is transmitted by the bite of infected mosquitoes of the Aedes species, primarily Aedes aegypti and Aedes albopictus. The word "chikungunya" comes from the Makonde language of Tanzania and means "to become contorted," which describes the characteristic bent posture of patients suffering from severe joint pain.

B. Historical background of Chikungunya:

Chikungunya was first recognized as a human disease in 1952 during an outbreak in Tanzania. Since then, the disease has spread to many regions of the world, including Southeast Asia, the Indian subcontinent, and the Americas. Outbreaks have occurred sporadically, but since 2004, large-scale epidemics have occurred in many countries. In 2013, chikungunya virus was introduced to the Caribbean, and within a year, the disease had spread to almost all countries in the region. The rapid spread of the disease and the severity of the symptoms have made chikungunya a significant public health concern.

C. Importance of chikungunya in public health

Chikungunya is an emerging mosquito-borne viral disease that poses a significant threat to global public health. The virus is transmitted to humans by the bite of infected mosquitoes, primarily Aedes aegypti and Aedes albopictus, which are widely distributed in tropical and subtropical regions of the world. The World Health Organization (WHO) estimates that there are between 1.3 and 4 million cases of chikungunya annually in over 100 countries, and the number of cases is increasing.

Chikungunya has a significant impact on public health due to its high morbidity rate and potential for outbreaks. The disease causes a range of debilitating symptoms, including fever, severe joint pain, muscle pain, headache, nausea, fatigue, and rash. In some cases, the symptoms can persist for several months or even years, leading to chronic joint pain and disability. Chikungunya outbreaks can also place a significant burden on healthcare systems, particularly in low- and middle-income countries, where resources are already limited.

The global impact of chikungunya was highlighted during the 2013-2014 outbreak in the Americas, which resulted in over 2 million suspected cases across 44 countries and territories. The outbreak also highlighted the potential for the virus to spread to new regions and the need for effective surveillance, prevention, and control measures.

Given the ongoing threat of chikungunya and the potential for future outbreaks, it is essential to raise awareness of the disease and develop effective strategies for prevention and control. This requires a coordinated global response involving governments, public health organizations, and communities, as well as ongoing research into the epidemiology, pathogenesis, and treatment of chikungunya.

II. Epidemiology

A. Global distribution of Chikungunya

The virus was first isolated in Tanzania in 1952, and since then, outbreaks of chikungunya have been reported in several countries across Asia, Africa, Europe, and the Americas. CHIKV is primarily transmitted by Aedes mosquitoes, which are also responsible for the transmission of other viral diseases such as dengue and Zika.

The first recorded outbreak of chikungunya occurred in Tanzania in 1952, and since then, outbreaks have occurred in more than 60 countries, including many tropical and subtropical regions of the world. In recent years, the incidence of chikungunya has increased globally, with major outbreaks reported in Asia, Africa, and the Americas.

B. Demographics of infected populations:

Chikungunya can affect individuals of all ages, genders, and ethnicities. However, certain populations may be at higher risk of infection and severe disease. In endemic regions, children and elderly individuals are often the most affected. This may be due to the fact that they have less immunity to the virus or that they are more likely to have other underlying health conditions that can worsen the severity of the disease.

Additionally, individuals who live in or travel to areas with ongoing outbreaks of chikungunya are at increased risk of infection. This includes individuals who work outdoors or engage in activities that increase their exposure to mosquito bites, such as camping or hiking. International travelers, especially those traveling to tropical and subtropical regions, are also at risk of infection.

C. Risk factors for contracting chikungunya:

Geographic location: Chikungunya virus is mainly found in tropical regions, so individuals living or traveling to these areas are at higher risk of infection.

Mosquito bites: The primary mode of transmission of chikungunya virus is through the bite of infected Aedes mosquitoes. Individuals who spend more time outdoors or live in areas with a high density of mosquitoes are at higher risk of contracting the virus.

Age and health status: Older adults, young children, and individuals with underlying health conditions such as diabetes, heart disease, or compromised immune systems may be more susceptible to severe forms of chikungunya infection.

Genetic factors: Certain genetic factors may increase an individual's susceptibility to chikungunya virus infection or influence the severity of the disease.

Occupational exposure: Individuals whose occupation involves outdoor activities, such as farming or construction work, may be at increased risk of exposure to mosquito bites and therefore chikungunya virus infection.

III. Pathophysiology

Chikungunya is a viral disease that is primarily transmitted through the bites of infected Aedes mosquitoes. Once the virus enters the human body, it can target a variety of tissues, including the skin, liver, muscles, and joints. The incubation period for the virus ranges from 2 to 12 days, after which the infected individual may experience a range of symptoms.

The initial symptoms of Chikungunya are typically similar to those of other viral infections, such as fever, headache, and muscle pain. However, as the virus progresses, it can cause more severe symptoms, particularly in the joints. The virus can infect the cells that make up the cartilage and synovium of the joints, leading to inflammation and damage. This can result in debilitating joint pain and stiffness that can last for months or even years.

The pathophysiology of Chikungunya is complex and not yet fully understood. However, research suggests that the virus may cause damage to the immune system, allowing the virus to replicate and spread more easily. Additionally, the virus may disrupt the normal functioning of the cells that line the blood vessels, leading to inflammation and tissue damage.

Despite the severity of the symptoms associated with Chikungunya, most people who contract the virus will recover fully. However, some individuals may experience persistent joint pain and stiffness that can last for years after the initial infection. There is currently no specific treatment for Chikungunya, but supportive care can help to manage symptoms and improve overall outcomes.

IV.Clinical Presentation

A. Acute phase symptoms: During the acute phase of chikungunya infection, patients may experience sudden onset of symptoms, including fever, headache, fatigue, joint pain, and muscle pain. Joint pain is typically the most severe and debilitating symptom and may last for weeks to months. Other symptoms may include rash, nausea, vomiting, and diarrhea.

B. Chronic phase symptoms: In some cases, patients with chikungunya may develop chronic symptoms that last for months or even years after the acute phase of the illness has resolved. These symptoms may include persistent joint pain, joint swelling, and stiffness, as well as fatigue and depression.

C. Neurological manifestations: Chikungunya can also affect the nervous system, leading to neurological symptoms such as encephalitis, meningitis, and myelitis. These symptoms may include headache, confusion, seizures, and paralysis, and can be particularly severe in older adults.

D. Ocular manifestations: In rare cases, chikungunya can cause ocular manifestations, including uveitis, retinitis, and optic neuritis. These symptoms may include eye pain, redness, and vision loss.

E. Other clinical presentations: Chikungunya infection has also been associated with other clinical presentations, such as hepatitis, myocarditis, and acute renal failure. However, these complications are relatively rare and typically occur in immunocompromised patients.

The clinical presentation of chikungunya can vary widely from patient to patient, and some individuals may experience mild or no symptoms at all. However, the most common and debilitating symptoms are joint pain and fatigue, which can persist for months or even years after the acute phase of the illness has resolved. It is important for healthcare providers to recognize the various clinical presentations of chikungunya in order to provide appropriate treatment and management of symptoms.

V. Diagnosis

The diagnosis of chikungunya infection is primarily based on the patient's clinical presentation, especially the characteristic symptoms of fever and joint pain. However, laboratory testing can be used to confirm the diagnosis and rule out other diseases with similar symptoms.

Serological Tests: Serological tests are used to detect the presence of antibodies against chikungunya virus in the patient's blood. The most commonly used serological test is the enzyme-linked immunosorbent assay (ELISA), which detects immunoglobulin M (IgM) and immunoglobulin G (IgG) antibodies against chikungunya virus. These antibodies are typically detectable in the blood 5-7 days after symptom onset and can remain detectable for several months. A fourfold or greater rise in antibody titer between acute and convalescent serum samples collected at least two weeks apart is considered diagnostic for chikungunya infection.

Viral Detection Tests: Viral detection tests are used to detect the presence of chikungunya virus in the patient's blood or other bodily fluids. The most commonly used viral detection tests are reverse transcription-polymerase chain reaction (RT-PCR) and virus isolation. RT-PCR is a molecular diagnostic test that detects the viral RNA in the patient's blood, while virus isolation involves culturing the virus from a patient's blood or other bodily fluids. Viral detection tests are most useful in the acute phase of the infection when the virus is present in high levels in the patient's blood.

VII. Treatment

Chikungunya treatment aims to relieve symptoms and support the body's natural healing processes. There are currently no specific antiviral drugs available for chikungunya, but several treatment options are available.

A. Symptomatic treatment

Symptomatic treatment focuses on alleviating the symptoms of chikungunya infection. This includes the use of nonsteroidal anti-inflammatory drugs (NSAIDs) such as ibuprofen and acetaminophen to relieve fever and pain. Rest, adequate hydration, and avoidance of strenuous activities are also recommended. In severe cases, hospitalization may be necessary to manage complications such as dehydration, severe joint pain, and neurological symptoms.

B. Antiviral therapy

Although there are currently no specific antiviral drugs approved for chikungunya, several antiviral drugs have been tested in preclinical and clinical studies. Some of these drugs include ribavirin, interferon-alpha, and chloroquine. However, their effectiveness in treating chikungunya infection is still being evaluated.

VIII. Chikungunya in Specific Populations

A. Chikungunya in pregnant women: Pregnant women infected with chikungunya may experience more severe symptoms, and there is a potential for adverse effects on the fetus. The risk of vertical transmission to the fetus has been reported to be low, but cases of congenital infection have been documented. Adequate management of chikungunya infection in pregnant women includes symptom management, close monitoring of maternal and fetal well-being, and delivery planning.

B. Chikungunya in children: Children are at risk of chikungunya infection, and they may experience similar symptoms as adults. However, children may be less able to communicate their symptoms, leading to delays in diagnosis and treatment. Management of chikungunya in children involves supportive care, including hydration, pain relief, and fever management.

C. Chikungunya in travelers: Chikungunya is primarily found in tropical regions, and travelers to these areas are at risk of infection. Prevention strategies for travelers include avoiding mosquito bites through the use of insect repellents, mosquito nets, and protective clothing. Travelers should also be aware of the signs and symptoms of chikungunya and seek medical attention if they become ill during or after their trip.

D. Chikungunya in non-endemic areas: Chikungunya has spread to non-endemic areas, including Europe and North America, through the importation of infected individuals and the establishment of local transmission cycles. These outbreaks pose a significant public health threat, and prevention efforts focus on mosquito control and surveillance to identify cases early and prevent further transmission. The diagnosis of chikungunya infection in non-endemic areas may be challenging due to limited awareness among healthcare providers and the overlap of symptoms with other viral infections such as dengue and Zika virus.

Dengue

I. Introduction

A. Definition of Dengue: Dengue is a viral infection caused by the dengue virus, which is transmitted to humans through the bites of infected Aedes mosquitoes. It is characterized by a sudden onset of high fever, severe headache, joint and muscle pain, and skin rash. In severe cases, dengue can progress to life-threatening complications such as dengue hemorrhagic fever and dengue shock syndrome.

B. Historical Background of Dengue: Dengue has been recognized as a clinical entity for over 200 years, with the first recorded epidemic occurring in Asia in the 1770s. The virus responsible for dengue was first isolated in 1944 during a dengue epidemic in the Philippines. Since then, dengue has become a major public health concern in tropical and subtropical regions around the world, with frequent outbreaks occurring in countries such as Brazil, India, Thailand, and the Philippines.

C. Importance of Dengue in Public Health: Dengue is one of the most important mosquito-borne viral diseases in the world, with an estimated 390 million infections and 20,000 deaths occurring each year. The incidence of dengue has increased dramatically in recent decades, with the disease now endemic in more than 100 countries in Africa, the Americas, the Eastern Mediterranean, Southeast Asia, and the Western Pacific. Dengue imposes a significant economic burden on affected communities and health systems, with costs related to treatment, surveillance, and vector control.

II. Epidemiology

A. Global distribution of dengue

1. **Dengue endemic regions:** Southeast Asia, Western Pacific, Africa, and the Americas
2. **Burden of disease:** approximately 390 million infections annually with 96 million resulting in illness and 20,000 deaths
3. Increasing incidence in recent years

B. Demographics of infected populations

1. All age groups are susceptible to dengue infection
2. Children under 15 years of age and adults over 60 years of age are at highest risk of severe dengue
3. Gender and genetic factors may also play a role in susceptibility

C. Risk factors for contracting dengue

1. Living in or traveling to dengue endemic areas
2. Exposure to infected mosquitoes
3. Lack of mosquito control measures
4. Previous dengue infection, as subsequent infections can lead to more severe disease
5. Immunological status and genetic factors

The pathophysiology of dengue fever

The pathophysiology of dengue fever involves a complex interplay between the dengue virus and the host immune system. The dengue virus is a single-stranded RNA virus that belongs to the Flaviviridae family. The virus is transmitted to humans through the bite of infected Aedes mosquitoes.

After the virus enters the host, it infects immune cells such as dendritic cells, macrophages, and monocytes. The virus then replicates in these cells, leading to the release of pro-inflammatory cytokines such as interleukin-6 (IL-6), interleukin-1β (IL-1β), and tumor necrosis factor-alpha (TNF-α).

The release of these cytokines triggers an immune response, leading to the activation of T cells, B cells, and natural killer cells. The activation of these cells leads to the production of antibodies against the virus. However, in some cases, the immune response is exaggerated and leads to the production of high levels of cytokines, a condition called cytokine storm. This can cause increased vascular permeability, which can lead to plasma leakage and subsequent shock, also known as dengue shock syndrome.

The pathophysiology of dengue fever also involves the interaction between the virus and the endothelial cells that line the blood vessels. The virus can infect these cells and cause apoptosis, leading to increased vascular permeability and leakage of plasma into the surrounding tissues. This can cause a range of clinical manifestations, including fever, headache, joint pain, rash, and bleeding.

The severity of dengue fever can vary from mild to severe, depending on the individual's immune response and the virulence of the virus strain. In severe cases, dengue fever can progress to dengue hemorrhagic fever and dengue shock syndrome, which can be life-threatening if not treated promptly.

IV. Clinical Presentation

A. Incubation period

The incubation period of dengue virus infection ranges from 4 to 10 days after the mosquito bite. However, most patients show symptoms within 4 to 7 days.

B. Symptoms of dengue infection

Dengue fever can present with a wide range of symptoms, ranging from mild to severe. Symptoms typically appear after the incubation period and can last for up to two weeks. The most common symptoms of dengue fever include:

1. High fever (over 101°F)
2. Severe headache, usually behind the eyes
3. Muscle and joint pain
4. Nausea and vomiting
5. Rash
6. Fatigue
7. Mild bleeding from the nose or gums

In severe cases, patients may experience dengue hemorrhagic fever or dengue shock syndrome. Symptoms of these severe forms of the disease may include:

- Severe abdominal pain
- Persistent vomiting
- Rapid breathing
- Bleeding under the skin or from the nose, mouth, or gums
- Blood in the urine, stools, or vomit
- Restlessness or irritability
- Cold, clammy skin
- Weak, rapid pulse

C. Complications of dengue infection

Most cases of dengue fever are self-limiting, and patients usually recover within a week or two without any complications. However, in some cases, dengue fever can progress to severe forms of the disease, such as dengue hemorrhagic fever or dengue shock syndrome. These severe forms of the disease can be life-threatening and require prompt medical attention.

Dengue hemorrhagic fever is characterized by bleeding under the skin or from the nose, mouth, or gums, as well as abdominal pain, persistent vomiting, rapid breathing, and restlessness or irritability. Dengue shock syndrome is a severe form of dengue hemorrhagic fever and is characterized by low blood pressure, weak rapid pulse, and cold, clammy skin. Without prompt and appropriate treatment, dengue hemorrhagic fever and dengue shock syndrome can be fatal.

V. Diagnosis

A. Diagnostic tests for dengue infection

Clinical diagnosis based on symptoms: Dengue infection can be clinically diagnosed based on symptoms such as high fever, headache, muscle and joint pains, and rash. This method of diagnosis is not specific to Dengue and can lead to misdiagnosis.

Serological tests: The Enzyme-Linked Immunosorbent Assay (ELISA) and Rapid Diagnostic Tests (RDTs) are commonly used serological tests for Dengue. ELISA is a highly sensitive test that can detect specific antibodies to the Dengue virus. RDTs are quick and easy to use but may not be as accurate as ELISA.

Molecular tests: The Reverse Transcriptase Polymerase Chain Reaction (RT-PCR) is a molecular test that can detect the presence of Dengue virus RNA in the blood. RT-PCR is highly sensitive and specific and can detect Dengue virus early in the course of infection.
B. Role of laboratory confirmation

Importance of laboratory confirmation: Laboratory confirmation is important for accurate diagnosis of Dengue and differentiation from other febrile illnesses with similar symptoms.

- Laboratory confirmation helps with disease surveillance and monitoring of Dengue outbreaks.
- Laboratory confirmation can guide appropriate management and treatment of Dengue cases.

B. Role of laboratory confirmation

The diagnosis of dengue fever is usually made based on clinical symptoms and findings, along with laboratory confirmation. The laboratory confirmation is important to differentiate dengue fever from other similar diseases like malaria, typhoid fever, and leptospirosis.

1. One commonly used laboratory test is the Dengue virus-specific IgM (immunoglobulin M) and IgG (immunoglobulin G) antibodies assay. These tests detect the presence of antibodies produced in response to dengue virus infection. IgM antibodies are produced early in the infection and are present for a few weeks, while IgG antibodies persist for a longer time after infection.

2. Another laboratory test used for the confirmation of dengue fever is the polymerase chain reaction (PCR) test, which detects the presence of the dengue virus RNA in blood or other body fluids. The PCR test is particularly useful in the early stages of infection when viral load is high.
3. In addition to these tests, other laboratory investigations like complete blood count (CBC), liver function tests, and electrolyte levels are performed to monitor the progression of the disease and detect any complications. Overall, laboratory confirmation plays a crucial role in the diagnosis and management of dengue fever.

VI. Prevention and Control

A. Vector control measures: Vector control is a critical strategy in the prevention and control of dengue. This includes environmental management, which involves reducing or eliminating the breeding sites of mosquitoes. This can be achieved through the removal of stagnant water, such as in discarded tires, cans, and other containers that can collect water. Insecticide-treated mosquito nets, indoor residual spraying, and larvicides are also effective tools in controlling mosquito populations.

B. Community-based interventions: Community participation is crucial in the prevention and control of dengue. Health education campaigns can increase awareness about the disease and promote preventive measures, such as covering water storage containers, wearing protective clothing, and using mosquito repellents. Community-based approaches to mosquito control, such as the use of mosquito traps and the elimination of mosquito breeding sites, have been successful in reducing dengue transmission in some areas.

C. Personal protective measures: Individuals can protect themselves from dengue by using mosquito repellents, wearing long-sleeved clothing, and sleeping under insecticide-treated mosquito nets. It is also important to avoid outdoor activities during peak mosquito biting hours, which are usually early in the morning and late in the afternoon.

D. Public health response to outbreaks of dengue: Early detection and prompt response to outbreaks of dengue are crucial in preventing the spread of the disease. This includes surveillance, case management, and laboratory confirmation of suspected cases. Health authorities may also implement emergency measures such as vector control, social mobilization, and communication campaigns to control the spread of the disease. In severe cases, hospitalization and supportive care are necessary, and timely treatment can reduce mortality rates.

VII. Treatment

A. Symptomatic treatment

Dengue is a self-limiting illness, and treatment is primarily supportive to manage symptoms such as fever, headache, and body aches. Patients are advised to get plenty of rest, stay hydrated, and use pain relievers such as acetaminophen (paracetamol) to alleviate fever and pain. However, nonsteroidal anti-inflammatory drugs (NSAIDs) such as aspirin or ibuprofen should be avoided, as they can increase the risk of bleeding.

B. Antiviral therapy

There is currently no specific antiviral therapy for dengue. However, several drugs have been tested in clinical trials, including chloroquine, ribavirin, and interferon, with mixed results. At present, these drugs are not routinely recommended for the treatment of dengue.

C. Experimental treatments

Researchers are currently exploring several experimental treatments for dengue. One promising approach is the use of monoclonal antibodies, which are engineered to target specific proteins on the surface of the dengue virus. Several clinical trials have shown that monoclonal antibodies can reduce the severity of dengue and prevent hospitalization. Another experimental treatment is the use of a drug called balapiravir, which inhibits the replication of the dengue virus. Clinical trials have shown that balapiravir can reduce the duration of fever and the amount of virus in the blood, but further research is needed to determine its effectiveness. Other potential treatments include the use of plant-derived compounds, such as papaya leaf extract, which has been shown to have antiviral properties against dengue in vitro. However, further research is needed to evaluate their safety and efficacy in clinical settings.

VIII. Dengue in Specific Populations

A. Dengue in pregnant women: Pregnant women are at an increased risk of severe dengue infection, especially during the third trimester. This is due to the changes in the immune system during pregnancy, which make women more susceptible to infections. Severe dengue infection in pregnant women can result in preterm labor, fetal distress, stillbirth, and maternal mortality. Therefore, early diagnosis and prompt management of dengue infection in pregnant women are crucial.

B. Dengue in children: Children are among the most vulnerable populations to dengue infection. They may develop severe dengue infection more frequently than adults, and the risk of severe dengue increases with younger age. Symptoms of dengue infection in children may be nonspecific, which makes diagnosis challenging. Early recognition of the disease, close monitoring, and prompt treatment can prevent complications and reduce mortality rates in children with severe dengue.

C. Dengue in travelers: Dengue is a significant concern for travelers visiting endemic areas, and travelers account for a significant proportion of dengue cases in non-endemic countries. Travelers can reduce their risk of contracting dengue by taking preventive measures such as using mosquito repellents, wearing protective clothing, and avoiding mosquito bites. Travelers who develop symptoms of dengue during or after their trip should seek medical attention promptly.

D. Dengue in non-endemic areas: Dengue has become a significant public health concern in non-endemic areas, where it is introduced by travelers or imported cases. The diagnosis and management of dengue in non-endemic areas can be challenging due to the lack of experience and infrastructure. Therefore, health care providers in non-endemic areas should be aware of the disease's clinical manifestations, risk factors, and diagnostic tests. Early diagnosis and prompt management can prevent the spread of the disease and reduce morbidity and mortality rates.

Summary of key points

- Dengue is a mosquito-borne viral disease that is endemic in many tropical and subtropical regions of the world.
- The virus is transmitted by the Aedes mosquito and can cause a wide range of symptoms, from mild fever to severe and potentially fatal dengue hemorrhagic fever.
- Dengue is a major public health concern due to its high incidence and potential to cause outbreaks and epidemics.
- Diagnosis is typically based on clinical symptoms and confirmed through laboratory testing.
- Prevention and control measures include vector control, community-based interventions, and personal protective measures.
- There is currently no specific antiviral treatment for dengue, and management is focused on symptomatic relief and supportive care.
- Dengue can affect specific populations such as pregnant women, children, and travelers, and requires special attention for diagnosis and management.

lymphatic filariasis

I. Introduction

Lymphatic filariasis (LF) is a parasitic disease caused by thread-like nematode worms that inhabit the lymphatic system, resulting in chronic and disabling conditions such as lymphedema and elephantiasis. It is considered a neglected tropical disease (NTD) and is one of the leading causes of disability worldwide. LF primarily affects the poorest and most marginalized populations in tropical and subtropical regions, where access to basic healthcare and sanitation is limited.

Historically, LF has been recognized as a disease since ancient times, with descriptions of elephantiasis found in ancient Hindu and Chinese texts. However, the first definitive descriptions of the disease were recorded in the 16th century by European travelers in India. During the 20th century, the global burden of LF increased rapidly, with the disease being prevalent in over 80 countries by the 1990s.

LF is of great importance in public health due to its high prevalence, chronic morbidity, and negative impact on socio-economic development in endemic areas. The disease can result in significant disability and stigma, leading to reduced productivity, social isolation, and a lower quality of life for those affected. LF is also a major economic burden, with estimates suggesting that the disease results in billions of dollars in lost productivity and healthcare costs every year.

II. Epidemiology

A. Global distribution of lymphatic filariasis

Lymphatic filariasis (LF) is a neglected tropical disease that is endemic in 73 countries, primarily in sub-Saharan Africa, the Indian subcontinent, Southeast Asia, and the Pacific. It is estimated that over 856 million people in these regions are at risk of LF infection, with over 120 million people infected and approximately 40 million people experiencing lymphedema or hydrocele due to LF. The highest burden of the disease is found in India, followed by Nigeria and Indonesia.

B. Demographics of infected populations

Lymphatic filariasis affects individuals of all ages and genders, but the disease burden is higher in adults due to the cumulative effects of long-term infection. In endemic regions, children can be infected at an early age, and many remain asymptomatic carriers of the disease. Individuals living in poverty, with limited access to clean water and sanitation, are at an increased risk of infection due to the presence of the disease-transmitting mosquitoes in their environment.

C. Risk factors for contracting lymphatic filariasis:

The primary risk factor for contracting lymphatic filariasis is living in an area with active transmission of the disease. The transmission of LF occurs through the bites of infected mosquitoes, primarily the Anopheles, Culex, and Aedes species. Other risk factors include poor hygiene, lack of access to clean water and sanitation facilities, and living in close proximity to standing water where mosquitoes can breed. Additionally, individuals who work outside or who sleep outdoors without bed nets are at a higher risk of contracting the disease.

III. Pathophysiology

The immune response to lymphatic filariasis infection is complex and multifaceted. The filarial parasites have evolved several mechanisms to evade host immune responses, leading to chronic infection in humans. The immune response to filarial parasites involves both innate and adaptive immunity.

Innate immunity is the first line of defense against filarial parasites, and is initiated when the parasite is recognized by pattern recognition receptors (PRRs) on immune cells such as dendritic cells, macrophages, and neutrophils. This recognition triggers the release of pro-inflammatory cytokines, such as interleukin-1 beta (IL-1β), tumor necrosis factor alpha (TNF-α), and interleukin-6 (IL-6), which activate other immune cells and recruit them to the site of infection. Innate immunity also plays a role in the activation of the complement system, which can aid in the destruction of the parasites.

Adaptive immunity is critical in the development of protective immunity against filarial parasites. The immune response to filarial parasites is characterized by a Th2-biased response, characterized by the production of cytokines such as interleukin-4 (IL-4), interleukin-5 (IL-5), and interleukin-13 (IL-13). These cytokines activate B cells to produce parasite-specific antibodies, which can help to neutralize the parasite and facilitate its destruction by other immune cells. The Th2 response also leads to the activation of eosinophils, which can help to kill the parasites through the release of cytotoxic granules.

However, the Th2 response can also lead to immunopathology and tissue damage, particularly in chronic infections. In addition, filarial parasites have developed several strategies to evade the immune response, such as the secretion of immunomodulatory molecules that can suppress immune activation and induce regulatory T cells (Tregs), which can inhibit immune responses and facilitate parasite survival.

IV. Clinical Presentation

Lymphatic filariasis can manifest in different ways, depending on the stage of the disease. The incubation period for lymphatic filariasis ranges from several months to years.

In the early stages, most people with lymphatic filariasis may not experience any symptoms or have mild symptoms, such as fever, lymphangitis (inflammation of lymphatic vessels), and lymphadenitis (inflammation of lymph nodes).

However, over time, the accumulation of the parasites in the lymphatic system can cause more severe symptoms. The most characteristic symptom of lymphatic filariasis is chronic lymphedema, which is a condition where the affected limb(s) become swollen and thickened due to the obstruction of lymphatic vessels. The swelling can cause discomfort, heaviness, and pain in the affected limb, as well as difficulty in moving the affected limb.

Another common manifestation of lymphatic filariasis is elephantiasis, which is the severe enlargement and hardening of the skin and subcutaneous tissue. This condition can occur in the limbs, breasts, genitals, and other parts of the body. The skin may become thickened, warty, and fissured, and can be prone to bacterial infections. The disfigurement caused by elephantiasis can result in social stigma, depression, and reduced quality of life for those affected.

In addition to lymphedema and elephantiasis, other complications of lymphatic filariasis can include chyluria (the presence of milky white urine due to the leakage of lymphatic fluid into the urinary system), hydrocele (the accumulation of fluid in the scrotum), and pulmonary tropical eosinophilia (a rare allergic manifestation of the disease). These complications can have a significant impact on the health and well-being of affected individuals.

V. Diagnosis

Lymphatic filariasis can be diagnosed by a combination of clinical examination, immunological tests, and parasitological tests. Diagnosis of lymphatic filariasis is important for both individual patient management and control of transmission at the population level.

Immunological tests for lymphatic filariasis include detection of circulating filarial antigens (CFA) and filarial-specific antibodies in serum or whole blood samples. CFA detection tests are highly specific and sensitive for the diagnosis of active infection. However, these tests may remain positive for several years after successful treatment, making them unsuitable for monitoring treatment efficacy. Antibody tests, on the other hand, may remain positive for several years after successful treatment and may not differentiate between current and past infection.

Parasitological tests involve the detection of microfilariae (immature forms of the parasite) in blood or other tissues. Microfilariae can be visualized using microscopy after concentration of the sample or using membrane filtration techniques. However, the sensitivity of these tests varies with the time of day, as microfilariae have a nocturnal periodicity, and may not be detectable during the day.

VI. Prevention and Control

A. Vector control measures: Vector control measures are the primary strategy for preventing the transmission of lymphatic filariasis. Control of the mosquito vector is the most effective method of preventing the transmission of the disease. Insecticide-treated bed nets and curtains can be used to prevent mosquito bites, and larval control methods such as the use of insecticides in breeding sites can help to reduce the number of mosquitoes.

B. Community-based interventions: Community-based interventions can also help to prevent the spread of lymphatic filariasis. Mass drug administration (MDA) programs have been implemented in many endemic areas to treat large populations with antifilarial drugs such as ivermectin and albendazole. This approach has been shown to be effective in reducing the prevalence and incidence of the disease. Health education campaigns can also be used to increase awareness of the disease and encourage people to adopt preventive measures.

C. Personal protective measures: Personal protective measures can also be used to prevent lymphatic filariasis. Individuals living in endemic areas can use insect repellents and wear protective clothing to reduce the risk of mosquito bites. People can also be encouraged to practice good hygiene, such as washing their hands frequently and avoiding contact with contaminated water.

D. Public health response to outbreaks of lymphatic filariasis: In areas where outbreaks of lymphatic filariasis occur, public health responses may include mass treatment with antifilarial drugs, enhanced vector control measures, and health education campaigns. The goal of these responses is to reduce the prevalence and incidence of the disease and prevent the spread of infection to other areas. In addition, surveillance systems can be established to monitor the incidence of the disease and identify outbreaks early, allowing for prompt intervention.

VII. Treatment

Relief of symptoms: Symptomatic treatment includes the relief of symptoms such as pain, inflammation, and fever. Pain relievers like paracetamol or ibuprofen may be prescribed to manage pain and fever. Bed rest and elevation of the affected limb may also help to reduce swelling and improve lymphatic flow.

Management of lymphedema: Compression bandages or garments may be used to help reduce swelling and improve lymphatic flow in patients with lymphedema. B. Antiparasitic therapy

Overview of antiparasitic therapy: Antiparasitic therapy is the primary treatment for lymphatic filariasis. The aim of antiparasitic therapy is to kill the adult worms responsible for lymphatic filariasis and prevent further transmission of the disease.

Medications used for antiparasitic therapy: The medications used for antiparasitic therapy include diethylcarbamazine (DEC), albendazole, and ivermectin. These medications are usually given in combination to increase their effectiveness.

DEC: DEC is the most commonly used medication for the treatment of lymphatic filariasis. It works by paralyzing the worms and making them more susceptible to the host's immune system. DEC is usually given in a single dose or in multiple doses over several days or weeks.

Albendazole: Albendazole is another medication used for the treatment of lymphatic filariasis. It works by preventing the worms from absorbing nutrients, leading to their eventual death. Albendazole is usually given in combination with DEC.

Ivermectin: Ivermectin is a newer medication used for the treatment of lymphatic filariasis. It works by paralyzing the worms and making them more susceptible to the host's immune system. Ivermectin is usually given in combination with albendazole.

Summary of key points

1. Lymphatic filariasis is a parasitic disease that affects the lymphatic system, causing severe swelling and disability.
2. The disease is endemic in many tropical and subtropical regions, with an estimated 120 million people infected worldwide.
3. Risk factors for contracting lymphatic filariasis include poverty, poor sanitation, and living in areas with high mosquito populations.
4. Diagnosis of lymphatic filariasis requires laboratory testing, and treatment includes antiparasitic medication and symptomatic management.
5. Prevention and control measures include vector control, community-based interventions, personal protective measures, and public health response to outbreaks.
6. Lymphatic filariasis disproportionately affects vulnerable populations such as pregnant women, children, and travelers, and can also occur in non-endemic areas among individuals who have traveled to or lived in endemic regions.
7. The Global Program to Eliminate Lymphatic Filariasis has made progress towards eradicating the disease through mass drug administration and other measures, but ongoing efforts are needed to achieve elimination goals.

Pneumonia

I. Introduction

Pneumonia is a common respiratory illness characterized by inflammation of the lungs, primarily affecting the air sacs known as alveoli. Historically, pneumonia has been recognized as a significant cause of morbidity and mortality worldwide, particularly in young children, elderly individuals, and those with weakened immune systems. The disease has been documented throughout history, with ancient Greek, Roman, and Chinese physicians describing symptoms consistent with pneumonia. In modern times, pneumonia remains a major public health concern, responsible for a significant burden of illness and mortality globally. The impact of pneumonia on public health is particularly pronounced in low- and middle-income countries, where limited access to healthcare and other social determinants of health can exacerbate the burden of disease.

II. Epidemiology

Pneumonia is a common infectious disease that can affect individuals of any age, but it is more common in certain populations. Some key demographics that are particularly vulnerable to pneumonia include young children, the elderly, individuals with weakened immune systems, and those with underlying health conditions such as chronic obstructive pulmonary disease (COPD), heart disease, or diabetes.

Other risk factors for contracting pneumonia include exposure to tobacco smoke, air pollution, or other environmental toxins, as well as close contact with individuals who have respiratory infections such as the flu. Additionally, individuals who have recently undergone surgery or who are hospitalized for another condition may be at increased risk for developing pneumonia due to the potential for bacterial infections to spread in healthcare settings. Socioeconomic factors such as poverty and overcrowding can also increase the risk of contracting pneumonia, particularly in developing countries with limited access to healthcare and sanitation facilities.

III. Pathophysiology

When pneumonia-causing pathogens enter the body, the immune system responds by launching a coordinated effort to eradicate the invader. The initial immune response is mediated by the innate immune system, which is comprised of non-specific cells and molecules that act quickly to contain and eliminate pathogens. The cells of the innate immune system, including neutrophils, macrophages, and dendritic cells, recognize conserved patterns on the surface of pathogens, called pathogen-associated molecular patterns (PAMPs), via pattern recognition receptors (PRRs) on their own surface.

Upon recognizing PAMPs, innate immune cells release inflammatory cytokines and chemokines that recruit additional immune cells to the site of infection. Neutrophils are the first cells to arrive at the site of infection, followed by macrophages, which phagocytose and destroy the invading pathogen. Dendritic cells act as antigen-presenting cells, displaying fragments of the pathogen on their surface to activate the adaptive immune response.

The adaptive immune response is mediated by antigen-specific cells, including B cells and T cells, which recognize and respond to specific epitopes on the surface of the pathogen. B cells produce pathogen-specific antibodies, which can bind to and neutralize the pathogen or target it for destruction by other cells of the immune system. T cells can also recognize and respond to specific epitopes, including viral antigens and bacterial peptides presented on the surface of infected cells.

In pneumonia caused by bacteria, the adaptive immune response is critical for clearance of the infection, while in viral pneumonia, the innate immune response plays a more important role. In severe cases of pneumonia, an excessive or dysregulated immune response can result in tissue damage and contribute to the development of acute respiratory distress syndrome (ARDS). Conversely, in immunocompromised individuals, a weak or impaired immune response can lead to persistent infection and chronic pneumonia.

IV. Clinical Presentation

Pneumonia can present in a variety of ways depending on the age and health status of the individual, as well as the causative organism. The classic symptoms of pneumonia include cough, fever, and shortness of breath. The cough may be productive or dry, and can produce phlegm that may be green or yellow in color. Fever is often present and can be high, although some people may not have a fever. Shortness of breath may be mild or severe, and may be accompanied by chest pain or discomfort. Other symptoms can include fatigue, weakness, headache, and muscle aches. In severe cases, confusion or changes in mental status may occur, particularly in older adults or those with weakened immune systems. Children with pneumonia may present with symptoms such as rapid breathing, wheezing, chest retractions, and grunting. Some may also have a fever or cough, although these symptoms may be less pronounced than in adults. In some cases, pneumonia can progress rapidly and cause life-threatening complications, such as sepsis or respiratory failure.

V. Diagnosis

A. Diagnostic tests for pneumonia:

The diagnosis of pneumonia is typically based on a combination of clinical symptoms, physical examination, and imaging studies. Common diagnostic tests for pneumonia include:

Chest X-ray: This imaging study is the most commonly used test for diagnosing pneumonia. It can reveal the presence of inflammation, fluid or other abnormalities in the lungs.

Sputum culture: This test involves analyzing a sample of sputum (phlegm) produced by coughing to identify the microorganism causing the pneumonia.

Blood tests: Blood tests can be used to detect the presence of infection and assess the severity of the illness. Elevated white blood cell count and C-reactive protein levels are indicative of infection.

Pulse oximetry: This test measures the oxygen saturation in the blood and is used to determine the severity of pneumonia and assess the need for supplemental oxygen.

B. Role of laboratory confirmation:

Laboratory confirmation of pneumonia is important in identifying the causative pathogen, guiding treatment, and preventing the spread of infection. Sputum culture and blood tests are commonly used to confirm the diagnosis of pneumonia. In some cases, further testing such as bronchoscopy or pleural fluid analysis may be necessary to identify the causative pathogen. Rapid diagnostic tests for pneumonia are also available, which can provide results within minutes to hours and aid in prompt diagnosis and treatment. However, it is important to note that not all cases of pneumonia require laboratory confirmation and diagnosis can often be made based on clinical symptoms and imaging findings alone.

VI. Prevention and Control

The response to outbreaks of pneumonia may vary depending on the underlying cause and the affected population. In general, public health officials work to quickly identify and control outbreaks, prevent transmission of the disease, and provide appropriate treatment to those affected.

One of the primary methods of controlling outbreaks of bacterial pneumonia is through vaccination. Vaccines can be used to prevent certain types of pneumonia, such as pneumococcal pneumonia, which is caused by the bacteria Streptococcus pneumoniae. In some cases, antibiotics may also be given prophylactically to individuals who have been exposed to the disease to prevent them from becoming infected.

In addition to vaccination and antibiotic prophylaxis, infection control measures are also important in preventing the spread of pneumonia. These may include isolating patients who are infected, wearing personal protective equipment (such as gloves and masks), and implementing strict hand hygiene protocols.

VII. Treatment

The treatment of pneumonia varies depending on the cause and severity of the infection. Bacterial pneumonia is typically treated with antibiotics, while antiviral medications may be prescribed for viral pneumonia. In cases of severe pneumonia, hospitalization may be necessary for intravenous antibiotic or antiviral therapy, oxygen therapy, and other supportive measures.

In addition to medication, treatment may also involve measures to relieve symptoms such as fever, cough, and shortness of breath. This can include over-the-counter pain relievers, cough suppressants, and expectorants. Patients with severe symptoms may also benefit from supplemental oxygen therapy.

Prevention is also an important aspect of pneumonia treatment. This may involve vaccination against common bacterial and viral strains, as well as lifestyle modifications to reduce the risk of respiratory infections, such as washing hands frequently and avoiding close contact with sick individuals. In addition, prompt treatment of other medical conditions, such as influenza or chronic obstructive pulmonary disease (COPD), can help prevent complications and reduce the risk of pneumonia.

Summary of key points for pneumonia:

1. Pneumonia is an acute respiratory infection that affects the lungs, causing inflammation in the air sacs.
2. Pneumonia is a major global public health problem, responsible for a significant proportion of morbidity and mortality worldwide.
3. The main risk factors for contracting pneumonia include age, underlying medical conditions, weakened immune system, and environmental factors such as smoking and air pollution.
4. Pneumonia can be caused by a variety of pathogens including bacteria, viruses, and fungi, which can be transmitted through respiratory droplets or contact with contaminated surfaces.
5. Clinical presentation of pneumonia includes symptoms such as fever, cough, chest pain, and difficulty breathing, and can lead to complications such as respiratory failure, sepsis, and death.
6. Diagnosis of pneumonia is based on clinical presentation, chest X-ray, and laboratory tests such as sputum culture and blood tests.
7. Prevention and control measures for pneumonia include vaccination, antibiotic prophylaxis, infection control measures, and public health response to outbreaks.
8. Treatment of pneumonia typically involves antibiotic therapy and supportive care.

Hypertension

I. Introduction:

A. Definition of hypertension: Hypertension, also known as high blood pressure, is a medical condition in which the blood pressure in the arteries is consistently elevated. Blood pressure is measured in millimeters of mercury (mmHg) and is expressed as two numbers: systolic blood pressure (SBP) and diastolic blood pressure (DBP). Normal blood pressure is defined as SBP < 120 mmHg and

DBP < 80 mmHg, while hypertension is defined as SBP ≥ 130 mmHg or DBP ≥ 80 mmHg.

B. Historical background of hypertension: The concept of high blood pressure has been recognized for centuries, but the modern understanding of hypertension began in the 19th century. In 1896, Italian physician Scipione Riva-Rocci invented the first practical device to measure blood pressure, called the sphygmomanometer. In the following years, physicians began to recognize the importance of hypertension as a risk factor for cardiovascular disease and stroke. The first effective drugs for hypertension, the thiazide diuretics, were introduced in the 1950s, and since then, many other medications have been developed to treat high blood pressure.

C. Importance of hypertension in public health: Hypertension is a major public health concern due to its high prevalence and significant impact on morbidity and mortality. According to the World Health Organization, hypertension is estimated to affect one billion people worldwide, and is responsible for approximately 9.4 million deaths per year. Hypertension is a major risk factor for cardiovascular disease, stroke, and kidney disease, and its complications place a significant burden on healthcare systems around the world. The prevention, detection, and treatment of hypertension are important public health priorities in order to reduce the incidence of cardiovascular disease and improve overall health outcomes.

II. Epidemiology

A. Global distribution of hypertension

Hypertension, also known as high blood pressure, is a global health issue. According to the World Health Organization (WHO), hypertension affects around one billion people worldwide, with an estimated global prevalence of 26%. The highest prevalence of hypertension is found in low- and middle-income countries, particularly in sub-Saharan Africa and South Asia.

B. Demographics of affected populations

Hypertension can affect individuals of any age, gender, or race, but certain demographic groups are more susceptible to developing the condition. These groups include older adults, individuals with a family history of hypertension, and people who are overweight or obese. Additionally, hypertension is more prevalent in men than in women before the age of 55, after which the prevalence becomes similar in both sexes.

C. Risk factors for developing hypertension

There are several risk factors associated with the development of hypertension. These include modifiable risk factors, such as unhealthy diet, physical inactivity, tobacco use, and alcohol consumption, as well as non-modifiable risk factors, such as age, genetics, and ethnicity. Other risk factors include stress, sleep apnea, and chronic kidney disease. Hypertension is also a common comorbidity in individuals with diabetes or cardiovascular disease.

III. Pathophysiology

Hypertension, or high blood pressure, is a chronic medical condition characterized by persistently elevated blood pressure levels in the arteries. The pathophysiology of hypertension is complex and involves several physiological mechanisms, including increased peripheral resistance, increased cardiac output, and abnormal activation of the renin-angiotensin-aldosterone system (RAAS).

Peripheral resistance is the resistance to blood flow in the small arteries and arterioles. In hypertension, there is an increase in peripheral resistance due to structural and functional changes in the blood vessels, such as thickening and narrowing of the vessel walls. This leads to an increase in the force required to pump blood through the vessels, resulting in an elevation in blood pressure.

Cardiac output is the amount of blood pumped by the heart per minute. In hypertension, there is an increase in cardiac output due to an increase in heart rate and stroke volume. This can be caused by several factors, such as stress, physical activity, and other medical conditions.

The RAAS plays an important role in regulating blood pressure. It is a complex hormonal system that involves several organs, including the kidneys, adrenal glands, and liver. The RAAS is activated in response to low blood pressure and leads to the production of angiotensin II, a potent vasoconstrictor that increases peripheral resistance and blood pressure. In hypertension, there is an abnormal activation of the RAAS, leading to excessive production of angiotensin II and perpetuating the cycle of elevated blood pressure.

Other factors that contribute to the pathophysiology of hypertension include genetic predisposition, obesity, sedentary lifestyle, and dietary factors such as high sodium intake. Understanding the complex pathophysiology of hypertension is critical for developing effective treatments and preventing long-term complications associated with this condition.

IV. Clinical Presentation of Hypertension:

Hypertension is often referred to as the "silent killer" because it often does not cause any symptoms, and the only way to diagnose it is to measure blood pressure. However, in severe cases or in long-term hypertension, some symptoms may develop. These symptoms may include:

Headaches: Hypertension can cause headaches, especially in the back of the head and in the morning.

Dizziness: Patients with hypertension may feel dizzy or lightheaded, especially when standing up.

Shortness of breath: Hypertension can cause shortness of breath, especially during physical activity or exertion.

Chest pain: Chest pain may occur in severe hypertension, but it is not common.

Vision changes: Blurred vision or other vision changes may occur due to hypertension, but this is rare.

Nausea and vomiting: Hypertension can cause nausea and vomiting, but this is rare.

It is important to note that these symptoms are not specific to hypertension and can be caused by other medical conditions as well. Therefore, a proper diagnosis by a healthcare provider is essential.

V. Diagnosis

Hypertension is typically diagnosed based on repeated measurements of elevated blood pressure. The current guideline for diagnosing hypertension is based on the American College of Cardiology/American Heart Association (ACC/AHA) 2017 hypertension guidelines, which define hypertension as a systolic blood pressure (SBP) of ≥130 mm Hg or diastolic blood pressure (DBP) of ≥80 mm Hg. Blood pressure should be measured in a calm environment, with the patient seated and resting for at least 5 minutes prior to measurement. At least two blood pressure readings should be obtained at each visit, separated by at least 1 minute. The average of these measurements should be used to determine the patient's blood pressure category.

In some cases, additional diagnostic tests may be ordered to determine the underlying cause of hypertension. These tests may include blood tests to assess kidney function, electrolyte levels, and lipid levels. Urine tests may also be used to evaluate kidney function. Other diagnostic tests that may be used include electrocardiogram (ECG) to evaluate heart function, echocardiogram to assess heart structure and function, and imaging tests such as computed tomography (CT) or magnetic resonance imaging (MRI) to evaluate for structural abnormalities in the cardiovascular system.

Laboratory confirmation of hypertension is not typically necessary, as the diagnosis is based on repeated blood pressure measurements. However, laboratory testing may be useful in certain cases, such as when assessing the underlying cause of secondary hypertension.

VI. Prevention and Control

A. Lifestyle modifications: Lifestyle modifications can help prevent hypertension and can also aid in controlling high blood pressure. These modifications include:

Maintaining a healthy weight: Being overweight or obese can increase the risk of developing hypertension. Losing weight through regular exercise and healthy diet can help lower blood pressure.

Engaging in regular physical activity: Regular exercise can help lower blood pressure and prevent hypertension. Exercise for at least 30 minutes a day, most days of the week, is recommended.

Eating a healthy diet: A diet that is rich in fruits, vegetables, whole grains, and low-fat dairy products and low in saturated and total fat can help lower blood pressure. The Dietary Approaches to Stop Hypertension (DASH) diet is a recommended eating plan to lower blood pressure.

Limiting alcohol consumption: Drinking too much alcohol can raise blood pressure. It is recommended that men should not drink more than two drinks per day and women should not drink more than one drink per day.

Quitting smoking: Smoking can raise blood pressure and increase the risk of heart disease. Quitting smoking can help lower blood pressure and improve overall health.

B. Pharmacologic interventions: In some cases, lifestyle modifications alone may not be enough to control hypertension. Medications may be needed to lower blood pressure. Common medications used to treat hypertension include:

Diuretics: Also known as water pills, these medications help the body get rid of excess sodium and water, which can lower blood pressure.

ACE inhibitors: These medications help relax blood vessels, which can lower blood pressure.

Angiotensin receptor blockers (ARBs): These medications block the action of angiotensin, a hormone that can raise blood pressure.

Calcium channel blockers: These medications help relax blood vessels, which can lower blood pressure.

Beta blockers: These medications help slow the heart rate and lower blood pressure.

C. Public health response to hypertension: Public health interventions can also aid in preventing and controlling hypertension. These interventions include:

Community-based interventions: Community-based interventions such as health education programs and support groups can help raise awareness about hypertension and promote healthy lifestyle choices.

Policy interventions: Policies such as taxes on unhealthy foods and beverages, restrictions on advertising of unhealthy foods and beverages, and workplace wellness programs can help prevent and control hypertension.

Clinical interventions: Clinical interventions such as regular blood pressure screenings, early diagnosis and treatment of hypertension, and effective medication management can help prevent and control hypertension.

VII. Treatment

The treatment of hypertension depends on the severity of the condition and the presence of any other comorbidities. Lifestyle modifications are recommended for all patients with hypertension, including weight reduction, regular exercise, reduction in dietary sodium intake, moderation of alcohol consumption, and smoking cessation.

For patients with stage 1 hypertension and low cardiovascular risk, lifestyle modifications may be the only necessary intervention. For patients with stage 2 hypertension, lifestyle modifications are recommended along with antihypertensive medications. The goal of treatment is to reduce blood pressure to below 140/90 mmHg, or below 130/80 mmHg for patients with diabetes or chronic kidney disease.

There are several classes of antihypertensive medications that can be used, including diuretics, ACE inhibitors, angiotensin II receptor blockers (ARBs), calcium channel blockers (CCBs), beta blockers, and aldosterone antagonists. The choice of medication depends on the patient's age, ethnicity, comorbidities, and medication side effect profile.

In addition to medications, lifestyle modifications and antihypertensive medications, hypertension can also be managed through regular blood pressure monitoring and patient education. Patients with hypertension should be educated about the importance of medication adherence, lifestyle modifications, and regular monitoring of blood pressure to prevent long-term complications of the condition.

Summary of key points

In conclusion, hypertension is a significant public health issue globally, affecting individuals of all ages and demographics. Hypertension is a complex disorder that arises from multiple physiological and environmental factors, and it can lead to severe complications if left untreated. Diagnosis and treatment of hypertension require a multidisciplinary approach, including lifestyle modifications and pharmacologic interventions. Furthermore, hypertension presents unique challenges in specific populations, such as older adults, children and adolescents, pregnant women, and individuals residing in non-endemic areas. Despite these challenges, effective prevention and control strategies, combined with ongoing research into experimental treatments, provide hope for reducing the burden of hypertension on global health.

Diabetes mellitus

I. Introduction:

Diabetes mellitus is a chronic metabolic disorder characterized by elevated blood glucose levels due to a defect in insulin secretion, insulin action, or both. The disease affects millions of people worldwide and is associated with various complications, including cardiovascular disease, nerve damage, kidney disease, and eye problems. Diabetes mellitus is classified into several types, with type 1 diabetes (T1D) and type 2 diabetes (T2D) being the most common.

T1D is caused by autoimmune destruction of pancreatic beta cells, resulting in a complete lack of insulin secretion.

T2D, on the other hand, is characterized by insulin resistance and impaired insulin secretion. Other less common types of diabetes include gestational diabetes, which occurs during pregnancy, and monogenic diabetes, which is caused by mutations in a single gene. Despite advances in diabetes management, the disease continues to pose a significant health burden worldwide.

II. Epidemiology

A. Global distribution of diabetes mellitus:

According to the International Diabetes Federation (IDF), as of 2021, approximately 537 million people worldwide have diabetes. The prevalence of diabetes is increasing rapidly, and it is estimated that by 2045, the number of people with diabetes will rise to 647 million. Diabetes is a significant global public health problem that affects people of all ages and ethnicities. The highest prevalence of diabetes is found in low- and middle-income countries, where access to healthcare and diabetes prevention programs is often limited.

B. Demographics of affected populations:

Diabetes affects individuals of all ages, genders, and ethnicities. However, some populations are at higher risk of developing diabetes than others. For example, the prevalence of diabetes is higher in older adults, individuals with a family history of diabetes, people who are overweight or obese, and individuals who lead sedentary lifestyles. Additionally, certain ethnic groups, such as African Americans, Hispanic/Latino Americans, and Native Americans, have a higher risk of developing diabetes compared to Caucasians.

C. Risk factors for developing diabetes mellitus:

Several risk factors contribute to the development of diabetes mellitus. These include lifestyle factors, such as physical inactivity, unhealthy eating habits, and obesity. Genetics also plays a role, and individuals with a family history of diabetes are at higher risk of developing the disease. Other risk factors include age, ethnicity, and certain medical conditions, such as high blood pressure and high cholesterol levels. Additionally, gestational diabetes, which occurs during pregnancy, increases a woman's risk of developing diabetes later in life.

III. Pathophysiology

Diabetes mellitus is a chronic metabolic disorder characterized by hyperglycemia, which results from defects in insulin secretion, insulin action, or both. There are two main types of diabetes: Type 1 and Type 2 diabetes. Type 1 diabetes, previously known as insulin-dependent diabetes, is characterized by the destruction of pancreatic beta cells that produce insulin, resulting in absolute insulin deficiency. In contrast, Type 2 diabetes, previously known as non-insulin-dependent diabetes, is characterized by insulin resistance, a condition in which the body's tissues become less responsive to insulin, and beta cell dysfunction, leading to relative insulin deficiency.

The pathophysiology of Type 1 diabetes involves the destruction of pancreatic beta cells by an autoimmune response, which is thought to be triggered by genetic and environmental factors. This destruction leads to an absolute deficiency of insulin, resulting in elevated blood glucose levels. In Type 2 diabetes, insulin resistance occurs due to various factors such as obesity, sedentary lifestyle, aging, and genetic predisposition. The body compensates for this resistance by increasing insulin secretion from beta cells. However, over time, the beta cells become exhausted and dysfunctional, resulting in relative insulin deficiency and hyperglycemia.

In both types of diabetes, chronic hyperglycemia leads to the development of microvascular and macrovascular complications such as retinopathy, nephropathy, neuropathy, cardiovascular disease, and stroke. The mechanisms underlying the development of these complications are complex and multifactorial and involve metabolic, hemodynamic, and inflammatory pathways.

The development of diabetes mellitus involves a complex interplay of various factors. In type 1 diabetes, an autoimmune response causes destruction of pancreatic beta cells, leading to insulin deficiency. This leads to hyperglycemia, as glucose cannot be taken up by cells in the absence of insulin. In type 2 diabetes, insulin resistance develops, where cells become less responsive to insulin, leading to hyperglycemia. Additionally, in type 2 diabetes, the pancreas may also fail to produce sufficient insulin to overcome the insulin resistance, further exacerbating hyperglycemia.

Other factors that can contribute to the development of diabetes mellitus include genetics, lifestyle factors such as physical inactivity and poor diet, obesity, and certain medical conditions such as pancreatic disease or hormonal disorders. Furthermore, gestational diabetes mellitus can develop during pregnancy due to hormonal changes and increased insulin resistance.

The chronic hyperglycemia associated with diabetes mellitus can lead to various complications, including cardiovascular disease, kidney disease, retinopathy, and neuropathy. The development of these complications is thought to be related to the damage caused by elevated glucose levels to small blood vessels and nerves throughout the body.

IV. Clinical Presentation

A. Types of diabetes mellitus: There are three main types of diabetes mellitus, including type 1 diabetes, type 2 diabetes, and gestational diabetes.

Type 1 diabetes: Type 1 diabetes is an autoimmune disorder that occurs when the body's immune system mistakenly attacks and destroys the beta cells in the pancreas that produce insulin. This type of diabetes typically develops in childhood or adolescence, although it can occur at any age.

Type 2 diabetes: Type 2 diabetes is the most common type of diabetes, accounting for about 90% of all cases. It occurs when the body becomes resistant to insulin or when the pancreas is unable to produce enough insulin to meet the body's needs. This type of diabetes is often associated with obesity, physical inactivity, and a family history of diabetes.

Gestational diabetes: Gestational diabetes is a type of diabetes that develops during pregnancy. It usually resolves after delivery, but women who have had gestational diabetes are at increased risk of developing type 2 diabetes later in life.

B. Symptoms of diabetes mellitus: The symptoms of diabetes mellitus can vary depending on the type and severity of the disease, but common symptoms include:

1. Increased thirst and urination
2. Unexplained weight loss
3. Fatigue
4. Blurred vision
5. Slow-healing sores or frequent infections
6. Tingling or numbness in the hands or feet

C. Complications of diabetes mellitus: Diabetes mellitus can cause a wide range of complications, both acute and chronic. Some of the most common complications include:

Diabetic ketoacidosis: This is a life-threatening complication that occurs when there is not enough insulin in the body, causing the blood to become too acidic.

Hypoglycemia: This is a condition in which blood sugar levels become too low, often as a result of insulin therapy or other medications used to treat diabetes.

Neuropathy: This is a type of nerve damage that can cause numbness, tingling, or pain in the hands and feet.

Retinopathy: This is a type of eye damage that can lead to vision loss or blindness.

Nephropathy: This is a type of kidney damage that can lead to kidney failure and the need for dialysis or a kidney transplant.

Cardiovascular disease: Diabetes mellitus is a major risk factor for cardiovascular disease, including heart attacks and strokes.

V. Diagnosis

A. Diagnostic tests for diabetes mellitus

There are several diagnostic tests used for diabetes mellitus. The most commonly used tests include blood glucose tests, glycated hemoglobin (A1C) test, and oral glucose tolerance test (OGTT).

The blood glucose test measures the level of glucose in the blood. The fasting plasma glucose (FPG) test measures blood glucose after an 8-hour fast, while the random plasma glucose (RPG) test measures blood glucose at any time of the day without fasting. The FPG and RPG tests are less reliable compared to the A1C test and OGTT.

The A1C test measures the percentage of glycated hemoglobin in the blood. It gives an average of blood glucose levels over the past 2-3 months, providing a more accurate picture of a person's blood glucose control.

The OGTT involves measuring blood glucose levels before and after consuming a sugary drink. It is used to diagnose gestational diabetes and in people suspected of having impaired glucose tolerance.

In addition to these tests, urine tests can also be used to detect the presence of glucose and ketones in the urine, which may indicate uncontrolled diabetes.

B. Role of laboratory confirmation

Laboratory tests are essential for the diagnosis and management of diabetes mellitus. There are several tests available for the diagnosis of diabetes mellitus, including glycated hemoglobin (A1C), fasting plasma glucose (FPG), and oral glucose tolerance test (OGTT). These tests are used to evaluate the levels of glucose in the blood and to determine if a person has diabetes mellitus.

Glycated hemoglobin (A1C)

Glycated hemoglobin (A1C) is a blood test that measures the average blood glucose levels over the past 2-3 months. It is used to diagnose diabetes mellitus and to monitor the effectiveness of diabetes treatment. A1C levels of 6.5% or higher indicate diabetes mellitus.

Fasting plasma glucose (FPG)

Fasting plasma glucose (FPG) is a blood test that measures the amount of glucose in the blood after an overnight fast of at least 8 hours. FPG levels of 126 mg/dL or higher indicate diabetes mellitus.

Oral glucose tolerance test (OGTT)

The oral glucose tolerance test (OGTT) is a blood test that measures the body's ability to use glucose. It involves drinking a sugary solution, and then measuring the blood glucose levels at specific intervals. OGTT levels of 200 mg/dL or higher indicate diabetes mellitus.

It is important to note that laboratory tests should always be interpreted in conjunction with the patient's medical history, physical examination, and other clinical findings. In some cases, a patient may have elevated glucose levels on one test, but not on others. Additionally, laboratory tests should be repeated to confirm the diagnosis of diabetes mellitus.

Laboratory tests are also used to monitor the effectiveness of diabetes treatment. Glycated hemoglobin (A1C) levels are typically measured every 3-6 months to assess the patient's blood glucose control. Fasting plasma glucose (FPG) and postprandial glucose (PPG) levels may also be monitored to evaluate the patient's response to treatment.

VI. Prevention and Control:

Preventing and controlling diabetes mellitus involves both lifestyle modifications and medical interventions.

A. Lifestyle Modifications:

Diet: A healthy diet is essential for controlling blood sugar levels in diabetic patients. It is important to avoid high-sugar, high-carbohydrate, and high-fat foods. Instead, diabetic patients should consume foods that are high in fiber, such as fruits, vegetables, whole grains, and legumes.

Exercise: Regular exercise can help improve insulin sensitivity and lower blood sugar levels in diabetic patients. It is recommended that diabetic patients engage in at least 150 minutes of moderate-intensity exercise per week.

Weight Management: Maintaining a healthy weight can reduce the risk of developing diabetes mellitus. Overweight and obese individuals are at a higher risk of developing diabetes mellitus, and losing weight can help improve blood sugar control.

Smoking Cessation: Smoking is a risk factor for diabetes mellitus, and quitting smoking can help reduce the risk of developing the disease.

B. Medical Interventions:

Medications: Medications such as metformin, sulfonylureas, and insulin can help control blood sugar levels in diabetic patients. The type and dosage of medication prescribed will depend on the individual patient's needs.

Blood Sugar Monitoring: Regular blood sugar monitoring is essential for diabetic patients to monitor their blood sugar levels and adjust their medication dosage accordingly.

Education and Support: Diabetic patients should receive education and support to help them manage their disease effectively. This can include diabetes self-management education, support groups, and counseling.

Screening: Screening for diabetes mellitus can help identify individuals who are at risk of developing the disease and allow for early intervention. Screening is recommended for individuals with risk factors such as obesity, family history of diabetes mellitus, and high blood pressure.

Preventing and controlling diabetes mellitus requires a multifaceted approach involving both lifestyle modifications and medical interventions. With proper management, diabetic patients can lead healthy and fulfilling lives while minimizing the risks associated with the disease.

Treatment:

The treatment of diabetes mellitus aims to control blood glucose levels, prevent complications, and improve overall health. Treatment plans may vary depending on the type and severity of diabetes, as well as the individual's health status and lifestyle factors.

For individuals with type 1 diabetes, insulin therapy is necessary to maintain normal blood glucose levels. Insulin can be administered through injections or insulin pumps, and dosages may need to be adjusted based on physical activity, diet, and other factors.

For individuals with type 2 diabetes, lifestyle modifications such as diet and exercise are often the first line of treatment. Additionally, oral medications or injectable medications such as insulin or glucagon-like peptide-1 receptor agonists may be prescribed to help regulate blood glucose levels.

In some cases, bariatric surgery may be recommended for individuals with type 2 diabetes who are obese and have difficulty controlling their blood glucose levels through other means.

Regardless of the type of diabetes, routine monitoring of blood glucose levels, blood pressure, and cholesterol levels is important for preventing complications such as heart disease, kidney disease, and nerve damage. Additionally, quitting smoking, maintaining a healthy weight, and managing stress can also help improve overall health outcomes for individuals with diabetes.

Cancer

I. Introduction

A. Definition of cancer Cancer is a group of diseases characterized by the uncontrolled growth and spread of abnormal cells in the body. These abnormal cells can invade and destroy surrounding tissues and organs, and can also spread to other parts of the body through the blood and lymphatic systems. There are many different types of cancer, each with its own unique set of symptoms, risk factors, and treatment options.

B. Overview of the incidence and prevalence of cancer worldwide Cancer is a major global health problem, with an estimated 19.3 million new cases and 10 million cancer-related deaths worldwide in 2020. The burden of cancer is expected to continue to rise, with an estimated 28.4 million new cancer cases projected by 2040. The most common types of cancer worldwide are lung, breast, colorectal, prostate, and stomach cancers.

C. Importance of cancer as a public health concern Cancer is a significant public health concern due to its high incidence and mortality rates, as well as the significant physical, emotional, and financial burden it places on individuals, families, and communities. Cancer can result in long-term disability, decreased quality of life, and significant healthcare costs. Additionally, cancer can disproportionately affect marginalized and vulnerable populations, highlighting the importance of addressing social determinants of health in cancer prevention and control efforts.

D. Goals of cancer prevention and control The goals of cancer prevention and control include reducing the incidence and mortality of cancer, improving cancer survival rates and quality of life for those affected by cancer, and addressing cancer-related health disparities. To achieve these goals, a comprehensive approach to cancer prevention and control is necessary, which includes a focus on primary prevention through lifestyle modifications, vaccination, and environmental and occupational health measures, as well as secondary prevention through early detection and screening. Additionally, effective cancer treatment and management, including multidisciplinary care and palliative care, are crucial components of cancer prevention and control efforts. Ongoing research, education, and advocacy are also important in advancing cancer prevention and control efforts.

II. Risk factors for cancer

A. Environmental factors

Environmental factors play a significant role in the development of cancer. Exposure to carcinogens, pollution, and radiation are among the most well-known environmental risk factors for cancer.

Exposure to carcinogens

Carcinogens are substances that have the potential to cause cancer. These can be naturally occurring, such as aflatoxins produced by certain molds, or synthetic, such as industrial chemicals or certain medications. Exposure to carcinogens can occur in the workplace, through the use of certain consumer products, or through environmental contamination.

Pollution

Pollution is another environmental risk factor for cancer. Air pollution, for example, has been linked to an increased risk of lung cancer and other respiratory diseases. Water pollution has also been associated with an increased risk of certain types of cancer, such as bladder cancer.

Radiation

Exposure to ionizing radiation is a well-known environmental risk factor for cancer. Sources of ionizing radiation include natural sources, such as cosmic radiation and radon gas, as well as human made sources, such as medical imaging and nuclear power plants.

Limiting exposure to ionizing radiation from both natural and human-made sources is an important strategy for cancer prevention and control. This can be achieved through measures such as using lower-dose imaging techniques when appropriate, implementing radiation safety protocols in medical settings, and regulating nuclear power plants and other sources of ionizing radiation. Public education and awareness campaigns can also be effective in promoting behaviors that reduce exposure to ionizing radiation, such as avoiding unnecessary medical imaging and testing homes for radon gas.

Other environmental factors

Other environmental factors that have been linked to an increased risk of cancer include dietary factors, such as a diet high in processed or red meat, and lifestyle factors, such as tobacco use and physical inactivity. Additionally, certain occupational exposures, such as working with asbestos or diesel exhaust, have been associated with an increased risk of cancer.

Overall, reducing exposure to environmental risk factors for cancer requires a comprehensive approach that involves regulatory measures, technological innovations, and individual behavior change. Efforts to promote public awareness of environmental risk factors for cancer and the importance of environmental health are also crucial in reducing the burden of cancer on individuals and communities.

II. Risk factors for cancer

B. Behavioral factors

Behavioral factors also play a significant role in the development of cancer. The following are some well-established behavioral risk factors:

Tobacco use

Tobacco use is the leading preventable cause of cancer and is responsible for a significant proportion of cancer deaths worldwide. Smoking cigarettes, cigars, or pipes, as well as using smokeless tobacco products, increases the risk of cancer in several organs, including the lungs, throat, mouth, pancreas, bladder, and kidney.

Alcohol consumption

Alcohol consumption is another well-established behavioral risk factor for cancer. Regular and excessive alcohol consumption has been linked to an increased risk of several cancers, including those of the breast, liver, colon, rectum, and mouth and throat.

Poor nutrition and physical inactivity

A diet high in processed and red meats, and low in fruits and vegetables, as well as physical inactivity, are associated with an increased risk of several types of cancer, including colon, breast, and endometrial cancer.

Unsafe sex Certain sexually transmitted infections, such as human papillomavirus (HPV) and hepatitis B and C, can increase the risk of several types of cancer, including cervical, liver, and some types of head and neck cancer.

C. Genetic factors

Genetic factors also play a role in the development of cancer. Inherited genetic mutations can increase the risk of certain types of cancer, including breast, ovarian, and colorectal cancer.

Family history of cancer Having a family history of certain types of cancer, such as breast, ovarian, or colorectal cancer, can increase an individual's risk of developing these cancers.

Inherited genetic mutations Inherited genetic mutations, such as mutations in the BRCA1 and BRCA2 genes, can significantly increase the risk of breast and ovarian cancer. Other inherited genetic mutations, such as those associated with Lynch syndrome, can increase the risk of colorectal and other types of cancer.

While genetic factors cannot be modified, individuals with a family history of cancer or known inherited genetic mutations can take steps to reduce their risk of developing cancer, such as undergoing regular cancer screenings and making lifestyle changes to reduce other modifiable risk factors, such as tobacco and alcohol use and physical inactivity.

Early detection and screening

A. Importance of early detection in cancer treatment

Early detection of cancer is crucial for successful treatment outcomes. When cancer is detected at an early stage, it is often easier to treat, and the likelihood of a full recovery is significantly higher. Early detection can also reduce the need for more aggressive treatments, such as surgery, radiation therapy, or chemotherapy.

B. Overview of cancer screening methods

Several screening methods are available for different types of cancer. The following are some of the most common screening methods:

Breast cancer screening

Mammography is the primary screening method for breast cancer. It is a low-dose X-ray that can detect changes in breast tissue that may indicate the presence of cancer. Women at average risk of breast cancer are recommended to start screening mammography at age 50 and continue every two years until age 74. Women with a higher risk of breast cancer, such as those with a family history of the disease, may need to start screening earlier and more frequently.

Colorectal cancer screening

Several screening methods are available for colorectal cancer, including colonoscopy, flexible sigmoidoscopy, fecal occult blood tests, and stool DNA tests. Colonoscopy is the most effective screening method, as it allows for the detection and removal of precancerous polyps before they develop into cancer. Screening for colorectal cancer is recommended starting at age 45 for average-risk individuals, and earlier for those with a family history of the disease.

Cervical cancer screening

Cervical cancer screening is typically performed using the Pap test, which involves collecting cells from the cervix and examining them for abnormalities that may indicate the presence of cancer or precancerous changes. The HPV test, which detects the presence of the human papillomavirus, which is the primary cause of cervical cancer, may also be used in conjunction with the Pap test. Screening for cervical cancer is recommended every three to five years for women aged 21 to 65 years.

Prostate cancer screening

The prostate-specific antigen (PSA) blood test is the primary screening method for prostate cancer. Elevated levels of PSA may indicate the presence of prostate cancer, although other conditions can also cause elevated PSA levels. Screening for prostate cancer remains controversial, as the benefits of early detection and treatment are still under debate. The American Cancer Society recommends that men discuss the potential benefits and risks of prostate cancer screening with their healthcare provider, starting at age 50 for those at average risk, or earlier for those at higher risk.

Cancer Prevention

A. Primary prevention strategies

Environmental and occupational health measures

Environmental and occupational health measures aim to reduce exposure to carcinogens and other cancer-causing substances in the environment and the workplace. This can be achieved through regulations, policies, and education campaigns aimed at reducing the use and emission of hazardous substances. Examples of environmental and occupational measures include:

1. Regulating the use of pesticides, industrial chemicals, and other hazardous substances.
2. Implementing workplace safety measures to reduce exposure to carcinogens, such as asbestos and silica dust.
3. Promoting clean air and water policies to reduce exposure to pollutants, such as radon and arsenic.

Behavioral interventions

Behavioral interventions aim to reduce modifiable risk factors for cancer, such as tobacco use, excessive alcohol consumption, poor diet, and physical inactivity. Examples of behavioral interventions include:

a. Tobacco control

Tobacco use is a major cause of cancer, responsible for around 22% of cancer deaths worldwide. Tobacco control measures include policies to reduce tobacco use and exposure to secondhand smoke, such as tobacco taxes, smoke-free laws, and tobacco advertising bans.

b. Alcohol control

Excessive alcohol consumption is also a risk factor for cancer, particularly for cancers of the breast, liver, and colon. Alcohol control measures include policies to reduce alcohol consumption, such as taxation, marketing restrictions, and education campaigns.

c. Healthy diet and physical activity promotion

Poor diet and physical inactivity are linked to an increased risk of cancer. Promoting healthy eating habits and regular physical activity can help reduce the risk of developing cancer. Examples of healthy diet and physical activity promotion include education campaigns, workplace wellness programs, and community-based initiatives.

Vaccination against cancer-causing viruses

Certain viruses, such as human papillomavirus (HPV) and hepatitis B and C viruses, are known to cause cancer. Vaccination against these viruses can prevent the development of cancer. Examples of cancer prevention vaccines include the HPV vaccine, which can prevent cervical, anal, and oropharyngeal cancers, and the hepatitis B vaccine, which can prevent liver cancer.

B. Secondary prevention strategies

Screening and early detection

Screening and early detection aim to detect cancer at an early stage when it is more treatable. Cancer screening tests can identify cancer before symptoms develop. Examples of cancer screening tests include mammography for breast cancer, colonoscopy for colorectal cancer, and Pap smear for cervical cancer.

Chemoprevention

Chemoprevention involves the use of drugs or other agents to prevent the development of cancer. Chemoprevention can be used for individuals at high risk of developing certain types of cancer. Examples of chemopreventive agents include tamoxifen and raloxifene, which can reduce the risk of breast cancer in high-risk women, and aspirin, which can reduce the risk of colorectal cancer.

Surgical prevention

Surgical prevention involves the removal of tissue that is at high risk of developing into cancer. Prophylactic surgery can be used for individuals with a high risk of developing certain types of cancer, such as a prophylactic mastectomy for women at high risk of developing breast cancer due to an inherited genetic mutation.

V. Cancer treatment and management

A. Overview of cancer treatment modalities

Cancer treatment typically involves a combination of different modalities that are tailored to the patient's specific type and stage of cancer. The four main cancer treatment modalities are surgery, radiation therapy, chemotherapy, and immunotherapy.

Surgery

Surgery involves the physical removal of cancerous tissue from the body. It is often the first treatment option for localized cancers and can be curative in some cases. Depending on the type and stage of cancer, surgery can be performed using traditional open techniques or minimally invasive procedures, such as laparoscopy or robot-assisted surgery.

Radiation therapy

Radiation therapy uses high-energy radiation to kill cancer cells by damaging their DNA. Radiation therapy can be delivered externally, using a machine outside the body, or internally, by placing a radioactive source inside the body near the cancer cells. Radiation therapy is often used in combination with other treatment modalities, such as surgery or chemotherapy.

Chemotherapy

Chemotherapy involves the use of drugs to kill cancer cells or prevent them from dividing. Chemotherapy drugs can be administered orally, intravenously, or topically, depending on the type of cancer being treated. Chemotherapy can be used as the primary treatment for some cancers or in combination with other modalities.

Immunotherapy

Immunotherapy is a newer cancer treatment modality that works by stimulating the body's immune system to attack cancer cells. Immunotherapy drugs target specific proteins on the surface of cancer cells or inhibit immune system checkpoints that prevent the immune system from attacking cancer cells.

B. Multidisciplinary cancer care

Multidisciplinary cancer care involves a team of healthcare professionals, including oncologists, surgeons, radiation therapists, nurses, and other specialists, who work together to develop a comprehensive treatment plan for each patient. Multidisciplinary cancer care can improve treatment outcomes and quality of life for patients by providing coordinated care that addresses all aspects of cancer treatment and management.

C. Survivorship and palliative care

Survivorship care focuses on the long-term management of cancer survivors, including monitoring for recurrence, managing treatment-related side effects, and promoting overall health and wellness. Palliative care is a type of supportive care that focuses on improving the quality of life for patients with advanced or terminal cancer by managing symptoms and providing emotional and spiritual support for patients and their families. Palliative care can be provided alongside curative treatment or as the primary focus of care for patients with advanced cancer.

Summary of keypoints

Cancer is a complex and multifactorial disease that poses a significant public health concern worldwide. Risk factors for cancer include environmental, behavioral, and genetic factors, and strategies for cancer prevention and control include primary and secondary prevention measures, early detection and screening, and various treatment modalities. Cancer treatment typically involves a multidisciplinary approach that includes surgery, radiation therapy, chemotherapy, and immunotherapy, and survivorship and palliative care are important aspects of cancer management. Overall, a comprehensive approach to cancer prevention, detection, and treatment is necessary to improve cancer outcomes and reduce the burden of this disease on individuals and society as a whole.

Drug addiction-drug substance abuse

I. Introduction

A. Definition of drug addiction and substance abuse:

Drug addiction, also known as substance use disorder, is a chronic, relapsing disorder characterized by compulsive drug seeking and use despite the harmful consequences. Substance abuse is the misuse of any substance that alters the normal functioning of the body, such as alcohol, tobacco, prescription drugs, and illegal drugs. B. Overview of the prevalence and impact of drug addiction and substance abuse worldwide: According to the World Health Organization (WHO), an estimated 35 million people worldwide suffer from drug use disorders. The impact of drug addiction and substance abuse is far-reaching, affecting not only the individual, but also their families, communities, and society as a whole. C. Importance of drug addiction and substance abuse as a public health concern: Drug addiction and substance abuse are major public health concerns due to their impact on physical and mental health, social functioning, and economic productivity. The burden of drug addiction and substance abuse falls heavily on healthcare systems and can result in increased healthcare costs, loss of productivity, and reduced quality of life. D. Goals of drug addiction prevention and control: The goals of drug addiction prevention and control are to reduce the incidence and prevalence of drug addiction and substance abuse, minimize the harm associated with drug use, and improve the overall health and well-being of individuals and society.

II. Types of Drugs

A. Depressants: Depressants are drugs that slow down the central nervous system, resulting in a range of effects from relaxation and sedation to unconsciousness and death. They include alcohol, benzodiazepines, barbiturates, and sleep aids. Depressant drugs are often misused for their calming and stress-relieving effects. Overuse or abuse of depressant drugs can lead to physical dependence, addiction, and fatal overdose.

B. Stimulants: Stimulants are drugs that increase activity in the central nervous system, leading to increased alertness, attention, and energy. They include cocaine, amphetamines, caffeine, and nicotine. Stimulant drugs are often misused for their euphoric and performance-enhancing effects. Overuse or abuse of stimulant drugs can lead to addiction, heart problems, seizures, and mental health problems such as anxiety and psychosis.

C. Hallucinogens:

Hallucinogens are drugs that alter perception, mood, and thought processes. They include LSD, psilocybin (magic mushrooms), and mescaline (peyote). Hallucinogenic drugs are often misused for their mind-altering and spiritual effects. Overuse or abuse of hallucinogenic drugs can lead to flashbacks, psychosis, and suicidal behavior.

D. Opioids: Opioids are drugs that are derived from opium or synthetically produced to mimic opium's effects on the body. They include prescription painkillers such as oxycodone and hydrocodone, as well as illegal drugs such as heroin and fentanyl. Opioid drugs are often misused for their pain-relieving and euphoric effects. Overuse or abuse of opioid drugs can lead to physical dependence, addiction, and fatal overdose.

Overall, drug addiction and substance abuse can have significant negative consequences for individuals and society. It is important to understand the types of drugs and their effects in order to prevent and treat drug addiction and substance abuse effectively.

III. Risk Factors for Drug Addiction and Substance Abuse

A. Biological factors

Several biological factors can increase the risk of drug addiction and substance abuse. These include genetics, gender, age, and underlying medical and mental health conditions. Genetic factors can affect an individual's susceptibility to drug addiction and substance abuse. Some people may inherit genetic variations that make them more prone to addiction. Gender can also play a role in drug addiction and substance abuse, as males are more likely to develop drug addiction than females. Age can also influence the risk of drug addiction and substance abuse, with younger individuals being more vulnerable to these conditions. Finally, underlying medical and mental health conditions, such as chronic pain, depression, and anxiety, can increase the risk of drug addiction and substance abuse.

B. Environmental factors

Environmental factors can also contribute to the development of drug addiction and substance abuse. These include exposure to drugs, peer pressure, access to drugs, socioeconomic status, and family dynamics. Exposure to drugs, whether through experimentation or prescription, can increase the likelihood of developing drug addiction and substance abuse. Peer pressure can also play a role, as individuals may feel pressured to use drugs to fit in with a particular social group. Access to drugs can also contribute to drug addiction and substance abuse, as individuals may be more likely to use drugs if they are readily available. Socioeconomic status can also influence the risk of drug addiction and substance abuse, as individuals from lower socioeconomic backgrounds may face more stressors and challenges that increase their susceptibility to these conditions. Finally, family dynamics, including family history of drug addiction, can contribute to drug addiction and substance abuse.

C. Behavioral factors

Several behavioral factors can also increase the risk of drug addiction and substance abuse. These include poor impulse control, thrill-seeking behavior, lack of coping skills, and social isolation. Poor impulse control can make it difficult for individuals to resist the temptation to use drugs, while thrill-seeking behavior may lead individuals to use drugs for the excitement or novelty. Lack of coping skills can also contribute to drug addiction and substance abuse, as individuals may turn to drugs to manage stress or emotional pain. Finally, social isolation can increase the risk of drug addiction and substance abuse, as individuals may turn to drugs as a way to alleviate loneliness or boredom.

IV. Impact of Substance Abuse

A. Physical health consequences

Substance abuse can have a significant impact on an individual's physical health. Chronic diseases such as liver disease, cardiovascular disease, and cancer can develop due to long-term substance abuse. In addition, substance abuse can weaken the immune system, making individuals more susceptible to infectious diseases such as HIV/AIDS and hepatitis.

One of the most severe physical consequences of substance abuse is overdose. An overdose occurs when an individual takes a toxic amount of a substance, resulting in a potentially fatal reaction. Overdoses can occur with any substance, including opioids, stimulants, and depressants.

B. Mental health consequences

Substance abuse can also have a significant impact on an individual's mental health. Substance-induced disorders can occur when an individual experiences mental health symptoms as a result of substance abuse. For example, individuals who abuse stimulants may experience symptoms such as paranoia and hallucinations.

In addition, substance abuse can contribute to the development of co-occurring mental health disorders such as depression, anxiety, and bipolar disorder. These conditions can be challenging to treat, as the substance abuse and mental health disorders can often exacerbate one another.

C. Social and economic consequences

Substance abuse can also have significant social and economic consequences. Relationship problems can develop due to substance abuse, as individuals may prioritize their drug use over their personal relationships. Additionally, substance abuse can lead to financial difficulties, as individuals may spend large amounts of money on drugs and may struggle to maintain employment.

Substance abuse can also lead to legal issues, as individuals may engage in criminal behavior to obtain drugs or may be arrested for drug possession. Legal issues can lead to further financial difficulties and can limit an individual's future opportunities for employment and education.

Substance abuse can have a significant impact on an individual's physical health, mental health, and social and economic well-being. It is essential to address substance abuse through prevention, early intervention, and effective treatment.

VI. Prevention of Drug Addiction and Substance Abuse

A. Primary prevention strategies

Education and awareness

Education and awareness programs are an essential component of primary prevention strategies. These programs aim to inform the public about the risks and consequences of drug addiction and substance abuse. Effective education and awareness programs should target all age groups and be delivered through various channels, such as schools, media, and community-based organizations. In addition, education and awareness programs should focus on reducing the stigma associated with drug addiction and substance abuse.

Public policies and regulations

Public policies and regulations can be effective in preventing and controlling drug addiction and substance abuse. Policies that limit the availability and accessibility of drugs can be effective in reducing drug use. For example, laws that restrict the sale of certain drugs, such as opioids, can be effective in preventing misuse and abuse of these drugs. Regulations that control the prescription and dispensing of drugs can also be effective in reducing drug abuse.

Community-based programs

Community-based programs can be effective in preventing and controlling drug addiction and substance abuse. These programs should be designed to meet the specific needs of the community and be delivered by trained professionals. Examples of community-based programs include peer support groups, community outreach programs, and substance abuse prevention coalitions.

B. Secondary prevention strategies

Early intervention and treatment

Early intervention and treatment can be effective in preventing drug addiction and substance abuse from progressing to a more severe condition. Early intervention involves identifying and addressing substance abuse problems as soon as they are detected. Treatment may involve medication-assisted treatment, behavioral therapies, or a combination of both.

Medication-assisted treatment

Medication-assisted treatment involves using medication to help manage withdrawal symptoms and reduce drug cravings. Medications used in medication-assisted treatment include methadone, buprenorphine, and naltrexone. This treatment approach is effective for opioid addiction.

Behavioral therapies

Behavioral therapies aim to modify an individual's behavior and teach them coping skills to manage stress and other triggers that may lead to substance abuse. Examples of behavioral therapies include cognitive-behavioral therapy, motivational interviewing, and contingency management.

C. Tertiary prevention strategies

Recovery support services

Recovery support services are designed to help individuals maintain their recovery from drug addiction and substance abuse. Examples of recovery support services include peer support groups, case management, and employment services.

Aftercare and relapse prevention

Aftercare and relapse prevention are essential components of tertiary prevention strategies. Aftercare involves providing ongoing support and treatment after an individual completes a treatment program. Relapse prevention involves teaching individuals strategies to avoid relapse and address any issues that may arise during recovery.

Harm reduction strategies

Harm reduction strategies aim to reduce the negative consequences associated with drug addiction and substance abuse. Examples of harm reduction strategies include needle exchange programs, overdose prevention education, and safe injection sites. These strategies do not aim to promote drug use but rather to reduce the harm associated with drug use.

VI

National Health Intervention Programe for Mother and Child

I. Introduction

A. Overview of the National Health Intervention Program for Mother and Child

The National Health Intervention Program for Mother and Child (NHIPMC) is a comprehensive program launched by the Government of India to provide maternal and child health services across the country. The program aims to reduce maternal and child mortality, promote health and nutrition among mothers and children, and enhance access to quality healthcare services for both.

B. Need for a national program for maternal and child health

Maternal and child health is a critical area that requires special attention in a country like India, where a significant proportion of the population lives in poverty and faces multiple health challenges. According to the World Health Organization (WHO), India accounts for 17% of global maternal deaths and 22% of global child deaths. The NHIPMC was launched to address these challenges and improve maternal and child health outcomes in the country.

C. Objectives of the National Health Intervention Program

- The National Health Intervention Program for Mother and Child has the following objectives:
- To reduce maternal and child mortality rates
- To improve access to and utilization of maternal and child health services
- To promote health and nutrition among mothers and children
- To enhance the quality of maternal and child health services
- To strengthen health systems and improve health infrastructure
- To promote community participation in maternal and child health programs

Components of the National Health Intervention Program for Mother and Child:

A. Maternal health services:

Antenatal care: The program aims to provide antenatal care to all pregnant women in the country, including screening and management of pregnancy-related complications and referral services where necessary.

Delivery care: The program promotes safe delivery practices and aims to ensure that all deliveries take place in a health facility with skilled birth attendants.

Postnatal care: The program aims to provide postnatal care to all mothers and newborns, including screening for and management of postpartum complications, counseling on infant care, and family planning services.

B. Child health services:

Immunization services: The program provides a range of vaccines to prevent common childhood illnesses, including polio, measles, and diphtheria. It aims to achieve high coverage rates and ensure that all children receive the recommended vaccines.

Nutrition services: The program provides nutrition education and counseling to parents and caregivers, and aims to prevent and manage malnutrition in children under five years of age.

Treatment of common childhood illnesses: The program aims to provide prompt and appropriate treatment to children with common illnesses such as diarrhea, pneumonia, and malaria.

C. Family planning and reproductive health services:

The program provides family planning services and aims to increase access to modern contraceptives, reduce maternal mortality and morbidity, and promote reproductive health.

D. Health education and behavior change communication:

The program includes health education and behavior change communication activities to promote healthy behaviors among mothers and caregivers, increase awareness of maternal and child health issues, and improve health-seeking behaviors. These activities may include community mobilization, media campaigns, and interpersonal communication with health providers.

The National Health Intervention Program for Mother and Child aims to provide comprehensive and integrated services to improve the health and well-being of mothers and children in India.

II. Services Provided by the National Health Intervention Program

A. Antenatal care services: Antenatal care (ANC) is a crucial component of the National Health Intervention Program, and aims to ensure the health of both the mother and the developing fetus. ANC services are typically provided by trained healthcare professionals and may include physical exams, ultrasounds, blood tests, and other diagnostic tests to identify and manage potential pregnancy complications.

B. Delivery and postnatal care services: Delivery and postnatal care services are essential for ensuring a safe and healthy childbirth experience for both the mother and newborn. These services may include skilled attendance during delivery, postpartum care, breastfeeding support, and screening for potential complications such as postpartum depression.

C. Immunization services for children: Immunization services are a critical component of the National Health Intervention Program and aim to protect children from vaccine-preventable diseases such as measles, polio, and pneumonia. These services are typically provided at health centers, hospitals, and outreach sites, and may include routine vaccinations, catch-up vaccinations, and special immunization drives.

D. Nutrition services for mothers and children: Nutrition services play an important role in promoting the health and well-being of mothers and children. These services may include the promotion of exclusive breastfeeding, education on appropriate complementary feeding practices, micronutrient supplementation, and treatment of malnutrition.

E. Treatment of common childhood illnesses: The National Health Intervention Program also provides treatment for common childhood illnesses such as diarrhea, pneumonia, and malaria. These services may include diagnosis and treatment with antibiotics, antimalarials, or other appropriate medications.

F. Family planning and reproductive health services: Family planning and reproductive health services are important components of the National Health Intervention Program and aim to provide women and families with the information and tools they need to make informed decisions about their reproductive health. These services may include counseling on family planning methods, provision of contraceptives, and treatment of reproductive health conditions.

G. Health education and behavior change communication: Health education and behavior change communication are crucial components of the National Health Intervention Program and aim to promote healthy behaviors and prevent disease through education and awareness-raising activities. These activities may include community health talks, radio broadcasts, or mass media campaigns on topics such as handwashing, hygiene, and nutrition.

IV. Financial Support Provided by the National Health Intervention Program

A. Budget allocation: The National Health Intervention Program for Mother and Child is funded by the Government of India, which allocates funds in its annual budget for the Ministry of Health and Family Welfare. The allocation of funds varies from year to year depending on the government's priorities and the needs of the program.

B. Funding for maternal and child health activities: The government provides funding for a range of maternal and child health activities, including the provision of antenatal, delivery, and postnatal care services, immunization services, nutrition services, treatment of common childhood illnesses, family planning and reproductive health services, and health education and behavior change communication.

C. Grants and schemes for institutions and individuals providing maternal and child health services: The government also provides grants and schemes to institutions and individuals providing maternal and child health services.

Janani Suraksha Yojana (JSY): This scheme provides financial assistance to pregnant women below the poverty line for institutional delivery, including the cost of transportation.

Pradhan Mantri Matru Vandana Yojana (PMMVY): This scheme provides financial assistance to pregnant and lactating mothers for their first live birth, with the aim of reducing maternal and neonatal mortality.

Integrated Child Development Services (ICDS): This scheme aims to provide a package of services, including nutrition, health, and education, to children under the age of 6 years and pregnant and lactating women.

National Iron Plus Initiative (NIPI): This scheme aims to prevent and control iron-deficiency anemia among pregnant and adolescent girls through the provision of iron and folic acid supplements.

National Rural Health Mission (NRHM): This scheme aims to improve the availability and accessibility of quality healthcare services in rural areas, including maternal and child health services.

Rashtriya Bal Swasthya Karyakram (RBSK): This scheme aims to provide early screening, detection, and management of birth defects, developmental delays, and common childhood illnesses among children up to 18 years of age.

Mission Indradhanush: This scheme aims to provide full immunization coverage to all children by 2020, including those who are hard to reach or have been left out of the routine immunization program

V. Achievements of the National Health Intervention Program

A. Reduction in maternal and child mortality rates

The National Family Health Survey (NFHS) reports a decline in India's maternal mortality rate from 178 per 100,000 live births in 2010 to 113 per 100,000 live births in 2016.

The infant mortality rate has declined from 50 per 1000 live births in 2016 to 32 per 1000 live births in 2019.

B. Increased coverage and accessibility of maternal and child health services

The Janani Shishu Suraksha Karyakram (JSSK) scheme launched in 2011 provides free services to all pregnant women and sick newborns accessing public health institutions.

The Pradhan Mantri Surakshit Matritva Abhiyan (PMSMA) launched in 2016 provides free antenatal check-ups to pregnant women on the 9th of every month at all government health facilities.

The National Health Mission has increased the number of accredited social health activists (ASHAs) who act as a bridge between the community and the health system.

C. Improved maternal and child health outcomes

The proportion of institutional deliveries has increased from 38.7% in 2005 to 79.9% in 2019.

The proportion of children under 5 years who are stunted has declined from 48% in 2006 to 34.7% in 2020.

D. Enhanced training and capacity building for health professionals

The Government of India has launched various initiatives such as the LaQshya program for improving the quality of maternal and newborn care and the Integrated Management of Neonatal and Childhood Illness (IMNCI) program for training healthcare providers in the diagnosis and management of common childhood illnesses.

E. Other notable achievements

The Mission Indradhanush launched in 2014 has increased immunization coverage in high priority districts of India.

The Beti Bachao Beti Padhao scheme launched in 2015 aims to address the declining child sex ratio and promote the education of girls.

VII

National Health Programs

Human Immunodeficiency Virus (HIV) is a virus that attacks and weakens the immune system, leaving the body vulnerable to infections and other diseases. Acquired Immunodeficiency Syndrome (AIDS) is the most advanced stage of HIV infection, characterized by severe immune deficiency and the presence of certain infections or cancers. HIV is transmitted through the exchange of bodily fluids, such as blood, semen, vaginal fluids, and breast milk. It can be spread through sexual contact, sharing needles or syringes, mother-to-child transmission during pregnancy, childbirth, or breastfeeding, and exposure to infected blood.

Global and Indian statistics on HIV/AIDS

According to the Joint United Nations Programme on HIV/AIDS (UNAIDS), there were approximately 38 million people living with HIV/AIDS globally in 2019. Of these, around 1.7 million were newly infected with HIV and 690,000 died from AIDS-related illnesses. India has the third-highest number of people living with HIV/AIDS in the world, with an estimated 2.4 million people affected. In 2019, there were around 69,000 new HIV infections in India, and around

56,000 deaths due to AIDS-related illnesses. The majority of people living with HIV/AIDS in India are concentrated in high-risk groups, including homosexuals, transgender individuals, people who inject drugs, and sex workers. However, HIV/AIDS also affects the general population, with a significant number of women and children also affected.

Importance of controlling HIV/AIDS Controlling the spread of HIV/AIDS is crucial for both individual and public health. HIV/ AIDS is a chronic and life-threatening condition that can significantly reduce the quality of life for those infected. It also has significant economic and social impacts, particularly in low-income countries where resources for healthcare and social services are limited. Additionally, HIV/AIDS can have a devastating impact on families and communities, particularly in cases of mother-to-child transmission or the loss of breadwinners. By controlling HIV/AIDS, individuals can live longer and healthier lives, and communities can thrive economically and socially. Controlling HIV/AIDS also requires a collective effort from individuals, communities, healthcare providers, and policymakers to prevent new infections and provide access to treatment and care.

The HIV/AIDS Control Program

The HIV/AIDS Control Program in India was launched in 1992 by the National AIDS Control Organization (NACO) under the Ministry of Health and Family Welfare. The program was initiated in response to the growing HIV/AIDS epidemic in India and aimed to reduce the spread of HIV, improve access to treatment and care, and address the social and economic impact of the disease. The program has since gone through several phases, with the current phase (Phase IV) running from 2017 to 2020, and focuses on four key strategic areas: prevention, testing and treatment, care and support, and enabling environment.

Objectives and goals

The primary objective of the HIV/AIDS Control Program in India is to reduce the spread of HIV/AIDS and improve the quality of life of those affected. The program has several goals, including:

To reduce new HIV infections by 75% by 2020

To provide antiretroviral therapy (ART) to at least 90% of people living with HIV/AIDS

To reduce AIDS-related deaths by 75% by 2020

To eliminate mother-to-child transmission of HIV by 2020

To empower and protect key populations, such as homosexuals, transgender individuals, people who inject drugs, and sex workers

Target population and coverage

The HIV/AIDS Control Program in India targets a range of population groups, including high-risk groups and the general population. The program focuses on providing prevention, testing, and treatment services to these groups, as well as addressing the social and economic factors that contribute to HIV/AIDS. The high-risk groups targeted by the program include homosexuals, transgender individuals, people who inject drugs, and sex workers. The program also provides services to women and children affected by HIV/AIDS, particularly those who are at risk of mother-to-child transmission.

Strategies and interventions

The HIV/AIDS Control Program in India employs a range of strategies and interventions to reduce the spread of HIV/AIDS and improve access to treatment and care. These include:

Prevention campaigns: The program uses various channels, such as mass media, community outreach, and social marketing, to promote HIV/AIDS prevention messages and encourage behavior change.

Condom distribution: The program provides free condoms to high-risk groups and promotes their use as an effective way to prevent HIV transmission.

HIV testing and counseling: The program offers free and confidential HIV testing and counseling services to encourage early detection and treatment of HIV/AIDS.

Antiretroviral treatment (ART): The program provides free ART to those living with HIV/AIDS and aims to increase access to treatment through decentralization and integration with primary healthcare services.

Prevention of mother-to-child transmission: The program provides antiretroviral drugs to pregnant women living with HIV/AIDS to prevent transmission to their babies.

Empowerment of key populations: The program works to empower and protect key populations, such as homosexuals, transgender individuals, people who inject drugs, and sex workers, by providing legal and social support, as well as access to health services.

Overall, the HIV/AIDS Control Program in India is a comprehensive and integrated approach that focuses on prevention, testing and treatment, care and support, and addressing social and economic factors that contribute to HIV/AIDS. The program has made significant progress in reducing the spread of HIV/AIDS and improving access to treatment and care, but there are still challenges to be addressed, particularly in reaching marginalized and remote populations.

Achievements of the HIV/AIDS Control Program in India

Reduction in new HIV infections

The HIV/AIDS Control Program in India has made significant progress in reducing new HIV infections in the country. According to NACO, the number of new HIV infections in India declined by approximately 37% between 2010 and 2019, from 120,000 to 75,000. This reduction can be attributed to various prevention strategies implemented by the program, such as condom distribution, HIV testing and counseling, and awareness campaigns. The program has also focused on reaching high-risk groups, such as homosexuals, transgender individuals, people who inject drugs, and sex workers, who are at a higher risk of HIV infection.

Improvement in access to treatment and care

The HIV/AIDS Control Program in India has significantly improved access to treatment and care for those living with HIV/AIDS. The program provides free ART to those in need and has decentralized treatment services to make them more accessible to those in remote and rural areas. As a result, the number of people living with HIV who are on ART has increased from 1.1 million in 2010 to 2.2 million in 2019, according to NACO. This has led to a reduction in AIDS-related deaths in India, with approximately 55% fewer deaths in 2019 than in 2010.

Empowerment of key populations

The HIV/AIDS Control Program in India has also focused on empowering key populations, such as homosexuals, transgender individuals, people who inject drugs, and sex workers, who are often marginalized and face stigma and discrimination. The program provides legal and social support to these groups and encourages their involvement in HIV/AIDS prevention and treatment efforts. For example, the program has established community-based organizations to provide peer support and information to high-risk groups, as well as to advocate for their rights and access to healthcare services. Additionally, the program has worked with law enforcement agencies to reduce harassment and violence against these groups.

Overall, the achievements of the HIV/AIDS Control Program in India are significant, and the program has contributed to a reduction in the burden of HIV/AIDS in the country. However, there are still challenges to be addressed, particularly in reaching marginalized and remote populations, and there is a need for sustained efforts to continue progress towards ending the HIV/AIDS epidemic in India.

Challenges in HIV/AIDS Control Program in India

Despite the progress made by the HIV/AIDS Control Program in India, there are still several challenges that need to be addressed to continue the fight against HIV/AIDS in the country. Some of these challenges are:

Stigma and discrimination

Stigma and discrimination continue to be major barriers in the HIV/AIDS Control Program in India. People living with HIV/AIDS face discrimination in many areas of life, including healthcare, education, employment, and social relationships. This often leads to reluctance to seek testing, treatment, and care, and can result in poor health outcomes. The program needs to continue efforts to reduce stigma and discrimination and promote acceptance and inclusion of people living with HIV/AIDS.

Limited funding and resources

The HIV/AIDS Control Program in India relies heavily on funding from international donors, such as the Global Fund and the US President's Emergency Plan for AIDS Relief (PEPFAR). However, these funds are limited and may not be sustainable in the long term. There is a need for increased domestic funding and resources for the program to continue its efforts towards controlling HIV/AIDS in the country.

Access to care in remote areas

Access to care remains a challenge in remote and rural areas of India. Many people living with HIV/AIDS live in these areas and may not have access to healthcare facilities that provide HIV testing, treatment, and care. The program needs to develop strategies to improve access to care in these areas, such as mobile clinics, community-based organizations,and telemedicine services. Additionally, efforts should be made to train and equip healthcare providers in these areas to effectively diagnose and treat HIV/AIDS.

Co-infection with other diseases

Co-infection with other diseases, such as tuberculosis and hepatitis, is a common challenge faced by people living with HIV/AIDS in India. This can complicate the management and treatment of HIV/AIDS, as well as increase the risk of poor health outcomes. The program needs to integrate screening and treatment for co-infections into its services to improve the health outcomes of people living with HIV/AIDS.

The HIV/AIDS Control Program in India has made significant progress in reducing the burden of HIV/AIDS in the country. However, there are still challenges that need to be addressed to continue this progress. The program needs to continue efforts to reduce stigma and discrimination, increase domestic funding and resources, improve access to care in remote areas, and integrate screening and treatment for co-infections into its services. By addressing these challenges, the program can continue to make progress towards ending the HIV/AIDS epidemic in India.

ꟹ

T.B

Introduction

Tuberculosis (TB) is an infectious disease caused by the bacterium Mycobacterium tuberculosis. It primarily affects the lungs but can also affect other parts of the body such as the brain, spine, and kidneys. TB is transmitted from person to person through the air when an infected person coughs, sneezes, or talks.

TB is a major public health problem worldwide, with an estimated 10 million cases and 1.4 million deaths in 2019, according to the World Health Organization (WHO). TB is also one of the top 10 causes of death globally and the leading cause of death from a single infectious agent.

TB situation in India:

India has the highest burden of TB in the world, with an estimated 2.7 million cases in 2019, which accounts for approximately one-quarter of the global TB burden. TB is prevalent in both urban and rural areas and affects people of all ages and genders.

The high burden of TB in India is due to various factors such as poverty, overcrowding, malnutrition, co-infection with HIV, and the emergence of drug-resistant strains of TB. The burden of TB in India is also compounded by limited resources and weak health systems, which have resulted in inadequate TB control and management.

The National Tuberculosis Elimination Program (NTEP)

The National Tuberculosis Elimination Program (NTEP) is a comprehensive TB control program implemented by the Government of India, with the goal of reducing the burden of TB in the country. The program was initially launched as the Revised National Tuberculosis Control Program (RNTCP) in 1997, and was later renamed as NTEP in 2018.

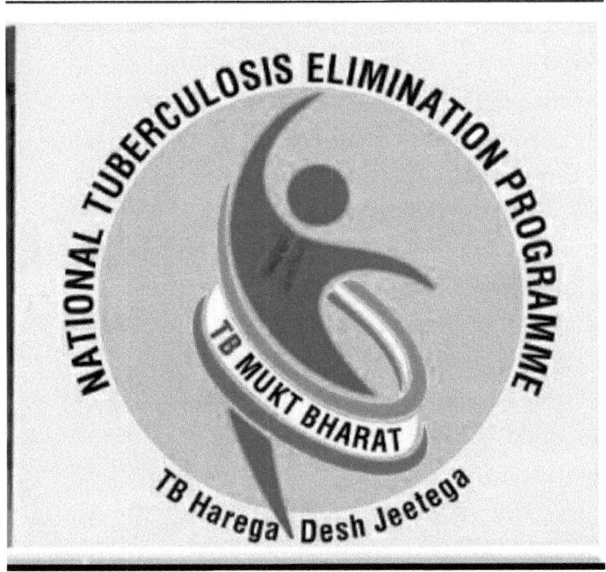

The emblem of the National Tuberculosis Elimination Program (NTEP) in India features a stylized image of a human lung, with a red ribbon wrapped around it. The red ribbon is a symbol of awareness and support for people living with TB, and is often used in campaigns to raise awareness about the disease.The image of the lung represents the focus of the NTEP on improving lung health and preventing TB, which primarily affects the lungs.The NTEP emblem is often used in official communications and documents related to the program, and is a visual representation of the program's mission to eliminate TB in India. It serves as a reminder of the importance of TB control efforts and the ongoing work that is needed to achieve a TB-free India.

History of NTEP

The National Tuberculosis Elimination Program (NTEP) in India has its origins in the Revised National Tuberculosis Control Program (RNTCP), which was launched in 1997. At that time, the burden of tuberculosis (TB) in India was very high, with an estimated 2.5 million new cases and 500,000 deaths annually.

The RNTCP was launched as a partnership between the Government of India and the World Health Organization (WHO), with the goal of achieving universal access to TB care services and reducing the morbidity and mortality due to TB in the country. The program was implemented in a phased manner, starting with pilot projects in selected areas, and gradually expanding to cover the entire country.

The RNTCP introduced several innovative strategies for TB control, including the use of the Directly Observed Treatment Short-course (DOTS) strategy, which involved the use of a standardized treatment regimen and direct observation of treatment by a healthcare worker or trained community member. The program also promoted public-private partnerships, to engage private healthcare providers in TB control efforts.

Over the years, the RNTCP made significant progress in TB control, with improved case detection rates and treatment success rates. The program was also successful in introducing new diagnostic tools, such as the GeneXpert MTB/RIF assay, which improved the accuracy and speed of TB diagnosis.

In 2018, the RNTCP was renamed as the National Tuberculosis Elimination Program (NTEP), to reflect the program's goal of eliminating TB from India by 2025. The NTEP continues to implement the DOTS strategy and other innovative strategies for TB control, and has scaled up efforts to address the challenges of drug-resistant TB and other forms of TB. The program is also working towards improving public awareness and reducing stigma associated with TB, to ensure that all TB patients receive timely and effective treatment.

Objectives of NTEP

NTEP has several key objectives

1. Achieving and maintaining universal access to TB care services, including diagnosis and treatment.
2. Reducing the morbidity and mortality due to TB.
3. Preventing the spread of TB through prompt diagnosis and treatment of active TB cases.
4. Addressing the challenges of drug-resistant TB and other forms of TB.
5. Promoting research and innovation in TB diagnosis, treatment, and prevention.

To achieve these objectives, NTEP has implemented several strategies

1. Universal access to quality-assured diagnosis and treatment for all TB patients, free of cost.
2. Use of the DOTS strategy for TB treatment, which includes intensive and continuation phases, and directly observed treatment by a healthcare worker or a trained community member.
3. Promotion of public-private mix (PPM) models, to engage private healthcare providers in TB control efforts.
4. Implementation of infection control measures in healthcare facilities to prevent the transmission of TB.
5. Provision of counseling and social support to TB patients and their families.
6. Use of molecular diagnostics, such as the GeneXpert MTB/RIF assay, to improve the accuracy and speed of TB diagnosis.

7. Scaling up efforts to detect and treat drug-resistant TB, including the use of second-line anti-TB drugs.

Success of NTEP

The National Tuberculosis Elimination Program (NTEP) in India has made significant progress in the fight against tuberculosis (TB) over the years. Here are some of the key successes of the program:

Improved case detection: The NTEP has increased the detection of TB cases through a variety of measures, including the use of sensitive diagnostic tests like the GeneXpert MTB/RIF assay, and active case finding through community-based initiatives. As a result, the program has been able to identify more TB cases than ever before, which is crucial for effective treatment and prevention of TB.

Increased treatment success: The NTEP has achieved high rates of treatment success for TB patients, with the most recent data showing a success rate of over 85%. This is due in part to the use of the Directly Observed Treatment Short-course (DOTS) strategy, which ensures that patients receive the full course of treatment under the supervision of a healthcare worker or trained community member.

Expansion of services: The NTEP has expanded access to TB care services across the country, including in remote and difficult-to-reach areas. This has been achieved through the establishment of TB diagnostic and treatment centers, and the use of mobile clinics and other innovative approaches to deliver TB care services.

Reduction in TB-related deaths: The NTEP has contributed to a significant reduction in the number of TB-related deaths in India. According to the World Health Organization (WHO), TB mortality in India has decreased by about 50% since 1990, which is a testament to the effectiveness of the NTEP.

Adoption of new tools and technologies: The NTEP has been at the forefront of adopting new tools and technologies for TB diagnosis and treatment. For example, the program was one of the first in the world to introduce the GeneXpert MTB/RIF assay, which is a highly sensitive diagnostic test that can detect TB and drug-resistant TB in a matter of hours.

The NTEP has been successful in improving TB control in India, and has set the country on a path towards TB elimination. However, there is still much work to be done, particularly in addressing the challenges of drug-resistant TB and improving access to TB care services for vulnerable populations.

Functioning of NTEP

A.Case detection:

NTEP primarily relies on passive case detection. The program relies on healthcare providers and private practitioners to identify and refer TB patients to the nearest government-run health facility for diagnosis and treatment. NTEP also conducts active case finding in high-risk populations such as slum dwellers, migrant workers, and people living with HIV.

B.Diagnosis and treatment:

NTEP provides free diagnosis and treatment for TB. The program uses a combination of diagnostic methods, including sputum microscopy, chest x-rays, and molecular tests. The program follows the WHO-recommended Directly Observed Treatment, Short-course (DOTS) strategy, which involves a combination of four first-line drugs administered under the supervision of a healthcare worker. The program also provides treatment for drug-resistant TB.

C.Patient support and care:

NTEP provides comprehensive patient support and care. The program provides nutritional support, psychosocial support, and financial assistance to TB patients and their families. It also provides adherence support to patients to ensure that they complete their treatment.

D.Monitoring and evaluation:

NTEP has a robust monitoring and evaluation system in place to track program performance and outcomes. The program uses an electronic reporting system to collect data on TB cases and treatment outcomes from health facilities across the country. The program also conducts regular program reviews and evaluations to identify areas for improvement.

E.Partnership and collaboration:

NTEP is implemented in partnership with various stakeholders, including state governments, non-governmental organizations, private healthcare providers, and community-based organizations. The program also collaborates with other government programs such as the National AIDS Control Program (NACP) and the National Rural Health Mission (NRHM) to strengthen TB control efforts.

VII.Molecular tests For diagnosis

There are several molecular tests used for the diagnosis of tuberculosis (TB), including:

GeneXpert MTB/RIF assay: This is a highly sensitive and specific test that can detect both Mycobacterium tuberculosis (MTB) and rifampicin resistance directly from sputum samples.

Line probe assays: These tests are similar to the GeneXpert assay and can detect MTB and rifampicin resistance from sputum samples. Examples include the Hain GenoType MTBDRplus and the Abbott RealTime MTB RIF/INH.

Loop-mediated isothermal amplification (LAMP): This is a relatively new molecular test that can detect MTB DNA directly from sputum samples in a short period of time.

Nucleic acid amplification tests (NAATs): These tests use polymerase chain reaction (PCR) technology to detect MTB DNA in sputum samples. Examples include the Cobas TaqMan MTB test and the BD ProbeTec ET system.

Molecular tests are highly sensitive and specific, and can provide rapid diagnosis of TB, which is important for timely initiation of treatment and control of the disease. However, these tests can be expensive and require specialized laboratory infrastructure and trained personnel.

Directly Observed Treatment Short-Course (DOTS)

The word "DOTS" stands for Directly Observed Treatment Short-Course, which is a standardized approach to TB treatment that was developed by the World Health Organization (WHO) in the 1990s. The DOTS strategy is based on five key components, including political commitment, diagnosis through quality-assured microscopy, standardized treatment with effective anti-TB drugs, direct observation of treatment, and a robust system for monitoring and evaluation.The DOTS emblem is often used in TB-related publications, posters, and other materials to promote awareness of the DOTS strategy and its importance in TB control efforts. It is a visual representation of the global effort to combat TB, and serves as a reminder of the ongoing work that is needed to achieve a TB-free world.

Directly Observed Treatment Short-Course (DOTS) is a key component of the Revised National Tuberculosis Control Program (RNTCP) in India and is a globally recognized strategy for the management and control of tuberculosis (TB). DOTS is a comprehensive and standardized approach to the diagnosis, treatment, and monitoring of TB patients. The key components of DOTS strategy are:

A.Diagnosis of TB:

The first step in the DOTS strategy is the prompt and accurate diagnosis of TB. RNTCP relies on a combination of diagnostic methods, including sputum microscopy, chest x-rays, and molecular tests, to diagnose TB. Patients suspected of having TB are referred to the nearest RNTCP-designated microscopy centers for diagnosis.

B.Standardized treatment:

DOTS strategy ensures that all TB patients receive standardized and effective treatment. The treatment regimen for TB in the DOTS strategy involves the administration of four first-line anti-TB drugs (isoniazid, rifampicin, pyrazinamide, and ethambutol) during the intensive phase, followed by two drugs (isoniazid and rifampicin) during the continuation phase. The treatment is given for a minimum of six months under the direct supervision of a healthcare worker.

C.Directly observed treatment:

One of the critical components of DOTS strategy is the direct observation of treatment. Healthcare workers supervise the administration of anti-TB drugs to ensure that patients take the correct medication at the right time and in the right dose. The aim of directly observed treatment is to ensure that patients complete their treatment, which is essential for curing TB, preventing relapse, and reducing the risk of developing drug resistance.

E.Patient support:

DOTS strategy provides comprehensive patient support to TB patients. This includes counseling, nutritional support, and psychosocial support. The program also provides financial assistance to patients who require it.

F.Recording and monitoring:

DOTS strategy maintains a comprehensive record of TB patients, their treatment, and outcomes. All patients who receive treatment under DOTS are registered, and their progress is monitored using a standardized recording and reporting system. Regular monitoring of treatment outcomes helps in the early detection of treatment failure and relapse.

G.Collaboration and partnership:

DOTS strategy involves collaboration and partnership with various stakeholders, including the government, non-governmental organizations, private healthcare providers, and community-based organizations. The program also collaborates with other government programs, such as the National AIDS Control Program (NACP), to strengthen TB control efforts.

H.Phases of DOTS Strategy

The intensive phase and the continuation phase are two distinct phases of treatment for tuberculosis (TB) that are part of the Directly Observed Treatment Short-Course (DOTS) strategy used in the Revised National Tuberculosis Control Program (RNTCP) in India.

The intensive phase of treatment is the initial phase of TB treatment that lasts for two months. During this phase, patients receive a combination of four first-line anti-TB drugs: isoniazid, rifampicin, pyrazinamide, and ethambutol. These drugs are taken together daily under the direct supervision of a healthcare worker. The goal of the intensive phase is to rapidly reduce the number of bacteria in the patient's body, improve symptoms, and prevent the development of drug resistance.

The continuation phase of treatment is the second phase of TB treatment that begins after the intensive phase is completed. The continuation phase typically lasts for four months and involves the use of two anti-TB drugs: isoniazid and rifampicin. These drugs are also taken daily under the direct supervision of a healthcare worker. The goal of the continuation phase is to eradicate any remaining bacteria and prevent relapse.

It is important for patients to complete both the intensive and continuation phases of treatment for TB to ensure complete recovery and prevent the development of drug resistance. The use of the DOTS strategy and directly observed treatment helps to ensure that patients complete their treatment and reduces the risk of treatment failure, relapse, and drug resistance.

Challenges faced in TB control in India

A. Delayed diagnosis and treatment initiation:

Delayed diagnosis and treatment initiation remain a major challenge in TB control in India. Patients often experience long delays in seeking healthcare, and healthcare providers may not diagnose TB in a timely manner. This delay in diagnosis and treatment initiation can lead to the spread of TB in the community and increase the risk of drug-resistant TB.

B. Inadequate resources and infrastructure:

Inadequate resources and infrastructure remain a significant challenge in TB control in India. Many health facilities lack the necessary resources and equipment to diagnose and treat TB effectively. There is also a shortage of trained healthcare workers, particularly in rural areas, which can lead to poor quality of care and low treatment success rates.

C. Limited public awareness and stigma:

Limited public awareness and stigma surrounding TB are major challenges in TB control in India. Many people in India are unaware of the signs and symptoms of TB and may not seek healthcare until the disease has progressed. Stigma surrounding TB can also lead to discrimination and social isolation for TB patients, which can further discourage people from seeking healthcare.

D. Drug-resistant TB and co-infection with HIV:

Drug-resistant TB and co-infection with HIV are major challenges in TB control in India. Drug-resistant TB is more difficult and expensive to treat than drug-susceptible TB, and there are limited treatment options available in India. Co-infection with HIV also increases the risk of TB and can lead to more severe forms of TB that are more difficult to treat.

E. Weak surveillance and monitoring systems:

Weak surveillance and monitoring systems remain a significant challenge in TB control in India. There is limited data available on TB incidence and prevalence, which can make it difficult to track the progress of TB control efforts. There is also a need for better monitoring of treatment outcomes to ensure that all TB patients receive timely and effective treatment.

TB control in India faces several challenges including delayed diagnosis and treatment initiation, inadequate resources and infrastructure, limited public awareness and stigma, drug-resistant TB and co-infection with HIV, and weak surveillance and monitoring systems. Addressing these challenges will require a multi-pronged approach that involves improving healthcare infrastructure, increasing public awareness of TB, reducing stigma, and strengthening surveillance and monitoring systems.

Possible solutions to overcome challenges

Tuberculosis (TB) control in India faces several challenges, including delayed diagnosis and treatment initiation, inadequate resources and infrastructure, limited public awareness and stigma, drug-resistant TB, and weak surveillance and monitoring systems. To overcome these challenges, the following possible solutions can be implemented:

A. Strengthening the health system: There is a need to improve the quality of healthcare services for TB patients. This can be achieved by training and providing adequate resources to healthcare workers, improving the availability and quality of diagnostic tools, ensuring the availability of essential drugs, and developing effective referral and linkage systems.

B. Increasing public awareness: There is a need to increase public awareness about TB, its causes, symptoms, and treatment. This can be done through community-based interventions, mass media campaigns, and social mobilization activities. It is also important to reduce the stigma associated with TB and encourage patients to seek early diagnosis and treatment.

C. Implementing innovative strategies: Innovative strategies such as active case-finding, targeted testing, and digital health technologies can be implemented to improve TB detection and treatment outcomes. These strategies can help in reaching out to high-risk populations, improving access to care, and ensuring better patient follow-up.

D. Scaling up efforts to detect and treat drug-resistant TB: There is a need to increase efforts to detect and treat drug-resistant TB. This can be achieved by improving access to drug susceptibility testing, ensuring the availability of second-line drugs, and developing effective treatment regimens for drug-resistant TB.

E. Improving surveillance and monitoring systems: There is a need to strengthen surveillance and monitoring systems for TB to track progress, identify gaps, and make evidence-based decisions. This can be achieved by developing and implementing robust surveillance systems, using digital technologies to improve data collection and analysis, and ensuring regular monitoring and evaluation of TB control programs.

National leprosy control programme

Hansen's disease, also known as leprosy, is caused by a slow-growing bacteria called Mycobacterium leprae, and can take up to 20 years to show symptoms. The disease affects the nerves, skin, eyes, and lining of the nose, and can cause loss of sensation and injury due to lack of pain response. If left untreated, the disease can result in paralysis of hands and feet, blindness, and disfigurement. Early diagnosis and treatment can prevent disability, and once treatment is started, the person is no longer contagious. It is important to complete the full course of treatment as directed by a doctor.

The National Leprosy Eradication Programme (NLEP) was initiated by the Government of India in 1954-55 with the aim of controlling leprosy in the country. Multi-Drug Therapy (MDT) was introduced in 1982 and the NLEP was established in 1983, with a strategy focused on reducing the incidence of the disease and breaking the chain of transmission. Initially implemented in endemic districts, the programme was extended to cover all districts in the country with assistance from the World Bank from 1993-94. As part of the programme, four research and training institutes were set up under the Directorate General of Health Services, including the Central Leprosy Training and Research Institute (CLTRI) in Chengalpattu and the Regional Leprosy Training and Research Institutes (RLTRI) in Raipur, Gauripur and Aska, as well as a Training Centre in Agra under the Indian Council of Medical Research (ICMR). The programme has made significant progress in reducing the burden of leprosy in India, achieving the goal set by the National Health Policy, 2002 of eliminating leprosy as a public health problem, defined as less than one case per 10,000 population, at the national level in December 2005.

Vision of NLEP:

The vision of the NLEP is to achieve a "Leprosy-free India", while its mission is to provide quality leprosy services free of cost to all sections of the population, with easy accessibility through the integrated healthcare system, including care for disability after cure of the disease. The objectives of the programme are to reduce the prevalence rate of leprosy to less than 1/10,000 population at sub-national and district levels, to reduce the percentage of new cases with Grade II disability to less than 1 at the national level, to reduce the number of Grade II disability cases to less than 1 per million population at the national level, to achieve zero disabilities among new child cases, and to eliminate stigma and discrimination against persons affected by leprosy.

Strategies Of NLEP to achieve its objectives

1. The provision of integrated anti-leprosy services through the general health care system.
2. Early detection and complete treatment of new leprosy cases.
3. Conducting household contact surveys to identify cases early.
4. Engaging Accredited Social Health Activists (ASHAs) in the timely detection and treatment of leprosy cases.
5. Strengthening Disability Prevention and Medical Rehabilitation (DPMR) services.
6. Implementing Information, Education, and Communication (IEC) activities in the community to improve self-reporting to Primary Health Centers (PHCs) and reduce stigma.
7. Ensuring intensive monitoring and supervision at Health and Wellness Centers and Block Primary Health Centre/Community Health Centre to enhance program effectiveness.

NLEP programme components

1. Case detection and management,
2. disability prevention and medical rehabilitation (DPMR),
3. information,
4. education and communication (IEC) including behaviour change communication (BCC),
5. human resource and capacity building,
6. Programme management.

Sapna,
campaign mascot

"Sapna" is a concept (mascot) designed and developed using a common girl living in community, who will help spread awareness in thecommunity, through key IEC messages.

Salient features of the National Leprosy Eradication Programme

1. The National Leprosy Eradication Programme (NLEP) is a centrally sponsored scheme launched by the Government of India, which functions under the umbrella of the National Health Mission (NHM).
2. The programme follows a decentralized health planning approach and funds are provided to the states through State Health Societies.
3. The main focus of the NLEP is on the quality of services and sustainability of the programme.
4. Disability Prevention and Medical Rehabilitation (DPMR) is given priority, and stigma and discrimination against persons affected by leprosy is addressed as a part of the strategy.

These salient features reflect the NLEP's commitment to eradicating leprosy in India through a comprehensive and integrated approach that involves both healthcare providers and the community.

NLEP - Milestones and Initiatives

Definite Cure for Leprosy:

Multi-Drug Therapy (MDT) in 1970
WHO study group recommendation in 1982
NLEP MDT initiation in 1983

Eradication Goals:

World Health Assembly resolution in 1991
World Bank support for NLEP1 in 1993

Elimination Status:

Nationwide evaluation in 2005
Prevalence rate dropped to 0.95/10000 population
Integration with General Health Care System:
National Rural Health Mission launch in 2005
Disability Prevention and Medical Rehabilitation Guidelines:
Introduced in 2007

Inclusion of Persons Affected with Leprosy:

Advocated in XI Five Year Plan (2007-2012)
Special Leprosy Action Plan:
Adopted in XII Five Year Plan (2012)
New Initiatives:

- Active Case Detection Campaigns (ACDC) in high endemic districts
- Focused Leprosy Campaign (FLC) in low endemic districts
- ASHA Based Surveillance for Leprosy Suspects (ABSULS)
- Grade II Disability Epidemiological Investigation
- Implementation of Post Exposure Prophylaxis (PEP)
- Sparsh Leprosy Awareness Campaigns
- NIKUSTH, a real-time leprosy reporting software

External Evaluation:
Conducted by WHO in 2019
Convergence with Other Programs:

- Ayushman Bharat for leprosy screening in adults
- Rashtriya Bal Swasthya Karyakram for leprosy screening in children
- Rashtriya Kishore Swasthya Karyakaram for counseling teenagers

ACD&RS Guidelines:

Active Case Detection and Regular Surveillance (ACD&RS) guidelines rolledout in 2020

Activities conducted under NLEP:

1. **Diagnosis and treatment of leprosy**: Free of cost services for diagnosis and treatment (Multi drug therapy) are provided by all public health care facilities throughout the country. Complicated cases are referred to district hospitals for further management.

All drugs, diagnostics, and surgical/non-surgical interventions are provided free of cost to all patients of leprosy.

2. **Capacity building:** Training of general health staff is conducted every year to develop adequate skills for diagnosis and management of leprosy cases.
3. **IEC and counseling:** Intensive IEC activities are conducted to generate awareness to help reduce stigma and discrimination associated with persons affected with leprosy. Major focus is also given on interpersonal communication.
4. **Disability prevention and medical rehabilitation**: Dressing material, supportive medicines, and MCR footwear are provided to leprosy patients for prevention and management of disability. Emphasis is also being placed on correction of permanent disability through reconstructive surgeries (RCS).
5. **Supervision and monitoring**: The programme is monitored at different levels through analysis of monthly progress reports, field visits by the supervisory officers, and programme review meetings held at central, state, and district level.
6. **NGO services under SET scheme**: NGOs are getting grants from the Government of India under Survey, Education, and Treatment (SET) scheme for various activities undertaken such as IEC, Prevention of Impairments and Deformities, Case Detection, and MDT Delivery.

NEW INITIATIVES OF NLEP

- Enhanced active and early case detection strategy through ACD&RS (Active Case Detection and Regular Surveillance strategy).
- Convergence of leprosy screening for different age groups under RBSK (0-18 yrs), RKSK (13-19 yrs), and CPHC-Ayushman Bharat (above 30+ yrs population).

- Timely referral and follow-up for treatment completion through Multi-Drug Therapy (MDT) available free of cost in all public health facilities.
- Post-Exposure Chemoprophylaxis administration (PEP) for the prevention of leprosy amongst contacts.
- Awareness activities, including routine IEC activities, Special Annual Mass Awareness Campaigns (Sparsh Leprosy Awareness Campaigns), and nationwide Gram Sabhas in villages to reduce stigma and discrimination against persons suffering from leprosy.

Achievements of the National Leprosy Eradication Programme (NLEP):

Reduction in Prevalence Rate: The prevalence rate of leprosy has decreased significantly in India from 57.8 per 10,000 population in 1983 to 0.2 per 10,000 population in 2020.

Elimination of leprosy as a public health problem: In 2005, India achieved the goal of eliminating leprosy as a public health problem, which means that the prevalence rate of leprosy fell below 1 case per 10,000 population at the national level.

Improved case detection and treatment: The NLEP has implemented several strategies to improve case detection and treatment, including active case detection, multi-drug therapy (MDT), and post-exposure prophylaxis (PEP) for contacts of leprosy patients.

Reduction in disability rate: The disability rate among new cases has decreased from 4.3% in 2005 to 1.7% in 2020, indicating that early detection and treatment has helped to prevent disability due to leprosy.

Stigma reduction: The NLEP has conducted several awareness campaigns and activities to reduce stigma and discrimination against persons affected by leprosy. This has helped to improve the quality of life of leprosy patients and their families.

National Mental Health Programme

I. Introduction

A. Overview of mental health in India

The prevalence of mental illness in India

1. According to the National Mental Health Survey (2015-16), nearly 15% of the Indian population (approximately 197 million people) is affected by mental illness.
2. The most common mental disorders in India are depression, anxiety, and substance use disorders.
3. Mental illness is a leading cause of disability and contributes to a significant burden of disease in India.

The impact of mental illness on individuals, families, and communities

1. Mental illness can have a significant impact on an individual's quality of life, daily functioning, and productivity.
2. It can also affect their relationships, social interactions, and economic well-being.
3. Mental illness not only affects the individual but also their families and communities, who may face stigma, discrimination, and financial burden.

The stigma and discrimination associated with mental illness

- Stigma and discrimination are major barriers to mental health care in India.
- The social stigma attached to mental illness can lead to isolation, exclusion, and discrimination.
- This stigma can prevent individuals from seeking help and can also affect their treatment and recovery.

B. Need for a national mental health program

The inadequacy of mental health services in India

- Mental health services in India are grossly inadequate, with a severe shortage of mental health professionals and facilities.
- According to the World Health Organization (WHO), India has only 0.3 psychiatrists and 0.07 psychologists per 100,000 population.
- The majority of mental health services are available in urban areas, with limited access in rural and remote areas.

The lack of access to mental health services in rural and remote areas

- The lack of mental health services in rural and remote areas is a major challenge in India.
- This results in a significant treatment gap for mental illness, with many individuals unable to access mental health care.
- Lack of awareness and stigma associated with mental illness also contribute to the treatment gap.

The high treatment gap for mental illness in India

- The treatment gap for mental illness in India is estimated to be around 70-90%.
- This means that the majority of individuals with mental illness in India do not receive adequate treatment or support.
- The high treatment gap is due to various factors, including lack of awareness, stigma, inadequate mental health services, and limited financial resources.

C. Objectives of the National Mental Health Programme

To provide accessible, affordable, and high-quality mental health care to all

- The primary objective of the National Mental Health Programme is to provide accessible, affordable, and high-quality mental health care to all individuals in need.
- The program aims to increase the availability and accessibility of mental health services, especially in rural and remote areas.

To promote mental health and prevent mental illness

- The program aims to promote mental health and prevent mental illness through awareness campaigns, community-based interventions, and early detection and intervention.
- It also aims to reduce stigma and discrimination associated with mental illness.

To enhance awareness and reduce stigma related to mental illness

The program aims to enhance awareness and reduce stigma related to mental illness through various initiatives, including media campaigns, community mobilization, and training of health professionals and volunteers.

To strengthen the mental health system in India

The program aims to strengthen the mental health system in India by improving the quality and availability of mental health services, enhancing the skills of mental health professionals, and developing a robust monitoring and evaluation system.

II. Components of the NMHP

A. Mental health infrastructure

The NMHP aims to strengthen the existing mental health infrastructure in the country by providing support for the establishment of new mental health facilities and upgradation of existing ones.

The program also aims to increase the number of beds for mental health patients and improve the quality of mental health care services provided.

B. Manpower development

The NMHP aims to address the shortage of mental health professionals in the country by providing training and support for the development of mental health manpower.

This includes training programs for psychiatrists, clinical psychologists, psychiatric social workers, and psychiatric nurses.

C. Community participation

The NMHP recognizes the importance of involving communities in mental health care and promoting awareness about mental health issues.

The program supports the establishment of community mental health centers and promotes community-based rehabilitation for mentally ill patients.

D. Promotion of mental health

The NMHP aims to promote mental health and prevent mental illnesses through various initiatives, including awareness campaigns, stress management programs, and suicide prevention efforts.

E. Treatment and rehabilitation of mentally ill patients

The NMHP provides support for the treatment and rehabilitation of mentally ill patients through various measures such as the provision of essential psychotropic drugs, support for electroconvulsive therapy (ECT), and support for aftercare services for discharged patients.

The program also promotes the integration of mentally ill patients into society and supports their rehabilitation through vocational training programs and other initiatives.

III. Various Mental Health Services Provided by NMHP

A. District Mental Health Program (DMHP)

The DMHP is a flagship program of the NMHP that aims to provide mental health services at the district level.

The program provides community-based mental health care services, including screening and treatment of mental illnesses, awareness campaigns, and training for health workers and community members.

B. National Institute of Mental Health and Neuro-Sciences (NIMHANS)

NIMHANS is a premier mental health institution in India that provides specialized services for the diagnosis, treatment, and rehabilitation of mental illnesses.

The NMHP provides support for the development and strengthening of NIMHANS and other mental health institutions in the country.

C. Suicide Prevention

The NMHP recognizes the high incidence of suicide in India and supports various initiatives for suicide prevention.

This includes the provision of training for health workers in the management of suicidal behavior, the establishment of crisis intervention centers, and the promotion of mental health awareness to prevent suicide.

D. National Toll-Free Helpline for Mental Health

The NMHP has set up a national toll-free helpline (1800-599-0019) for mental health to provide counseling and support to individuals in distress.

The helpline is available 24/7 and provides support in multiple languages.

E. Other initiatives and programs

The NMHP supports various other initiatives and programs for mental health, including the provision of essential psychotropic drugs, support for the rehabilitation of mentally ill patients, and the promotion of mental health awareness in schools and colleges.

Note: The NMHP provides financial support for the implementation of these various programs and services at the state and district levels. The program also provides technical guidance and training for the effective implementation of these initiatives.

IV. Financial Support Provided by NMHP

A. Budget allocation

The NMHP is a centrally sponsored scheme, and the budget for the program is allocated by the Ministry of Health and Family Welfare, Government of India.

The budget for the program is allocated on an annual basis and is based on the requirements and proposals submitted by the states.

B. Funding for mental health services

The NMHP provides financial support for the implementation of various mental health services, including the DMHP and the provision of essential psychotropic drugs.

The program also supports the development and strengthening of mental health institutions in the country, including NIMHANS and other mental health centers.

C. Grants and schemes for mental health institutions

The NMHP provides grants and schemes for mental health institutions to improve the quality of care and services provided.

The program supports the development of new mental health institutions and the upgradation of existing facilities.

The program also provides funding for the procurement of equipment and other resources necessary for the provision of quality mental health services.

V. Achievements of NMHP

A. Reduction in treatment gap for mental illness

One of the major achievements of the NMHP has been a significant reduction in the treatment gap for mental illness.

The program has helped to increase the availability and accessibility of mental health services, particularly in rural and remote areas of the country.

B. Increased availability of mental health services

The NMHP has led to an increase in the availability of mental health services in the country.

The program has supported the development and strengthening of mental health institutions, the training of mental health professionals, and the provision of essential psychotropic drugs.

C. Improved awareness and attitudes towards mental health

The NMHP has played an important role in improving awareness and attitudes towards mental health in the country.

The program has conducted various awareness campaigns, including the observance of World Mental Health Day, to reduce stigma and discrimination associated with mental illness.

D. Enhanced training and capacity building for mental health professionals

The program has supported the training and capacity building of mental health professionals in the country.

This has helped to improve the quality of care and treatment provided to mentally ill patients and has increased the availability of trained mental health professionals in the country.

E. Other notable achievements

The NMHP has contributed to the development of various policies and guidelines related to mental health in the country.

The program has also supported research and innovation in the field of mental health.

Note: The achievements of the NMHP have been significant, but there is still a long way to go in addressing the mental health needs of the country's population. The program needs to be strengthened and scaled up to reach more people and provide comprehensive mental health services to all sections of society.

National programme for control of blindness

Introduction:

A. Overview of blindness and visual impairment in India:

Blindness and visual impairment is a major public health concern in India. According to the World Health Organization (WHO), India is home to the largest number of blind people in the world, accounting for one-third of the world's total blind population. The main causes of blindness in India are cataract, refractive errors, glaucoma, corneal opacities, and other age-related eye diseases. The burden of blindness is not limited to the elderly population but also affects the younger population.

B. Need for a national program to control blindness and visual impairment:

In India, blindness and visual impairment have a significant impact on the socio-economic development of individuals and the country. Blindness and visual impairment are not only a health issue but also a social and economic issue that affects productivity and quality of life. There is a need for a comprehensive program to control blindness and visual impairment in India that addresses the issue at various levels such as prevention, treatment, and rehabilitation.

C. Objectives of the National Programme for Control of Blindness and Visual Impairment:

The National Programme for Control of Blindness and Visual Impairment (NPCB&VI) was launched in India in 1976 with the objective of reducing the prevalence of blindness and visual impairment by providing comprehensive eye care services to the population. The key objectives of NPCB&VI are:

- To reduce the prevalence of blindness and visual impairment by providing eye care services to the population.
- To provide comprehensive eye care services to all sections of the population, especially the underprivileged.
- To develop human resources for eye care and to provide training and capacity building for eye care professionals.
- To promote the use of technology for eye care services and to improve the quality of eye care services.
- To create awareness about eye health and prevention of blindness and visual impairment.

The NPCB&VI is implemented through a network of eye care facilities, both government and non-governmental, across the country. The program focuses on providing preventive, promotive, curative, and rehabilitative services for various eye diseases and disorders.

II. Components of NPCB&VI

A. Eye care infrastructure development: The NPCB&VI aims to strengthen and improve the existing infrastructure for eye care in India. This includes the establishment of new eye care facilities and the renovation and upgradation of existing ones. The program also provides financial assistance for the purchase of equipment and supplies for these facilities.

B. Human resource development: The program focuses on training and capacity building of ophthalmic personnel at all levels, from primary health care workers to ophthalmologists. The training includes clinical, surgical, and managerial skills development, as well as training on the use of new technology and equipment.

C. Disease control activities: The NPCB&VI aims to reduce the prevalence of preventable blindness and visual impairment caused by diseases such as cataract, refractive error, glaucoma, and corneal blindness. The program provides free or subsidized treatment for these diseases, including surgery, medications, and corrective lenses.

D. Eye banking and corneal transplantation: The NPCB&VI promotes the establishment of eye banks and the retrieval, processing, and distribution of corneas for transplantation. The program also provides financial assistance for corneal transplantation surgeries for eligible patients.

E. Promotion of eye health education and awareness: The NPCB&VI aims to promote eye health education and awareness among the general public and healthcare providers. The program conducts awareness campaigns and provides educational materials and training programs to increase awareness about eye health, preventable blindness, and the importance of early diagnosis and treatment.

III. Various Services Provided by NPCB&VI

A. Screening and detection of eye diseases: NPCB&VI provides a comprehensive screening and detection program for eye diseases such as cataracts, glaucoma, and refractive errors. This is done through various camps, outreach programs, and screening facilities at primary health centers and hospitals.

B. Free treatment and surgeries for eye diseases: NPCB&VI provides free treatment and surgeries for various eye diseases to those who cannot afford them. This includes surgeries for cataracts, glaucoma, corneal transplant, and other eye-related surgeries.

C. Provision of spectacles and other assistive devices: NPCB&VI provides free or subsidized spectacles, low vision aids, and other assistive devices to those with visual impairment. This helps them to lead a more normal life and carry out their daily activities with greater ease.

D. Rehabilitation and training for visually impaired individuals: NPCB&VI provides rehabilitation services and training for visually impaired individuals to help them lead independent lives. This includes training in mobility, daily living skills, and vocational training to enable them to earn a livelihood.

E. Other services and initiatives: NPCB&VI also conducts research and surveys on the prevalence of blindness and visual impairment, and advocates for policies and programs to improve eye health in India. They also collaborate with national and international organizations to share knowledge, resources, and best practices in the field of eye health.

IV. Achievements of NPCB&VI

The National Programme for Control of Blindness and Visual Impairment (NPCB&VI) has achieved significant success since its inception. Some of the notable achievements of NPCB&VI are:

A. Reduction in prevalence of blindness and visual impairment:

- According to the NPCB&VI, the prevalence of blindness has reduced from 1.49% in 2006-07 to 1.11% in 2019-20.
- The prevalence of moderate to severe visual impairment has also decreased from 1.88% in 2006-07 to 1.07% in 2019-20.

B. Increased availability and accessibility of eye care services:

- The number of functional eye units has increased from 7,401 in 2006-07 to 26,050 in 2019-20.
- The number of cataract surgeries performed has increased from 29.06 lakh in 2006-07 to 72.25 lakh in 2019-20.
- More than 5.5 crore people have been screened for various eye diseases under NPCB&VI.

C. Improved awareness and understanding of eye health:

- NPCB&VI has conducted various awareness campaigns and programs to educate people about the importance of eye health and prevention of blindness.
- The program has also worked towards reducing the stigma associated with blindness and visual impairment.

D. Enhanced training and capacity building for eye care professionals:

- NPCB&VI has conducted various training programs and workshops for eye care professionals to improve their skills and knowledge.
- The program has also established various institutes and centers for training and capacity building.

E. Other notable achievements:

- NPCB&VI has successfully implemented several initiatives such as the School Eye Health Program, the National Program for Control of Retinopathy of Prematurity, and the National Program for Control of Childhood Blindness.
- The program has also established a National Eye Donation Fortnight to promote eye donation and facilitate corneal transplantation.

The NPCB&VI has made significant progress in reducing the burden of blindness and visual impairment in India through various initiatives and services.

The National Programme for Prevention and Control of Deafness (NPPCD)

I. Introduction

A. Overview of deafness and hearing loss in India:

According to the World Health Organization (WHO), over 5% of the world's population or 466 million people have disabling hearing loss, and approximately one-third of people over 65 years of age are affected by disabling hearing loss. In India, it is estimated that around 63 million people suffer from significant auditory impairment. Additionally, the incidence of hearing loss is higher in rural areas and among low-income populations due to lack of awareness, access to healthcare, and exposure to noise pollution.

B. Need for a national program to prevent and control deafness:

The high prevalence of deafness and hearing loss in India highlights the need for a national program to prevent and control these conditions. The impact of hearing loss can be profound and includes communication difficulties, social isolation, and reduced quality of life. Moreover, the economic burden of untreated hearing loss is substantial, including loss of income, unemployment, and increased healthcare costs.

C. Objectives of the National Programme for Prevention and Control of Deafness (NPPCD):

The National Programme for Prevention and Control of Deafness (NPPCD) was launched by the Government of India in 2006 with the following objectives:

- To prevent the occurrence of deafness and hearing impairment through public health measures such as ear hygiene, immunization, and screening.
- To promote early identification and treatment of ear diseases and hearing impairment through regular ear screening and

provision of hearing aids.

- To improve the rehabilitation of people with hearing impairment through the provision of appropriate interventions, including hearing aids, cochlear implants, and sign language training.
- To develop human resources for ear care services, including training of ear care professionals.
- To enhance the capacity of the health system to prevent and manage ear diseases and hearing impairment.
- The NPPCD aims to reduce the prevalence of deafness and hearing impairment and to improve the quality of life of people with hearing loss in India.

II. Components of NPPCD

A. Infrastructure and technology development: The NPPCD aims to strengthen the infrastructure and technology for ear and hearing care services. This includes setting up of specialized ear care centers, audiology centers, and speech therapy centers, and providing them with necessary equipment and supplies.

B. Human resource development: The program focuses on developing a skilled and trained workforce to provide ear and hearing care services. This includes training of ear surgeons, audiologists, speech therapists, and other healthcare professionals involved in ear and hearing care.

C. Prevention and early identification of hearing loss: The program emphasizes the need for early identification and prevention of hearing loss. This includes conducting screening programs for school children, newborns, and high-risk populations, as well as providing ear care services in remote and underserved areas.

D. Treatment and rehabilitation services: The program aims to provide comprehensive treatment and rehabilitation services for people with hearing loss. This includes the provision of hearing aids, cochlear implants, and other assistive devices, as well as speech therapy and counseling services.

E. Advocacy, communication, and social mobilization: The program aims to create awareness about ear and hearing care among the general public and healthcare professionals. This includes conducting campaigns and programs to promote ear and hearing care, and collaborating with other organizations and stakeholders to address the issue of deafness and hearing loss.

III. Various Services Provided by NPPCD

A. Screening and detection of hearing loss:

NPPCD provides screening and detection services for individuals of all ages, including newborns and school-aged children.

The program uses various screening methods, including otoacoustic emissions (OAE), auditory brainstem response (ABR), and pure tone audiometry.

The goal of screening and detection services is to identify hearing loss at an early stage and provide appropriate intervention.

B. Hearing aids and cochlear implant services:

NPPCD provides hearing aids and cochlear implant services to individuals with hearing loss.

The program provides hearing aids of different types and models, including behind-the-ear (BTE), in-the-ear (ITE), and completely-in-the-canal (CIC) hearing aids.

NPPCD also provides cochlear implant services, which are surgical procedures that can help individuals with severe to profound hearing loss.

C. Rehabilitation and training for individuals with hearing loss:

NPPCD provides rehabilitation and training services for individuals with hearing loss to help them adapt and cope with their condition.

Rehabilitation services include speech and language therapy, auditory-verbal therapy, and sign language training.

The program also provides vocational training and job placement services for individuals with hearing loss.

D. Early intervention services for children with hearing loss:

NPPCD provides early intervention services for children with hearing loss to help them achieve their full potential.

Early intervention services include parent counseling, speech and language therapy, and special education services.

The program also supports the inclusion of children with hearing loss in regular schools through the provision of assistive devices and teacher training.

E. Other services and initiatives:

NPPCD conducts community-based awareness campaigns to promote ear and hearing care.

The program also supports research and development in the field of audiology and hearing care.

NPPCD collaborates with other government agencies and NGOs to implement and coordinate hearing care services across the country.

IV. Financial Support Provided by NPPCD

A. Budget allocation:

The NPPCD is a centrally sponsored scheme, meaning that funding is provided jointly by the central government and the state governments.

The budget allocation for NPPCD has increased over the years, from Rs. 52 crore in 2010-11 to Rs. 215 crore in 2021-22.

The increased budget allocation has enabled the program to expand its reach and provide more comprehensive services.

B. Funding for deafness prevention and control activities:

The NPPCD provides funding for various activities related to deafness prevention and control, such as screening and detection, treatment and rehabilitation, and capacity building of professionals.

The funding is provided to both government and non-governmental organizations that provide deafness services.

The program also supports research and development activities related to deafness prevention and control.

C. Grants and schemes for institutions and individuals providing deafness services:

The NPPCD provides grants and schemes to institutions and individuals that provide deafness services, such as hearing aid centers, cochlear implant centers, and speech therapy centers.

These grants and schemes are aimed at improving the accessibility and affordability of deafness services, particularly for low-income and marginalized communities.

The program also provides financial assistance to individuals with hearing loss for purchasing hearing aids and cochlear implants.

Overall, the financial support provided by NPPCD has been instrumental in expanding the reach and improving the quality of deafness services in India.

IV. Achievements of NPPCD

A. Reduction in prevalence of deafness and hearing loss: Since the inception of NPPCD, there has been a significant reduction in the prevalence of deafness and hearing loss in India. According to the National Sample Survey conducted in 2014, the prevalence of deafness and hearing loss has decreased from 6.3% to 4.6% over the past decade.

B. Increased availability and accessibility of ear care services: The NPPCD has helped in establishing and strengthening ear care facilities across the country. This has led to an increase in the availability and accessibility of ear care services for people living in remote and underserved areas.

C. Improved awareness and understanding of ear health: The NPPCD has played a crucial role in creating awareness and understanding about ear health among the general public. The program has organized various awareness campaigns and health education programs to promote ear health and prevent hearing loss.

D. Enhanced training and capacity building for ear care professionals: The NPPCD has provided training and capacity building programs for ear care professionals to improve their skills and knowledge in the prevention, diagnosis, and treatment of ear diseases. This has helped in improving the quality of ear care services across the country.

E. Other notable achievements: The NPPCD has successfully implemented various initiatives such as the school health program, which aims to screen school children for ear diseases and provide them with early intervention services. The program has also established a National Resource Centre for deafness, which provides technical support and expertise to various ear care institutions and professionals.

Universal Immunization Programme

I. Introduction

A. Overview of the Universal Immunization Programme in India

The Universal Immunization Programme (UIP) is a flagship program of the Government of India launched in 1985 to provide free vaccines against several vaccine-preventable diseases to all children under the age of one year, and pregnant women. The program has since been expanded to include vaccines for other age groups, such as children up to five years old and adolescents.

B. Need for a national immunization program

Immunization is one of the most effective and cost-effective public health interventions to prevent infectious diseases and their associated morbidity and mortality. In India, infectious diseases are a major public health problem, and immunization is a key strategy to control the burden of these diseases. The national immunization program was initiated to ensure that all children, regardless of their economic status, have access to vaccines to protect them from vaccine-preventable diseases.

C. Objectives of the Universal Immunization Programme

The objectives of the Universal Immunization Programme are:

- To provide free and universal access to vaccines against vaccine-preventable diseases to all children and pregnant women in India
- To reduce morbidity and mortality due to vaccine-preventable diseases
- To increase immunization coverage and reach every child in India
- To maintain the quality of vaccines and immunization services
- To strengthen the immunization supply chain and cold chain management
- To monitor and evaluate the immunization program to ensure its effectiveness and efficiency.

The Universal Immunization Programme is an essential component of India's public health system, and it plays a crucial role in preventing infectious diseases and promoting child health.

II. Components of the Universal Immunization Programme

A. Vaccine procurement and management: The procurement and management of vaccines are done through the Central Vaccine Depot and State Vaccine Stores, which procure the vaccines from both domestic and international sources. The vaccines are then distributed to different levels of health facilities based on the demand and need.

B. Cold chain infrastructure: The cold chain is a temperature-controlled supply chain that ensures the safety and efficacy of vaccines from the time of manufacture to the administration to the patient. The Universal Immunization Programme has a well-established cold chain infrastructure that maintains the quality of vaccines throughout the supply chain.

C. Vaccination service delivery: The vaccination service delivery is done through a network of health facilities, including primary health centers, community health centers, and hospitals. The vaccination schedule is followed as per the guidelines issued by the Ministry of Health and Family Welfare.

D. Vaccine safety surveillance: The vaccine safety surveillance system in India monitors adverse events following immunization (AEFI) and investigates and reports any serious AEFIs. The National AEFI Committee and State AEFI Committees oversee the vaccine safety surveillance activities.

E. Immunization data management: The immunization data management system maintains and monitors the immunization status of individuals through a network of health facilities. The data is collected, compiled, and analyzed for monitoring and evaluation of the program.

The above components of the Universal Immunization Programme ensure that the vaccines are available, stored, transported, and administered safely and efficiently to the targeted population.

III. Vaccines Included in the Universal Immunization Programme

A. Polio vaccine: The polio vaccine is administered to infants and children to protect them against the poliovirus which can cause paralysis. India was certified as polio-free in 2014.

B. Measles vaccine: The measles vaccine is given to children to prevent the measles virus which can lead to serious complications such as pneumonia, brain damage, and death.

C. Hepatitis B vaccine: The hepatitis B vaccine is given to infants to prevent hepatitis B infection which can cause liver disease and liver cancer.

D. Pentavalent vaccine: The pentavalent vaccine protects against five diseases - diphtheria, pertussis, tetanus, hepatitis B, and Haemophilus influenzae type b (Hib).

E. Other vaccines included in the program: The program also includes vaccines such as the inactivated polio vaccine, measles-rubella vaccine, and tetanus toxoid vaccine for pregnant women.

F. Rotavirus vaccine: The rotavirus vaccine is given to infants to protect them from severe diarrhoea caused by rotavirus which can lead to dehydration and death.

G. BCG vaccine (for tuberculosis): The BCG vaccine is given to infants to prevent tuberculosis, a bacterial infection that primarily affects the lungs.

H. Japanese Encephalitis vaccine (JE): The JE vaccine is given to children living in areas with a high incidence of Japanese encephalitis, a viral infection that can cause inflammation of the brain.

I. Human Papillomavirus vaccine (HPV): The HPV vaccine is given to adolescent girls to protect against HPV infection which can lead to cervical cancer.

J. Pneumococcal Conjugate Vaccine (PCV): The PCV vaccine is given to protect infants and young children against pneumonia, meningitis, and sepsis caused by pneumococcal bacteria.

K. Typhoid Conjugate Vaccine (TCV): The TCV vaccine is given to children to protect against typhoid fever, a bacterial infection that can cause fever, stomach pain, and diarrhoea.

IV. Services Provided by the Universal Immunization Programme

A. Routine immunization services: The UIP provides routine immunization services to infants and children, which includes administering the required doses of vaccines at the recommended ages to protect them against vaccine-preventable diseases.

B. Special immunization drives: The UIP also conducts special immunization drives for certain vaccines, such as measles, polio, and rubella, to cover areas with low immunization coverage or during outbreaks of vaccine-preventable diseases.

C. Immunization services for high-risk populations: The program provides immunization services to high-risk populations such as pregnant women, health care workers, and those living in areas with a high burden of vaccine-preventable diseases.

D. Maternal immunization services: The UIP also offers maternal immunization services to protect pregnant women and their unborn children against certain vaccine-preventable diseases, such as tetanus and influenza.

E. Other immunization services: The program also provides immunization services to refugees, displaced populations, and those affected by natural disasters or emergencies to prevent outbreaks of vaccine-preventable diseases in these vulnerable populations.

V. Achievements of the Universal Immunization Programme

The Universal Immunization Programme (UIP) has made significant achievements since its inception in 1985. Some of the notable achievements are:

A. Reduction in vaccine-preventable diseases: The UIP has played a crucial role in reducing the burden of vaccine-preventable diseases in India. Diseases such as polio, measles, and neonatal tetanus have been significantly reduced due to the program's efforts. India was declared polio-free in 2014, a significant milestone for the UIP.

B. Increased coverage and accessibility of vaccines: The UIP has made significant strides in increasing the coverage and accessibility of vaccines across the country. As of 2020, India's immunization coverage was 90%, and over 26 million infants were immunized annually. The program has also expanded its reach to cover underserved areas through mobile and outreach immunization services.

C. Improved vaccine safety and quality: The UIP has implemented several measures to ensure the safety and quality of vaccines administered in the program. The program follows strict protocols for vaccine procurement, storage, and transportation to maintain the vaccine's potency and efficacy. Adverse events following immunization (AEFI) are monitored and reported to ensure the vaccine's safety.

D. Enhanced training and capacity building for immunization professionals: The UIP has played a critical role in training and building the capacity of immunization professionals, including doctors, nurses, and vaccinators. The program provides regular training and support to healthcare workers to ensure the effective implementation of the program's goals.

E. Other notable achievements: In addition to the above, the UIP has contributed to the development of new vaccines and technologies, such as the introduction of the pentavalent vaccine in 2011, which protects against five diseases, and the development of a rotavirus vaccine, which was introduced in 2016. The program has also launched several campaigns to increase awareness about immunization, such as the "Mission Indradhanush" campaign, which aims to vaccinate all children and pregnant women by 2020.

The Pulse Polio Immunization programme

- Polio is a highly infectious disease caused by the poliovirus, which can lead to paralysis or even death in severe cases. The global initiative for polio eradication was launched by the World Health Assembly in 1988, with the aim of eradicating polio from the world by the year 2000. The Pulse Polio Immunization programme was launched in India in 1995 as part of this global initiative.

- The Pulse Polio Initiative aimed to achieve 100% coverage under Oral Polio Vaccine (OPV) in children aged 0-5 years. The programme was launched to immunize children through improved social mobilization, plan mop-up operations in areas where poliovirus has almost disappeared, and maintain a high level of morale among the public.
- The programme was implemented through National and Sub-national immunization rounds in high-risk areas every year. During each National Immunization Day (NID), approximately 172 million children were immunized.
- The objective of the Pulse Polio Initiative was to stop the transmission of the poliovirus in India and eventually eradicate the disease from the country. The initiative aimed to achieve this objective by ensuring that every child in the country received OPV and was protected against polio. The Pulse Polio programme in India was one of the largest public health initiatives in the world, and it played a crucial role in the global effort to eradicate polio.Implementation of the Programme
- The Pulse Polio Immunization programme in India targeted children in the age group of 0-5 years. The programme was implemented through National and Sub-national immunization rounds, which were conducted twice a year. During these rounds, children were administered polio drops, which were easily administered orally.
- The programme also involved an extensive social mobilization campaign to improve coverage. Health workers, community leaders, and volunteers played a crucial role in creating awareness about the importance of polio vaccination and encouraging parents to bring their children for vaccination.
- Mop-up operations were conducted in areas where poliovirus had almost disappeared. These operations involved vaccinating children in the affected area to prevent the spread of the virus. High-risk areas were identified based on the history of polio

cases and immunization coverage.

- Monitoring and evaluation of the programme was an integral part of its implementation. The government worked closely with WHO and other partner agencies to monitor the progress of the programme and ensure that it was meeting its objectives. The programme was regularly evaluated to identify areas for improvement and make necessary changes to improve its effectiveness.

Challenges Faced

- The implementation of the Pulse Polio Programme in India faced a number of challenges. Some of the major challenges include:
- Lack of awareness: Lack of awareness about the importance of polio vaccination was a major challenge. Many parents were hesitant to get their children vaccinated due to misconceptions and misinformation about the vaccine.
- Difficult terrain: India is a vast country with diverse geography and difficult terrain. Reaching remote and inaccessible areas was a major challenge.
- Resistance from some communities: In some communities, there was resistance to vaccination due to religious or cultural beliefs.
- Logistics: The programme required a massive logistical effort to ensure that vaccines were transported to all corners of the country and distributed efficiently.

To overcome these challenges, the following strategies were implemented:

- Intensive social mobilization efforts: The government and other stakeholders carried out intensive social mobilization efforts to create awareness about the importance of polio vaccination. This included campaigns using mass media, community mobilization, and the involvement of religious and community leaders.

- Innovative vaccination strategies: To reach remote and difficult-to-access areas, innovative strategies were used. These included the use of mobile vaccination teams, vaccination camps, and reaching out to nomadic communities.
- Community engagement: Engaging with communities and understanding their beliefs and concerns was crucial in addressing resistance to vaccination. Community leaders and influencers were involved in the vaccination process to build trust and increase acceptance.
- Robust monitoring and evaluation: A robust monitoring and evaluation system was put in place to track progress and identify gaps in the programme. Regular surveys were conducted to measure coverage and identify areas that needed additional attention.
- Despite the challenges, the Pulse Polio Programme in India was successful in achieving its objective of polio eradication. The strategies implemented can serve as a model for other countries in their efforts to eradicate polio.

Overview of the achievements of the Pulse Polio Programme in India

- The Pulse Polio Programme in India has been one of the most successful public health initiatives in the world, with significant achievements in eradicating polio. Since its inception in 1995, the programme has achieved the following:
- Total number of children vaccinated: As of 2021, more than 2.5 billion doses of the oral polio vaccine have been administered to children in India under the Pulse Polio Programme.
- Coverage achieved in high-risk areas: The programme has successfully achieved high coverage rates in high-risk areas,

which has been crucial in reducing the incidence of polio. During each National Immunization Day (NID), which is a part of the Pulse Polio Programme, about 172 million children in the age group of 0-5 years are vaccinated.

- Reduction in polio cases in India: The impact of the programme can be seen in the remarkable reduction in polio cases in India. The last polio case in the country was reported from Howrah district of West Bengal with date of onset 13th January 2011. Thereafter, no polio case has been reported in the country (25th May 2012). This is a significant achievement, considering that India was once considered to be one of the most challenging countries in the world for polio eradication.
- Recognition received by India for its successful polio eradication efforts: India's success in eradicating polio has been recognized by various international organizations, including the World Health Organization (WHO), United Nations Children's Fund (UNICEF), and Rotary International. In 2014, the WHO declared India as a polio-free country, a major milestone in the global effort to eradicate polio.
- Before the implementation of the Pulse Polio Programme in India, the country had a high incidence of polio cases. In 1995, the year the programme was launched, India reported 28,252 cases of polio, the highest in the world. The incidence of polio in India remained high in the subsequent years, with 9,357 cases reported in 2002.
- However, the implementation of the Pulse Polio Programme led to a significant reduction in the number of polio cases in the country. By 2010, the number of reported cases had decreased to 42, and the last case of wild polio virus was reported in January 2011. Since then, no new cases of polio have been reported in India.
- The success of the Pulse Polio Programme in India has been recognized globally, and the country has become an example for other countries to follow. The programme has also helped to reduce the global incidence of polio, and India's success has

contributed to the worldwide efforts to eradicate the disease.

- As of 2021, there are only two countries in the world where wild polio virus is still endemic - Afghanistan and Pakistan. The success of the Pulse Polio Programme in India has encouraged other countries to adopt similar initiatives to achieve the goal of polio eradication.

India's successful polio eradication efforts received numerous awards and accolades from various organizations and countries.

- In 2014, India was certified as polio-free by the World Health Organization (WHO) after no new cases were reported for three consecutive years. This was a major achievement considering India was once considered one of the most challenging countries in the world for polio eradication due to its large population, difficult terrain, and poor sanitation.
- The government of India and healthcare workers involved in the Pulse Polio Programme received several awards and recognition for their efforts. Some of the notable awards include:
- The National Polio Eradication Award in 2006, presented by the President of India, for achieving more than 90% coverage during the NID rounds
- The Rotary International's Polio Eradication Champion Award in 2011, presented to Indian Health Minister Ghulam Nabi Azad for his leadership and commitment to polio eradication
- The Gates Vaccine Innovation Award in 2012, presented to the Indian Ministry of Health and Family Welfare for its successful efforts in polio eradication
- The Excellence in Public Health award by the Harvard School of Public Health in 2014, presented to Indian Health Minister Dr. Harsh Vardhan for his leadership in polio eradication and other public health initiatives
- India's successful polio eradication efforts have also been recognized by international organizations like the WHO. India's achievement in eradicating polio has been described as a major

milestone in the global fight against the disease. The WHO has commended India's efforts and its strategies that have been successful in reaching and vaccinating high-risk populations. India has also been recognized as a model for other countries in the fight against polio.

ꕥ

IDSP

Introduction:

The Integrated Disease Surveillance Project (IDSP) is a program launched by the Ministry of Health and Family Welfare in India in 2004 to strengthen disease surveillance activities in the country. The aim of IDSP is to develop a decentralized, state-based surveillance system that can detect and respond to outbreaks of diseases at an early stage. The project is implemented by the National Centre for Disease Control (NCDC) in collaboration with state health departments.

Objectives of IDSP:

The objectives of IDSP are as follows:

Early detection and response to outbreaks of diseases: The IDSP aims to detect outbreaks of diseases at an early stage and respond quickly to prevent their spread.

Timely and accurate reporting of disease data: The IDSP aims to ensure timely and accurate reporting of disease data from various parts of the country.

Strengthening of public health systems: The IDSP aims to strengthen the public health systems at the district and state levels to effectively respond to outbreaks of diseases.

Components of IDSP:

The IDSP has several components that work together to achieve its objectives. These components are as follows:

Disease surveillance:

Disease surveillance is an essential component of the Integrated Disease Surveillance Project (IDSP) in India. The IDSP is a nationwide program implemented by the Ministry of Health and Family Welfare to monitor, detect and respond to infectious disease outbreaks. The IDSP is designed to enhance disease surveillance activities by integrating and strengthening existing disease surveillance systems at the national, state, and district levels.

Disease surveillance is the systematic collection, analysis, and interpretation of health-related data, with the aim of identifying disease trends and outbreaks in a timely manner. The IDSP collects data from various sources, including hospitals, laboratories, and other health facilities, and analyzes this information to detect any unusual or unexpected trends. The data is then used to inform public health interventions and disease control measures.

One of the key components of disease surveillance under the IDSP is the reporting of notifiable diseases. Notifiable diseases are those that are required by law to be reported to public health authorities. This includes diseases such as tuberculosis, malaria, dengue, and cholera, among others. The IDSP ensures that all cases of notifiable diseases are reported in a timely and accurate manner, which helps to identify outbreaks early and prevent further transmission of the disease.

The IDSP also monitors non-communicable diseases, such as cancer, diabetes, and cardiovascular diseases, through its Non-Communicable Disease (NCD) component. The NCD component of the IDSP focuses on the early detection and prevention of these diseases, which are a growing public health concern in India.

Another important aspect of disease surveillance under the IDSP is the use of laboratory-based surveillance. This involves the collection of samples from patients with suspected infectious diseases, which are then tested in laboratories to identify the causative agent. This information is used to identify and respond to outbreaks in a timely manner, and to monitor the effectiveness of disease control measures.

Disease surveillance is a critical component of the IDSP, and plays an important role in protecting the health of the population in India. By monitoring disease trends and responding quickly to outbreaks, the IDSP helps to prevent the spread of infectious diseases and reduce their impact on public health.

Laboratory surveillance:

Laboratory surveillance is an important component of the Integrated Disease Surveillance Project (IDSP), which is a national program implemented by the Ministry of Health and Family Welfare in India. The objective of laboratory surveillance is to ensure timely detection and confirmation of disease outbreaks, monitor disease trends, and evaluate the effectiveness of control measures.

The laboratory surveillance system under IDSP is designed to be comprehensive and integrated with other components of the project. The system is structured to collect and analyze laboratory data from different levels of the healthcare system, including public and private laboratories, hospitals, and clinics. The laboratory data is then integrated with clinical and epidemiological data to provide a comprehensive understanding of disease patterns.

The laboratory surveillance system under IDSP relies on a network of laboratories, both public and private, that are equipped and capable of testing for a range of diseases. The laboratories are required to report all positive results to the designated health authorities in a timely manner. The data is then analyzed to identify disease outbreaks and trends, which enables rapid response to contain the spread of the disease.

In addition to disease detection and confirmation, laboratory surveillance under IDSP also provides important data on the antimicrobial susceptibility patterns of bacterial pathogens. This data is critical for guiding treatment decisions and developing appropriate treatment guidelines.

The laboratory surveillance system under IDSP also includes capacity building activities for laboratory personnel, including training on quality assurance, biosafety, and biosurveillance. These activities aim to improve the quality of laboratory testing and ensure that laboratories adhere to international standards.

Laboratory surveillance is a crucial component of the IDSP program in India. It plays a critical role in disease detection, monitoring disease trends, evaluating the effectiveness of control measures, and guiding treatment decisions. The system is designed to be comprehensive and integrated with other components of the project, and includes capacity building activities for laboratory personnel to ensure the quality of laboratory testing.

Outbreak response:

Outbreak response is one of the key components of the Integrated Disease Surveillance Project (IDSP) which was launched by the Government of India in 2004. The main objective of this component is to ensure prompt and effective response to disease outbreaks in order to prevent their spread and minimize their impact on the population.

The outbreak response component of IDSP is designed to provide a systematic approach for detection, investigation, and management of outbreaks. This involves the development of outbreak response plans, training of healthcare workers, and establishment of communication networks for timely reporting and response.

Under the outbreak response component of IDSP, there are several activities that are undertaken in order to achieve the desired outcomes. These include:

Rapid Response Teams (RRTs): RRTs are established at the district, state, and national levels. These teams are responsible for the investigation of outbreaks, collection of samples, and management of patients.

Outbreak Investigation: The first step in outbreak response is the identification and investigation of outbreaks. This involves the collection of information on the affected population, the nature and extent of the outbreak, and the possible source of infection.

Laboratory Support: Laboratory support is critical for the identification and confirmation of outbreak pathogens. IDSP has established a network of laboratories across the country that provide diagnostic and testing services for outbreak investigation.

Communication: Effective communication is key to the success of outbreak response. IDSP has established a communication network that facilitates timely reporting of outbreaks and response activities.

Training and Capacity Building: Training and capacity building of healthcare workers is essential for effective outbreak response. IDSP provides training to healthcare workers on outbreak investigation, management, and infection control.

Surveillance and Monitoring: IDSP continuously monitors the disease situation in the country through its surveillance system. This helps in the early detection of outbreaks and timely response., the outbreak response component of IDSP is an important mechanism for the prevention and control of infectious diseases. It involves a coordinated effort between various stakeholders, including healthcare workers, laboratories, and government agencies. The success of outbreak response depends on timely detection, effective investigation, and prompt management of outbreaks.

The outbreak response component of IDSP is an important mechanism for the prevention and control of infectious diseases. It involves a coordinated effort between various stakeholders, including healthcare workers, laboratories, and government agencies. The success of outbreak response depends on timely detection, effective investigation, and prompt management of outbreaks.

Capacity building:

Capacity building is a crucial component of the Integrated Disease Surveillance Project (IDSP), which is a flagship program of the Government of India aimed at strengthening disease surveillance and response in the country. Capacity building refers to the process of enhancing the skills, knowledge, and resources of public health professionals to improve their ability to detect, diagnose, and respond to disease outbreaks effectively.

Under the IDSP, capacity building is achieved through a variety of activities, including training programs, workshops, and seminars. These activities are designed to provide public health professionals with the necessary skills and knowledge to carry out their roles effectively. The capacity-building activities of IDSP are implemented at the national, state, and district levels, with the aim of building a strong and resilient public health workforce across the country.

One of the key activities of capacity building under the IDSP is the training of surveillance officers, laboratory personnel, and epidemiologists. These professionals are trained to conduct disease surveillance, collect and analyze data, and respond to disease outbreaks. The training programs cover a wide range of topics, including epidemiology, disease diagnosis, outbreak investigation, data management, and communication skills.

In addition to training, IDSP also provides technical assistance to the public health workforce to improve their capacity. This includes support for laboratory infrastructure, equipment, and supplies, as well as assistance in data management, analysis, and reporting. Technical assistance also includes support for the development of guidelines and protocols for disease surveillance and response.

Another important component of capacity building under the IDSP is the establishment of a network of public health professionals across the country. This network facilitates the sharing of knowledge, experience, and best practices, which can help to strengthen the response to disease outbreaks.

Capacity building is a critical component of the IDSP, which aims to improve the capacity of the public health workforce to detect, diagnose, and respond to disease outbreaks effectively. The program's capacity-building activities are essential to building a strong and resilient public health system in India, which can effectively prevent and control the spread of infectious diseases.

Advocacy, communication, and social mobilization (ACSM):

Advocacy, communication, and social mobilization (ACSM) is a critical component of the Integrated Disease Surveillance Project (IDSP) in India. The ACSM component of IDSP focuses on creating awareness among the general public and key stakeholders about various infectious diseases and the importance of early detection and reporting. ACSM activities also aim to promote healthy behavior and practices to prevent the spread of diseases.

The ACSM component of IDSP involves a range of activities, including community mobilization, awareness campaigns, and health education. One of the key strategies used in the ACSM component is to involve the community in disease surveillance and response activities. This is done through the establishment of community-based surveillance systems, which involve community members in the identification and reporting of suspected cases of infectious diseases.

Another important aspect of the ACSM component is the development and dissemination of health education materials. These materials are designed to educate the public about infectious diseases, their symptoms, and ways to prevent their spread. The materials are distributed through various channels, including mass media, community meetings, and outreach activities.

The ACSM component also plays a critical role in promoting public health policies and practices. This is done through advocacy activities that aim to create an enabling environment for disease surveillance and response. Advocacy activities involve engaging with policymakers, civil society organizations, and other stakeholders to promote policies and practices that support disease surveillance and response efforts.

The ACSM component of IDSP is an essential component of India's public health system. It plays a critical role in creating awareness among the general public and key stakeholders about infectious diseases and the importance of early detection and reporting. Through community mobilization, health education, and advocacy activities, the ACSM component helps to prevent the spread of infectious diseases and promote the overall health and well-being of communities.

Implementation of IDSP:

The IDSP is implemented at the district and state levels. At the district level, the district surveillance unit (DSU) is responsible for disease surveillance activities. The DSU is headed by the district surveillance officer (DSO), who is responsible for the overall management of disease surveillance activities in the district.

At the state level, the state surveillance unit (SSU) is responsible for coordinating disease surveillance activities in the state. The SSU is headed by the state surveillance officer (SSO), who is responsible for the overall management of disease surveillance activities in the state.

The IDSP also has a national level coordination unit (NCU) that provides technical assistance and support to the state and district level units.

VIII

National Family Welfare Program

India holds the distinction of being the **first country in the world** to implement a **family welfare program** at the government level.

The National Family Welfare Programme (NFWP) is a government initiative in India aimed at promoting and providing family planning services, maternal and child health care, and reproductive health education to the population.

1. The National Family Welfare Programme was initiated in India in 1952 as the **National Family Planning Program (NFPP)** making it the first of its kind in the world.
2. The program was redesigned and renamed the "National Family Welfare Program" in 1977. The Ministry of Health and Family Welfare is responsible for the program, which is 100% centrally sponsored.

The objective of the program is to achieve population stabilization at the level of 130 million by the year 2050 AD through small family norms, while improving the quality of life of the people. The concept of welfare is broader in scope than family planning, encompassing education, safe drinking water, and other aspects that relate to the quality of life.

Some key events year-wise related to the National Family Welfare Programme

1952: The National Family Planning Programme (NFPP) is launched by the government of India.

1961: The first family planning research center is established in Mumbai.

1977:The National Family Welfare Programme (NFWP) was launched, which focused on promoting family planning services, maternal and child health, and other reproductive health services.

1983: The National Population Policy is launched with the aim of stabilizing India's population by the year 2045.

1996:The NFPP was rebranded as the National Family Welfare Program (NFWP) to focus on maternal and child health in addition to family planning services.

2005: The government launches the National Rural Health Mission (NRHM) to provide accessible, affordable, and quality health care to rural populations, including family planning services.

2013: The National Health Mission (NHM) is launched, which includes the Reproductive, Maternal, Newborn, Child, and Adolescent Health (RMNCH+A) initiative to address the health needs of mothers, children, and adolescents.

These are some of the key events in the timeline of the National Family Welfare Programme in India.

Throughout its history, the National Family Welfare Programme has faced a number of challenges, including low levels of awareness and access to family planning services, inadequate funding and infrastructure, and resistance from some religious and cultural groups. Despite these challenges, the programme has achieved a number of significant successes, including a decline in the country's total fertility rate from 5.9 in 1951 to 2.2 in 2017, and an increase in the use of modern contraceptives from 13% in 1970 to 48% in 2017.

Background information on India's population growth and family planning initiatives.

1. India, with a population of over 1.3 billion, is the second-most populous country in the world after China. The country's population is expected to reach 1.7 billion by 2050, making it the world's most populous country.
2. The rapid growth of the population has led to a range of challenges, including increased demand for resources such as food, water, and energy, as well as increased pressure on the environment.
3. In response to these challenges, India has implemented a number of family planning initiatives over the past several decades.
4. These initiatives aim to provide couples with the knowledge and resources they need to make informed decisions about family planning and to ensure that they have access to a range of contraceptive options.
5. The National Family Planning Program (NFPP) was launched in 1952 as India's first family planning initiative. The program focused on providing clinical services, such as sterilization, to couples who wished to limit the size of their families. Over the years, the program has evolved to include a range of services, including education and counseling on family planning, as well as the provision of a variety of contraceptive methods.

In 1996, the NFWP was rebranded again as the National Health and Family Welfare Programme (NHFWP) to reflect a broader focus on health and family welfare issues, including maternal and child health. Eventually, the program was further restructured and renamed as the National Health Mission (NHM) in 2013, which includes the Reproductive, Maternal, Newborn, Child, and

Adolescent Health (RMNCH+A) initiative. The RMNCH+A initiative aims to address the health needs of mothers, children, and adolescents through a range of interventions and services, including family planning.

Despite these initiatives, India continues to face significant challenges in managing its population growth. The country's total fertility rate (TFR), which is the average number of children born to a woman during her lifetime, remains higher than many other countries, at around 2.2. Additionally, there are significant disparities in the use of family planning services across different states and socioeconomic groups.

Given the ongoing challenges, there is a need for continued investment in family planning and reproductive health initiatives in India

History of Family Planning in India

India's efforts towards family planning dates back to the early 1950s, when the government started promoting family planning and birth control measures to address the issue of rapidly growing population. **The First Five Year Plan (1951-56)** identified family planning as a key priority for the country's development, and the government established the **Family Planning Division in 1952** to oversee the implementation of the program. However, the early initiatives were not very successful due to lack of awareness, resistance from some religious and cultural groups, and inadequate infrastructure.

In 1961, India's population crossed the 400 million mark, which further highlighted the urgency of implementing effective family planning policies. The government launched the **National Family Planning Programme (NFPP)** in 1952 with the aim of promoting family planning measures, such as contraceptives and sterilization, to control population growth. The program initially focused on maternal and child health, but later expanded to include broader reproductive health services.

Over time, the NFPP evolved to include newer policies and measures to address the changing needs of the population. The government introduced a number of measures to improve access and availability of contraceptives, including the establishment of family planning clinics and distribution of free contraceptives. The government also started incentivizing couples who underwent sterilization, which resulted in a significant increase in sterilization rates.

In 1977, the **National Family Welfare Programme (NFWP)** was introduced as a comprehensive program to provide integrated services for maternal and child health, family planning, and reproductive health. The NFWP sought to provide a range of services to promote safe motherhood, reduce infant and maternal mortality, and promote family planning measures.

Since then, India has continued to make efforts to improve its family planning programs and policies. The focus has shifted towards improving access to quality services, increasing awareness and education, and reducing inequities in service delivery across different regions and socio-economic groups. The government has also recognized the need to involve community-based organizations and civil society in implementing and monitoring family planning programs.

Policy Framework

India has a long history of implementing family planning policies, and the government has been the primary driver of these initiatives. The Indian government's family planning efforts have been guided by a range of policy documents, including the **National Population Policy (NPP) and the National Health Policy (NHP)**. The NPP, which was first introduced in 1976 and updated in 2000 and 2020, outlines the government's goals and strategies for population control and family planning. The policy has had a significant impact on family planning programs in India, and it has helped to shape the country's approach to family planning.

In addition to government-led initiatives, non-governmental organizations (NGOs) have also played a key role in promoting family planning in India. NGOs have focused on increasing awareness about family planning methods and encouraging individuals and communities to take control of their reproductive health. These organizations have also worked to improve access to family planning services, particularly in rural areas where government services may be limited.

Programme Implementation

The government has adopted a range of strategies and approaches to implement the NFWP, including community-based interventions, outreach services, and mobile clinics.

The National Rural Health Mission (NRHM), launched in 2005, has also played a key role in expanding access to family planning services in rural areas. The NRHM has focused on strengthening primary health care systems and improving the quality of health care services, including family planning services.

State and district level initiatives have also been important for implementing family planning programs in India. Many states have developed their own family planning strategies and programs, and district level authorities have been responsible for implementing these programs at the local level.

Services and Interventions

The NFWP provides a range of family planning methods, including male and female sterilization, intrauterine devices (IUDs), oral contraceptive pills, condoms, and injectable contraceptives. The government has also introduced newer methods, such as emergency contraceptive pills and subdermal contraceptive implants, to increase the range of choices available to individuals.

Access to family planning services has been a major focus of the NFWP, particularly in rural areas. The government has established a network of family planning clinics and mobile clinics to provide services to underserved areas. The NFWP also provides family planning education and counseling services to individuals and communities to increase awareness and understanding of different family planning methods and their benefits.

Components of the National Family Welfare Programme:

Maternal and Child Health: The National Family Welfare Programme focuses on improving the health of mothers and children through measures such as prenatal care, safe delivery practices, and child immunization. The programme aims to reduce maternal and infant mortality rates and improve the overall health of women and children.

Family Planning: The family planning component of the programme aims to provide access to contraceptive methods and family planning education to individuals and couples. The programme promotes the use of modern contraceptive methods, such as intrauterine devices (IUDs), oral contraceptive pills, and male and female sterilization. The programme also emphasizes the importance of spacing births and limiting family size.

Adolescent Health: The National Family Welfare Programme also addresses the health needs of adolescents, including issues related to sexual and reproductive health. The programme provides education and services related to contraception, sexually transmitted infections (STIs), and menstrual hygiene management.

Infrastructure and Training: The programme focuses on improving the infrastructure and training of healthcare providers in order to increase access to quality family planning and reproductive health services. The programme also aims to strengthen the capacity of community health workers and volunteers to deliver services and education in remote and under-served areas.

Public-Private Partnership: The National Family Welfare Programme collaborates with private healthcare providers to increase the availability and accessibility of family planning services. The programme also works with non-governmental organizations (NGOs) to provide outreach and education to communities.

The National Family Welfare Programme has also implemented a range of innovative approaches to improve access to family planning and reproductive health services. These include the use of mobile health clinics, community-based distribution of contraceptives, and the provision of postpartum family planning services.

Achievements and Challenges

India's National Family Welfare Programme has achieved significant success in reducing the country's population growth rate and improving maternal and child health. Since the programme's inception, the total fertility rate in India has declined from 5.9 in the 1950s to 2.2 in 2021, and the maternal mortality ratio has decreased from 437 per 100,000 live births in 1990 to 113 per 100,000 live births in 2021. The programme has also expanded access to family planning services, with 53% of married women of reproductive age using a modern contraceptive method in 2021.

However, the National Family Welfare Programme still faces several challenges in its implementation. One of the main challenges is the persistence of gender-based discrimination and violence, which can limit women's access to family planning services and contribute to high rates of unintended pregnancy. Additionally, there are disparities in access to family planning services between urban and rural areas, with rural areas having lower rates of contraceptive use and limited access to health facilities. There are also issues with the quality of family planning services and the availability of certain types of contraceptive methods, particularly long-acting and permanent methods.

Future Directions and Recommendations

To address the remaining challenges and continue the progress made by the National Family Welfare Programme, several recommendations can be made. These include:

Addressing gender-based discrimination and violence: Efforts should be made to promote gender equality and women's empowerment, including through education and economic opportunities, to improve access to family planning services and reduce unintended pregnancy.

Improving access to family planning services in rural areas: Strategies should be developed to improve access to health facilities and increase awareness of family planning services in rural areas, including through mobile clinics and outreach programs.

Expanding the range of family planning methods available: Efforts should be made to expand the availability of long-acting and permanent contraceptive methods, which can provide more effective and convenient options for women.

Improving the quality of family planning services: Efforts should be made to improve the quality of family planning counseling and services, including through training of healthcare providers and monitoring and evaluation of services.

Increasing investment in family planning: Greater investment is needed to sustain and expand the National Family Welfare Programme, including through increased funding for health facilities and programs, as well as increased public awareness of the importance of family planning.

IX

National Tobacco control Programme

Background information

1. Tobacco use is a major public health issue globally and in India
2. India is the third-largest tobacco-producing country and the second-largest consumer of tobacco in the world
3. Tobacco use causes a wide range of health problems, including cancer, heart disease, and respiratory diseases
4. The World Health Organization (WHO) has identified tobacco control as a top priority for public health

The problem of tobacco use in India

Prevalence of tobacco use in India

a. According to the Global Adult Tobacco Survey (GATS) India 2016-17, the prevalence of tobacco use in India is 28.6%

b. This is a significant decrease from the prevalence rate of 34.6% in 2009-10
c. However, tobacco use still remains a major public health problem in India, with millions of people still using tobacco products.

Health effects of tobacco use in India

a. Tobacco use is the leading cause of preventable deaths in India
b. It causes a wide range of health problems, including cancer, heart disease, and respiratory diseases c. Tobacco use also leads to economic costs, as it increases the burden on the healthcare system and reduces productivity

Factors contributing to tobacco use in India

a. The tobacco industry is a powerful force in India, with strong political connections and significant economic clout
b. Low levels of awareness about the health effects of tobacco use and inadequate enforcement of tobacco control laws also contribute to the problem

Overview of the National Tobacco Control Programme (NTCP)

A. Background information

1. The NTCP was launched by the Government of India in 2007-08 during the 11th Five-Year-Plan
2. Its primary aim is to reduce the prevalence of tobacco use in India and create awareness about the harmful effects of tobacco consumption
3. The NTCP is implemented through a three-tier structure, including the National Tobacco Control Cell (NTCC), State Tobacco Control Cells (STCCs), and District Tobacco Control Cells (DTCCs)

B. Objectives of the NTCP

1. To create awareness about the harmful effects of tobacco consumption
2. To reduce the production and supply of tobacco products
3. To ensure effective implementation of the provisions under the Cigarettes and Other Tobacco Products (Prohibition of Advertisement and Regulation of Trade and Commerce, Production, Supply and Distribution) Act, 2003 (COTPA)
4. To help people quit tobacco use
5. To facilitate implementation of strategies for prevention and control of tobacco advocated by WHO Framework Convention of Tobacco Control

C. Components of the NTCP

1. Training of health and social workers, NGOs, school teachers, and enforcement officers
2. Information, education, and communication (IEC) activities
3. School programs
4. Monitoring of tobacco control laws
5. Coordination with Panchayati Raj Institutions for village level activities
6. Setting up and strengthening of cessation facilities, including provision of pharmacological treatment facilities at the district level

Achievements

The National Tobacco Control Programme (NTCP) has achieved several significant milestones since its inception in 2007-08. Here are some of the key achievements of NTCP:

1. Increased Awareness: NTCP has played a vital role in creating awareness about the harmful effects of tobacco consumption among the general public, especially youth and adolescents.

Through mass media campaigns, school programs, and other IEC activities, NTCP has succeeded in informing people about the dangers of tobacco use.

2. Reduction in Prevalence of Tobacco Use: The prevalence of tobacco use in India has decreased by six percentage points from 34.6% to 28.6% from 2009-10 to 2016-17, which is a significant achievement. The reduction in the prevalence of tobacco use can be attributed to the implementation of NTCP initiatives like tobacco cessation services and effective implementation of the Cigarettes and Other Tobacco Products Act (COTPA).
3. Establishment of Three-Tier Structure: The establishment of National Tobacco Control Cell (NTCC), State Tobacco Control Cell (STCC), and District Tobacco Control Cell (DTCC) has ensured the effective implementation of tobacco control initiatives at all levels. The three-tier structure has helped in creating a network of dedicated personnel who work towards achieving the goals of NTCP.
4. Provision of Cessation Services: NTCP has set up and strengthened tobacco cessation services at district level. These services provide pharmacological treatment facilities for those who want to quit tobacco use. The provision of cessation services has helped many tobacco users to quit the habit.
5. Mainstreaming Research and Training: NTCP has mainstreamed research and training on alternative crops and livelihood with other nodal ministries. This has not only helped in finding alternatives to tobacco farming but has also provided new livelihood opportunities for farmers.
6. Integration with National Health Mission: NTCP has been integrated with the National Health Mission (NHM) framework, which has helped in effective implementation and monitoring of tobacco control initiatives. The state and district tobacco control components have been subsumed in the Flexi-pool for Non-Communicable Disease (NCDs) under NHM, which has ensured the availability of funds and manpower for the implementation of the programme.

In conclusion, NTCP has achieved significant success in creating awareness about the harmful effects of tobacco consumption, reducing the prevalence of tobacco use, and establishing a network of dedicated personnel working towards tobacco control initiatives at all levels. The provision of cessation services, mainstreaming research and training, and integration with NHM have further strengthened the programme.

X

National Malaria Prevention Program

Introduction

Malaria is a serious infectious disease caused by the Plasmodium parasite that is transmitted through the bites of infected female Anopheles mosquitoes. It is one of the major public health challenges in India, with more than 80% of the country's population at risk of contracting the disease. The National Malaria Prevention Programme (NMCP) was launched in 1953 by the Government of India, with the objective of reducing the burden of malaria in the country. The programme has been implemented by the National Vector Borne Disease Control Programme (NVBDCP) under the Ministry of Health and Family Welfare.

Objectives:

1. The main objectives of the NMCP are to reduce the incidence and mortality due to malaria in India.

2. The programme aims to **reduce the incidence of malaria** by at least **75% by 2022,** as compared to the 2015 levels.
3. It also aims to **reduce the mortality due to malaria by at least 75% by 2022.**
4. The programme aims to **eliminate malaria from India by 2030**.
5. The objectives of the programme are aligned with the global goals of the World Health Organization's Global Technical Strategy for Malaria 2016-2030.

Strategy:

The NMCP has adopted a multi-pronged strategy to achieve its objectives. The main components of the strategy are:

Early diagnosis and prompt treatment: The programme aims to ensure that all cases of malaria are diagnosed and treated promptly. This is achieved through the distribution of rapid diagnostic test (RDT) kits and the provision of free treatment for all cases of malaria.

Insecticide-treated bed nets (ITNs): The programme promotes the use of ITNs, which are treated with insecticide to kill mosquitoes that come in contact with them. This is an effective way to reduce the transmission of malaria.

Indoor residual spraying (IRS): IRS involves spraying insecticide on the walls and ceilings of houses to kill mosquitoes that come into contact with them. This is another effective way to reduce the transmission of malaria.

Behaviour change communication (BCC): The programme conducts BCC activities to raise awareness about malaria and its prevention. This includes the use of mass media, interpersonal communication and community mobilization.

Surveillance and monitoring: The programme monitors the incidence of malaria through a surveillance system and conducts regular surveys to assess the impact of its interventions.

Achievements:

Reduction in malaria cases and deaths: The NMCP has contributed to a significant reduction in malaria cases and deaths in India. According to the National Vector Borne Disease Control Programme (NVBDCP), there has been a 50% reduction in malaria cases and deaths in India from 2013 to 2019.

Improved access to diagnosis and treatment: The programme has improved access to diagnostic tools such as Rapid Diagnostic Tests (RDTs) and Microscopy, and effective anti-malarial treatment, which has helped in reducing malaria-related morbidity and mortality.

Increase in coverage of insecticide-treated bed nets (ITNs): The NMCP has significantly increased the coverage of ITNs in high malaria transmission areas. This has helped in reducing the transmission of malaria by preventing mosquito bites.

Strengthening of surveillance and monitoring: The programme has strengthened the surveillance and monitoring of malaria cases, enabling early detection and prompt response to outbreaks.

Capacity building of healthcare providers: The programme has focused on capacity building of healthcare providers, including training in diagnosis, treatment, and management of malaria cases, which has improved the quality of care for patients.

Partnerships and collaborations: The NMCP has established partnerships and collaborations with various stakeholders, including civil society organizations, private sector, and academia, which has helped in achieving its objectives and scaling up its interventions.

The NMCP has contributed significantly to reducing the burden of malaria in India. However, the programme faces several challenges, including drug resistance, vector resistance, and inadequate funding, which need to be addressed for sustained progress in malaria control and elimination.

XI

National Program for Health Care of The Elderly

Introduction:

The National Programme for Health Care of the Elderly (NPHCE) was launched by the Ministry of Health and Family Welfare, Government of India, in the year 2010. The programme was launched in response to the growing needs of the elderly population in the country. According to the 2011 Census of India, the population of elderly people aged 60 years and above in the country was around 100 million, which is expected to triple by 2050.

The elderly population in India faces a number of health issues such as chronic diseases, mental health problems, disabilities, and social isolation. In addition, there is a lack of adequate health care facilities and trained health care professionals to address the health needs of this population. The NPHCE was designed to address these issues and improve the overall health status of the elderly population in the country.

The NPHCE is a comprehensive health care programme for the elderly that focuses on providing promotive, preventive, curative and rehabilitative services to this population. The programme aims to provide accessible, affordable and quality health care services to the elderly population in the country. The programme also aims to build capacity among health care professionals to provide effective and efficient health care services to the elderly

The National Programme for Health Care of the Elderly (NPHCE) is a government initiative aimed at providing comprehensive health care services to the elderly population in India. The programme was launched in 2010 and is implemented through primary health care facilities, community health centres, district hospitals, and specialized geriatric centres.

Objectives:

The objectives of NPHCE are:

1. To provide accessible, affordable, and quality health care services to the elderly population.
2. To promote healthy ageing and improve the quality of life of the elderly.
3. To build capacity in health care professionals for providing geriatric care.
4. To promote research on geriatric health issues and develop evidence-based treatment protocols.

Components of NPHCE:

The National Programme for Health Care of the Elderly (NPHCE) has two components to provide geriatric health care services: the district and sub-district level component and the tertiary level component.

The district and sub-district level component focuses on providing health care services to the elderly population through primary health care facilities, community health centres, and district hospitals. The package of services provided to elderly people at these levels includes health education related to healthy ageing, domiciliary visits for attention and care to home-bound/bedridden elderly persons, suitable callipers and supportive devices from the PHC to the elderly disabled persons to make them ambulatory, linkage with other support groups and day care centres, weekly geriatric clinic run by a trained medical officer, routine health assessment of the elderly persons based on simple clinical examination, provision of medicines and proper advice on chronic ailments, public awareness on promotional, preventive and rehabilitative aspects of geriatrics during health and village sanitation day/camps, referral for diseases needing further investigation and treatment, and more.

The district hospital also has a geriatric clinic for regular dedicated OPD services to the elderly, facilities for laboratory investigations for diagnosis and provision of medicines for geriatric medical and health problems, and a ten-bedded geriatric ward for in-patient care of the elderly. Existing specialities like General Medicine, Orthopaedics, Ophthalmology, ENT services, etc. will provide services needed by elderly patients, and the hospital provides services for the elderly patients referred by the CHCs/ PHCs, etc.

The tertiary level component provides specialized health care services to the elderly population through regional geriatric centres and the National Centre for Ageing. The regional geriatric centre has a geriatric clinic (Specialized OPD for the Elderly), 30-bedded geriatric ward for in-patient care, and dedicated beds for the elderly patients in various specialties such as surgery, orthopedics, psychiatry, urology, ophthalmology, neurology, and other medical fields. The centre also conducts research on geriatric diseases prevalent in the country, develops evidence-based treatment protocols for these conditions, and focuses on human resource development in all sub-specialties of Geriatric Medicine.

Acievements

The National Programme for Health Care of the Elderly (NPHCE) has achieved significant milestones since its inception in 2010. Some of the major achievements of the programme are:

Establishment of Geriatric Clinics: The NPHCE has established geriatric clinics in various health facilities across the country, which provide comprehensive health care services to the elderly population. These clinics are equipped with trained medical officers and staff, and provide a range of services such as health education, screening, diagnosis, treatment, and rehabilitation.

Training of Health Care Providers: The programme has provided training to health care providers in geriatric care, including medical officers, nurses, physiotherapists, and community health workers. The training covers various aspects of geriatric care such as assessment, diagnosis, management, and rehabilitation.

Development of Standard Treatment Guidelines: The NPHCE has developed standard treatment guidelines for common geriatric conditions such as hypertension, diabetes, osteoporosis, and dementia. These guidelines provide evidence-based recommendations for the diagnosis and management of these conditions.

Strengthening of Health Care Infrastructure: The programme has strengthened the health care infrastructure for geriatric care, by providing funds for the establishment of geriatric wards in district hospitals, and for the procurement of equipment and supplies needed for geriatric care.

Community Participation: The programme has encouraged community participation in geriatric care, by involving local NGOs, self-help groups, and community health workers in the implementation of the programme. This has helped to increase awareness about geriatric care, and has facilitated the delivery of services to the elderly population.

Monitoring and Evaluation: The programme has put in place a robust monitoring and evaluation system, which tracks the progress of the programme and provides feedback for improvement. This system includes regular reviews and assessments, data collection and analysis, and feedback from stakeholders.

The National Programme for Health Care of the Elderly has made significant contributions to the health and well-being of the elderly population in India, by improving access to quality health care services, strengthening the health care infrastructure, and promoting community participation in geriatric care.

XII

Social Health Programs

India has implemented various social health programs over the years to improve the health and wellbeing of its population, particularly the vulnerable and marginalized sections of society. These programs are designed to address various health issues, from infectious diseases to non-communicable diseases, maternal and child health, and mental health.

The government of India has launched numerous social health programs with the aim of providing accessible, affordable, and quality healthcare services to all, especially those who are economically and socially disadvantaged. These programs are implemented through the public healthcare system, and in collaboration with various stakeholders, including non-governmental organizations, community-based organizations, and private healthcare providers.

The focus of these programs is on preventive healthcare, early detection, and management of diseases, as well as improving healthcare infrastructure, healthcare workforce, and health literacy among the population. They also aim to address the social determinants of health such as poverty, education, sanitation, and access to clean water.

Some of the key social health programs implemented by the government of India include the National Rural Health Mission, Ayushman Bharat, National Program for Prevention and Control of Cancer, Diabetes, Cardiovascular Diseases and Stroke, Swachh Bharat Abhiyan, and the National Nutrition Mission. These programs have made significant contributions to improving the health and wellbeing of the population, but there are still challenges that need to be addressed, such as improving the quality of healthcare services, addressing the shortage of healthcare professionals, and ensuring universal access to healthcare services.

National Cancer Control Program:

The National Cancer Control Program was launched in 1975 with the objective of preventing and controlling cancer in India.

- The program focuses on prevention, early detection, diagnosis, treatment, and palliative care of cancer.
- The program provides a range of services such as cancer screening, diagnosis, treatment, and rehabilitation, with a special emphasis on the underserved and rural areas.
- The program has established a network of cancer hospitals, regional cancer centers, and district cancer centers across the country, which provide comprehensive cancer care services to the population.
- The program also focuses on creating awareness about cancer prevention and early detection, promoting healthy lifestyle practices, and reducing the risk factors for cancer.
- The program has several sub-programs such as the National Tobacco Control Program and the National Program for Prevention and Control of Cancer, Diabetes, Cardiovascular Diseases, and Stroke (NPCDCS), which aim to address specific aspects of cancer prevention and control.

- The program has been successful in improving cancer care services in the country, with an increase in the number of cancer hospitals and the availability of cancer drugs and technologies. According to the National Health Profile of India 2021, cancer accounted for 6.7% of all deaths in India in 2019 compared to 7.2% in 2018.

National AIDS Control Program:

The National AIDS Control Program (NACP) was launched in 1987 with the objective of preventing and controlling the spread of HIV/AIDS in India. The program is implemented by the National AIDS Control Organization (NACO), which is a division of the Ministry of Health and Family Welfare.

- The program focuses on prevention, care, and support for people living with HIV/AIDS.
- The program has a multi-sectoral approach, involving various government departments, civil society organizations, and international partners.
- The program provides free HIV testing and counseling services, as well as free antiretroviral therapy (ART) for people living with HIV/AIDS.
- The program also focuses on preventing mother-to-child transmission of HIV, through the provision of antiretroviral drugs and counseling to pregnant women living with HIV.
- The program has been successful in reducing the spread of HIV/AIDS in India. According to the UNAIDS report of 2020, India has achieved significant progress in reducing the new HIV infections by 37% and AIDS-related deaths by 56% since 2010. However, there is still a need to strengthen the program to ensure that it reaches all those in need.

National Program for Prevention and Control of Deafness:

The National Program for Prevention and Control of Deafness was launched in 2006 with the aim of preventing and controlling hearing loss and deafness in India.

- The program focuses on the prevention and early detection of hearing loss, and the provision of rehabilitation services to those affected by deafness.
- The program provides a range of services such as ear screening, diagnosis, treatment, and rehabilitation, with a special emphasis on the underserved and rural areas.
- The program has established a network of deafness prevention and control centers, hearing aid banks, and school health programs across the country, which provide comprehensive deafness care services to the population.
- The program also focuses on creating awareness about deafness prevention and early detection, promoting healthy lifestyle practices, and reducing the risk factors for deafness.
- The program has been successful in improving deafness care services in the country, with an increase in the number of deafness prevention and control centers and the availability of hearing aids and technologies. According to the National Health Profile of India 2021, hearing impairment accounted for 0.1% of all deaths in India in 2019 compared to 0.2% in 2018.

National Mental Health Program:

The National Mental Health Program was launched in 1982 with the objective of providing mental health services to the people of India. The program focuses on providing mental health care at the primary health care level, creating awareness about mental health issues, and reducing stigma associated with mental illness.

- The program focuses on promoting mental health, preventing mental illness, and providing treatment and rehabilitation services to those affected by mental illness.
- The program provides a range of services such as community mental health care, mental health education and awareness, psychiatric treatment facilities, and rehabilitation services for persons with mental illness, with a special emphasis on the underserved and rural areas.
- The program has established a network of mental health centers, psychiatric hospitals, and community mental health teams across the country, which provide comprehensive mental health care services to the population.
- The program also focuses on creating awareness about mental health, reducing the stigma associated with mental illness, and promoting healthy lifestyle practices to prevent mental illness.

The program has been successful in improving mental health care services in the country, with an increase in the number of mental health centers and the availability of mental health professionals and drugs. According to the National Health Profile of India 2021, mental and behavioral disorders accounted for 1.3% of all deaths in India in 2019 compared to 1.4% in 2018.

National Cancer Registry:

The National Cancer Registry is a nationwide program that was launched in 1982. The registry collects data on cancer cases and provides information for research, planning, and policy-making. The program also provides information on the incidence and prevalence of different types of cancer in India.

- The program collects data on cancer cases and deaths from various sources such as hospitals, cancer centers, and pathology laboratories across the country.

- The program uses this data to estimate the incidence, prevalence, and mortality rates of various types of cancers in different regions of the country.
- The program also conducts research on the risk factors, prevention, and treatment of cancer, and provides technical assistance and training to healthcare professionals involved in cancer care and control.
- The program has established a network of population-based cancer registries (PBCRs) and hospital-based cancer registries (HBCRs) across the country, which collect and report data on cancer cases and deaths.
- The program has been successful in generating reliable data on cancer burden in India, which is essential for policy planning and resource allocation for cancer care and control. According to the National Health Profile of India 2021, cancer accounted for 5.5% of all deaths in India in 2019 compared to 5.7% in 2018.

National Leprosy Eradication Program:

The National Leprosy Eradication Program was launched in 1983 with the objective of eliminating leprosy from India. The program focuses on early detection and treatment of leprosy cases, providing disability care services, and reducing stigma associated with leprosy.

- The program focuses on early detection and prompt treatment of leprosy cases, prevention of disabilities due to leprosy, and social and economic rehabilitation of persons affected by leprosy.
- The program provides multi-drug therapy (MDT) free of cost to all leprosy patients, which is a combination of three drugs - rifampicin, clofazimine, and dapsone - that is highly effective in curing leprosy and preventing its transmission.

- The program also conducts active surveillance for leprosy cases, which involves periodic screening of high-risk populations such as household contacts of leprosy patients, slum dwellers, and migrant workers.
- The program has established a network of leprosy clinics and hospitals across the country, which provide comprehensive leprosy care services such as diagnosis, treatment, and rehabilitation.
- The program has been successful in reducing the burden of leprosy in the country, with a decline in the number of new cases from 126,164 in 2016-17 to 89,463 in 2019-20, according to the Ministry of Health and Family Welfare.

Universal Immunization Program:

The Universal Immunization Program was launched in 1985 with the aim of providing immunization services to all children in India. The program focuses on preventing vaccine-preventable diseases such as measles, polio, tetanus, and hepatitis B.

The program provides free vaccines to children against 12 vaccine-preventable diseases such as tuberculosis, polio, measles, diphtheria, pertussis, tetanus, hepatitis B, haemophilus influenzae type b (Hib), rotavirus, pneumococcal disease, rubella, and Japanese encephalitis.

The program provides immunization services through a network of public health facilities such as primary health centers, community health centers, and district hospitals, as well as through outreach sessions in schools, anganwadi centers, and other community settings.

The program also provides vaccines to pregnant women against tetanus, which is an important cause of maternal and neonatal mortality in the country.

The program has been successful in reducing the burden of vaccine-preventable diseases in the country. For instance, the country has been declared polio-free since 2014, and there has been a significant decline in the incidence of measles and other vaccine-preventable diseases in recent years.

National Vector Borne Disease Control Program:

The National Vector Borne Disease Control Program was launched in 2003 with the objective of controlling vector-borne diseases such as malaria, dengue, and chikungunya. The program focuses on vector control measures such as indoor residual spraying, insecticide-treated bed nets, and larval control.

- The program focuses on the prevention and control of six major vector-borne diseases in the country, namely malaria, dengue, chikungunya, lymphatic filariasis, kala-azar, and Japanese encephalitis.
- The program provides insecticide-treated bed nets (ITNs) and long-lasting insecticidal nets (LLINs) to prevent malaria and other mosquito-borne diseases. It also conducts indoor residual spraying (IRS) with insecticides to kill mosquitoes and other vectors in high-risk areas.
- The program promotes community mobilization and behavior change communication (BCC) to create awareness about vector-borne diseases and their prevention. It also strengthens the capacity of health workers and laboratories to diagnose and treat vector-borne diseases.
- The program also focuses on integrated vector management (IVM), which involves a combination of different strategies such as environmental management, source reduction, and use of insecticides to control vectors.
- The program has been successful in reducing the burden of malaria and other vector-borne diseases in the country. For instance, the incidence of malaria has declined from 2.03 million cases in 2000 to 5.59 lakh cases in 2019, according to the Ministry of Health and Family Welfare.

National Tobacco Control Program:

The National Tobacco Control Program was launched in 2007 with the aim of reducing the prevalence of tobacco use in India. The program focuses on creating awareness about the health hazards of tobacco use, enforcing tobacco control laws, and promoting tobacco cessation services.

- The program focuses on implementing the provisions of the Cigarettes and Other Tobacco Products Act (COTPA), which includes measures such as prohibition of smoking in public places, sale of tobacco products to minors, and sale of tobacco products within 100 yards of educational institutions.
- The program also aims to create awareness about the harmful effects of tobacco use through mass media campaigns, health warnings on tobacco products, and community mobilization activities.
- The program promotes smoking cessation services such as counseling and nicotine replacement therapy (NRT) to help people quit tobacco use.
- The program also focuses on strengthening the capacity of health workers and laboratories to diagnose and treat tobacco-related diseases, and on surveillance and monitoring of tobacco use and its effects on health.
- The program has made some progress in reducing tobacco use in the country. For instance, the prevalence of tobacco use among adults (aged 15 years and above) has declined from 34.6% in 2009-10 to 28.6% in 2016-17, according to the Global Adult Tobacco Survey (GATS).

National Program for Healthcare of the Elderly:

The National Program for Healthcare of the Elderly was launched in 2011 with the objective of providing comprehensive healthcare services to the elderly population in India. The program focuses on providing preventive, promotive, curative, and rehabilitative services to the elderly. The key components of the program include health promotion and education, community-based care, and long-term care.

- The program focuses on promoting healthy aging and preventing and managing chronic diseases and disabilities among the elderly population.
- The program provides geriatric health services at various levels of the healthcare system, including primary health centers (PHCs), community health centers (CHCs), district hospitals, and medical colleges. These services include screening and management of chronic diseases, rehabilitation services, palliative care, and counseling services.
- The program also aims to create awareness about healthy aging and to promote community participation in the care of elderly people. It provides training to health workers, community volunteers, and caregivers on geriatric care and management.
- The program also focuses on strengthening the capacity of health facilities and laboratories to provide quality geriatric health services, and on research and development in the field of geriatric care.
- The program has made some progress in improving the healthcare services for the elderly population in the country. For instance, the number of geriatric clinics and day care centers for the elderly has increased, and the number of elderly people receiving health services has also increased.

National Rural Health Mission (NRHM):

The National Rural Health Mission (NRHM) was launched in 2005 by the Ministry of Health and Family Welfare with the aim of improving the health status of people living in rural areas of the country.

Key points:

The program focuses on providing accessible, affordable, and quality healthcare services to people living in rural areas, especially women and children.

The program aims to strengthen the primary healthcare system in rural areas by improving infrastructure, human resources, and management systems. It also promotes community participation in healthcare planning and management.

The program provides financial and technical support to states and union territories for implementing various health interventions such as immunization, maternal and child health services, family planning, and communicable disease control.

The program also focuses on addressing the social determinants of health such as nutrition, safe drinking water, sanitation, and hygiene.

The program has made some progress in improving the health status of people living in rural areas of the country. For instance, there has been an increase in the number of institutional deliveries and in the coverage of immunization among children in rural areas.

Pradhan Mantri Jan Arogya Yojana (PMJAY):

PMJAY is another health insurance scheme launched in 2018. It provides free healthcare to the poorest families in India, covering hospitalization costs for up to Rs. 5 lakhs per family per year.

- Pradhan Mantri Jan Arogya Yojana (PMJAY) is another name for Ayushman Bharat, which is a flagship health insurance scheme launched by the Government of India in 2018. The scheme aims to provide financial protection to vulnerable families against catastrophic health expenditures.

- Under the scheme, health insurance cover of up to Rs. 5 lakh per family per year is provided for secondary and tertiary care hospitalization to over 10 crore vulnerable families in the country. This includes families from both rural and urban areas who are identified as per the Socio-Economic Caste Census (SECC) data. The scheme covers more than 1,500 medical and surgical procedures, including pre-existing conditions, and has a network of empanelled public and private hospitals across the country for providing cashless treatment to the beneficiaries.
- The scheme also includes the establishment of Health and Wellness Centers (HWCs) to provide primary healthcare services such as screening and management of non-communicable diseases, maternal and child health services, and basic diagnostic services.
- PMJAY aims to reduce out-of-pocket expenditure on healthcare, improve access to quality healthcare services, and reduce the financial burden of catastrophic health expenditures on vulnerable families. It has made significant progress in expanding health insurance coverage and improving access to healthcare services for vulnerable families in the country. As of 2021, over 3 crore hospital admissions and medical procedures have been availed under the scheme.

Swachh Bharat Abhiyan:

Launched in 2014, Swachh Bharat Abhiyan is a cleanliness campaign that aims to improve sanitation and hygiene in India. It focuses on constructing toilets, promoting safe sanitation practices, and creating awareness about the importance of hygiene.

- The campaign aims to eliminate open defecation and ensure the construction of toilets in every household, school, and public places across the country. It also aims to promote the adoption of safe sanitation practices and behavior change among the people.

- The campaign includes the construction of community toilets, public toilets, and solid waste management systems in urban and rural areas.
- The campaign also focuses on creating awareness and educating people about the benefits of sanitation, cleanliness, and hygiene through various communication and behavior change campaigns.
- The campaign has made significant progress in improving the sanitation coverage and cleanliness in the country. According to the government data, the sanitation coverage has increased from 39% in 2014 to over 100% in 2021, and over 100 million toilets have been constructed across the country.

National Nutrition Mission (Poshan Abhiyan):

Launched in 2018, Poshan Abhiyan aims to reduce malnutrition in India. It focuses on improving the nutritional status of pregnant and lactating women and children under the age of five.

- The program aims to reduce stunting, under-nutrition, and low birth weight among children, as well as anemia and under-nutrition among women and adolescent girls.
- The program focuses on the first 1,000 days of a child's life, which is the critical period for growth and development, and aims to provide targeted interventions to address the nutritional needs of pregnant women, lactating mothers, and children under two years of age.
- The program uses a convergent approach, which involves the convergence of various sectors such as health, water and sanitation, education, and social protection, to address the underlying causes of malnutrition.
- The program includes various components such as the identification and tracking of children and pregnant women, the provision of nutritional supplements and counseling, the

promotion of breastfeeding and complementary feeding practices, the improvement of hygiene and sanitation, and the strengthening of health and nutrition services.

- The program also aims to create awareness and promote behavior change through various communication and community mobilization activities.
- The program has made significant progress in reducing malnutrition and improving the nutritional status of women and children in the country. According to government data, the prevalence of stunting among children under five years of age has reduced from 38.4% in 2005-06 to 34.7% in 2019-20, and the prevalence of anemia among women has reduced from 55% in 2005-06 to 50% in 2019-20.

Mission Indradhanush:

Launched in 2014, Mission Indradhanush is a vaccination program that aims to increase the coverage of immunization in India. It focuses on vaccinating children against seven preventable diseases.

- The program aims to achieve full immunization coverage of all children and pregnant women by 2020, with a focus on reaching the unvaccinated and partially vaccinated children in the underserved areas of the country.
- The program targets seven vaccine-preventable diseases - diphtheria, whooping cough, tetanus, polio, tuberculosis, measles, and hepatitis B - and provides vaccination against these diseases free of cost at the government health facilities.
- The program uses a targeted approach, which involves the identification and mapping of the areas and populations with low immunization coverage and the implementation of intensive vaccination campaigns in these areas.
- The program uses innovative strategies such as the use of mobile vans, increased community engagement and awareness, and the

involvement of stakeholders such as civil society organizations, media, and celebrities, to improve the reach and coverage of the program.

- The program has made significant progress in improving immunization coverage in the country. According to government data, the coverage of fully immunized children has increased from 61% in 2009-10 to 84% in 2018-19, and the coverage of pregnant women receiving tetanus toxoid vaccine has increased from 53% in 2009-10 to 90% in 2018-19.

National Program for Control of Blindness and Visual Impairment:

The National Program for Control of Blindness and Visual Impairment was launched in 1976 with the aim of reducing the prevalence of blindness and visual impairment in India. The program focuses on providing comprehensive eye care services, including cataract surgery, screening for refractive errors, and treatment of other eye diseases

- The program aims to provide eye care services, including prevention, early detection, treatment, and rehabilitation of blindness and visual impairment, to all sections of the population, especially the underprivileged and marginalized.
- The program targets the major causes of blindness and visual impairment in the country, including cataract, refractive error, glaucoma, corneal blindness, childhood blindness, and low vision, and provides free or highly subsidized treatment for these conditions.
- The program uses a multi-pronged approach, which includes the strengthening of eye care infrastructure, human resource development, community participation, and advocacy and awareness generation.

- The program also aims to eliminate avoidable blindness by the year 2020 and has set specific targets for each state in the country.
- The program has made significant progress in reducing the burden of blindness and visual impairment in the country. According to government data, the prevalence of blindness has decreased from 1.1% in 2001 to 0.36% in 2019, and the number of cataract surgeries has increased from 1.17 million in 2006-07 to 6.3 million in 2019-20.

National Program for Filaria Control:

The National Program for Filaria Control was launched in 1955 with the objective of controlling and eliminating lymphatic filariasis in India. The program focuses on mass drug administration, morbidity management, and disability prevention.

- Filaria, also known as lymphatic filariasis, is a parasitic disease caused by the filarial worm that affects the lymphatic system and can cause swelling, disability, and disfigurement.
- The program aims to eliminate filariasis as a public health problem by reducing the transmission of the disease through mass drug administration, improving the management of cases, and reducing the morbidity associated with the disease.
- The program provides free treatment with safe and effective drugs to all eligible individuals, including those in endemic areas, and conducts surveillance to monitor the prevalence and transmission of the disease.
- The program also focuses on improving the hygiene and sanitation in endemic areas, as poor sanitation can increase the transmission of the disease.
- The program has made significant progress in reducing the burden of filariasis in the country. According to government data, the prevalence of microfilaria, the immature form of the

parasite, has decreased from 1.24% in 2004 to 0.22% in 2019.

National Program for Control of Non-Communicable Diseases:

The National Program for Control of Non-Communicable Diseases was launched in 2010 with the aim of reducing the burden of non-communicable diseases such as diabetes, hypertension, and cardiovascular diseases in India. The program focuses on creating awareness about the risk factors for these diseases, promoting healthy lifestyles, and providing early diagnosis and treatment.

- NCDs are non-infectious diseases that are not transmitted from one person to another, such as cardiovascular diseases, diabetes, cancer, and chronic respiratory diseases. These diseases are responsible for a significant proportion of morbidity and mortality in India.
- The program aims to reduce the burden of NCDs by promoting healthy lifestyles, early detection and management of NCDs, and strengthening the healthcare system to provide better services for NCDs.
- The program focuses on creating awareness about NCDs and their risk factors, such as tobacco use, unhealthy diet, physical inactivity, and alcohol consumption, and promoting healthy behaviors such as regular exercise, healthy eating, and tobacco cessation.
- The program also aims to strengthen the health system for the prevention and control of NCDs by training healthcare professionals, improving the availability and accessibility of essential medicines and technologies, and promoting research and innovation in the field.
- The program targets the population aged 30 years and above in urban and rural areas, with a special focus on high-risk groups such as those with a family history of NCDs, elderly people, and

those living in slums and low-income areas.

- The program has made significant progress in reducing the burden of NCDs in the country, but there are still challenges such as the need for better coordination among different stakeholders, improving the availability and affordability of essential medicines, and addressing the social and environmental determinants of NCDs.
- The program needs to be further strengthened to achieve the goal of reducing the burden of NCDs in the country and improving the quality of life of the people.

National Program for Oral Health Care:

The National Program for Oral Health Care was launched in 1974 with the objective of improving the oral health status of the population in India. The program focuses on providing oral health services, including preventive and curative care, to the rural and urban population.

- The program focuses on providing preventive, promotive, and curative oral health services to the population, with a special emphasis on the rural and underserved areas.
- The program aims to create awareness about oral health and hygiene, promote healthy habits, and provide early diagnosis and treatment of oral diseases.
- The program provides a range of services, including oral health education, fluoride supplementation, dental check-ups, treatment of dental caries and gum diseases, and oral cancer screening.
- The program has a network of primary health centers, community health centers, and district hospitals that provide oral health services to the population.
- The program also focuses on capacity building of health professionals, including dentists, dental hygienists, and dental

assistants, to provide quality oral health services.

- The program has been successful in improving the oral health status of the population, with a significant reduction in the prevalence of dental caries and gum diseases. However, there is still a need to strengthen the program to ensure that it reaches all those in need, particularly in the underserved and rural areas.

National Program for Palliative Care:

The National Program for Palliative Care was launched in 2012 with the aim of improving the quality of life of patients with life-limiting illnesses and their families. The program focuses on providing palliative care services, including pain and symptom management, psychosocial support, and spiritual care.

- Palliative care is specialized medical care for people with serious illnesses that focuses on providing relief from symptoms, pain, and stress. It aims to improve the quality of life of patients and their families.
- The program aims to improve access to palliative care services for patients with life-limiting illnesses such as cancer, HIV/AIDS, and chronic organ failure, and to strengthen the healthcare system to provide better services for palliative care.
- The program focuses on creating awareness about palliative care and its benefits among healthcare professionals, patients, and the public, and on training healthcare professionals in palliative care.
- The program aims to improve the availability and accessibility of essential medicines for pain relief and symptom management, and to ensure that palliative care services are integrated into the existing healthcare system.
- The program targets the population with life-limiting illnesses and their families, and aims to provide palliative care services at all levels of the healthcare system, from primary health centers

to tertiary care hospitals.

- The program has made significant progress in improving access to palliative care services in the country, but there are still challenges such as the need for better coordination among different stakeholders, improving the availability and affordability of essential medicines, and addressing the stigma associated with palliative care.

National Organ Transplant Program:

The National Organ Transplant Program (NOTP) was launched in 1995 with the aim of promoting organ donation and transplantation in India. The program is implemented by the Ministry of Health and Family Welfare.

- The program focuses on creating awareness about organ donation and transplantation, and establishing a regulatory framework for organ donation and transplantation in the country.
- The program aims to increase the availability of organs for transplantation, reduce the waiting time for transplantation, and improve the success rate of transplant procedures.
- The program has established a network of transplant centers across the country, which provide services for various organ transplants such as liver, kidney, heart, lungs, and pancreas.
- The program has also set up a National Organ and Tissue Transplant Organization (NOTTO) to coordinate and regulate organ donation and transplantation activities in the country.
- The program provides financial assistance to the needy patients for their transplantation through various schemes like Rashtriya Arogya Nidhi and Prime Minister's National Relief Fund.
- The program has been successful in increasing the number of organ donations and transplantations in the country. According to the NOTTO annual report of 2020-21, India witnessed an

increase in organ donation rate by 8.5% in the last year.

XIII

Role of World Health Organization (WHO) in Indian National Programs

Introduction:

The World Health Organization (WHO) is a specialized agency of the United Nations that is responsible for providing leadership on global health issues. It plays a significant role in supporting countries in developing and implementing national health programs, including India. India has been a member of the WHO since 1948 and has collaborated with the organization on numerous health initiatives.

National Health Programs in India: India has implemented several national health programs over the years with the aim of improving the health and wellbeing of its population. These programs cover various health issues such as infectious diseases, non-communicable diseases, maternal and child health, and mental health. The government of India, in collaboration with various stakeholders, implements these programs through the public healthcare system.

Role of WHO in Indian National Health Programs:

Technical Assistance:

The WHO provides technical assistance to the government of India in the development and implementation of national health programs. It provides guidance on various aspects of these programs such as planning, implementation, monitoring, and evaluation. For example, the WHO has provided technical assistance to the government of India in the development of the National Cancer Control Program.

Capacity Building:

The WHO also plays a significant role in building the capacity of healthcare professionals in India. It provides training programs, workshops, and other capacity-building initiatives for healthcare professionals to improve their knowledge and skills in various areas of healthcare. For example, the WHO has supported the government of India in building the capacity of healthcare professionals to manage and prevent the spread of COVID-19.

Advocacy and Awareness:

The WHO supports advocacy and awareness campaigns to improve the health and wellbeing of the population in India. It collaborates with the government of India and other stakeholders to raise awareness of various health issues and promote healthy behaviors. For example, the WHO has supported the government of India in the promotion of the National Tobacco Control Program.

Research and Innovation:

The WHO promotes research and innovation in healthcare to improve the health outcomes of the population in India. It collaborates with various research institutions in India to conduct research studies and develop innovative solutions to address various health issues. For example, the WHO has supported research studies in India to develop vaccines for various infectious diseases.

Let us discuss each role with more information

Technical Assistance:

The World Health Organization (WHO) plays a crucial role in supporting the Indian government's efforts to improve the health of its citizens. One of the key ways in which the WHO supports India is through the provision of technical assistance for the development and implementation of national health programs. This technical assistance encompasses a wide range of areas such as planning, implementation, monitoring, and evaluation.

Technical Assistance for National Health Programs: The WHO provides technical assistance to the government of India in the development and implementation of several national health programs. For instance, the WHO has provided technical assistance in the development of the National Cancer Control Program. The program aims to prevent and control cancer in India through early detection, diagnosis, and treatment. The WHO has helped in the development of guidelines for cancer control, training programs for healthcare professionals, and the establishment of cancer registries.

Another example of the WHO's technical assistance is in the development of the National Program for Prevention and Control of Deafness. The program aims to prevent and control hearing loss in India through early detection, diagnosis, and treatment. The WHO has helped in the development of guidelines for deafness prevention and control, training programs for healthcare professionals, and the establishment of a national database for deafness.

The WHO has also provided technical assistance in the development of the National Mental Health Program. The program aims to provide accessible, affordable, and quality mental healthcare to all individuals in need in India. The WHO has helped in the development of guidelines for mental healthcare, training programs for healthcare professionals, and the establishment of a national mental health surveillance system.

Monitoring and Evaluation: The WHO also provides technical assistance in monitoring and evaluating the progress of national health programs. For example, the WHO has assisted in the development of the National Vector Borne Disease Control Program's monitoring and evaluation framework. The program aims to control vector-borne diseases such as malaria, dengue, and chikungunya in India. The WHO has helped in the development of a surveillance system for vector-borne diseases, training programs for healthcare professionals, and the establishment of a reporting system for vector-borne diseases.

Case Study: One of the successful collaborations between the WHO and the Indian government is the Polio Eradication Program. The program aimed to eliminate polio from India through a nationwide immunization campaign. The WHO provided technical assistance to the Indian government in the planning, implementation, monitoring, and evaluation of the program. The program was successful, and India was declared polio-free in 2014.

The WHO plays a critical role in supporting the Indian government's efforts to improve the health of its citizens. The technical assistance provided by the WHO is a crucial element in the development and implementation of national health programs. The WHO's expertise and guidance have helped the Indian government in the successful implementation of several health programs, including the Polio Eradication Program. The WHO's continued technical assistance is essential for the success of national health programs in India.

Capacity Building:

Capacity building is another crucial area where the World Health Organization (WHO) has been actively involved in supporting India's national health programs. The WHO's capacity-building initiatives aim to improve the skills, knowledge, and competencies of healthcare professionals, particularly those working in resource-limited settings.

The WHO provides various training programs and workshops to healthcare professionals in India to enhance their capacity in various areas of healthcare, including disease management, prevention, and control. For instance, the WHO has conducted capacity-building workshops and training programs for healthcare workers to improve their knowledge and skills in managing tuberculosis, malaria, HIV/AIDS, and other communicable diseases.

In addition, the WHO has supported the Indian government in building the capacity of healthcare professionals to respond to emergencies and disasters. For example, in response to the COVID-19 pandemic, the WHO has collaborated with the Indian government to provide technical assistance, training, and guidance to healthcare workers on infection prevention and control measures, clinical management of COVID-19, and risk communication.

Another significant aspect of the WHO's capacity-building initiatives is the development of guidelines, standards, and protocols for healthcare professionals. These guidelines aim to promote evidence-based practices and improve the quality of healthcare services delivered in India. For instance, the WHO has developed guidelines for the prevention and management of non-communicable diseases, such as diabetes, cancer, and cardiovascular diseases.

The WHO's capacity-building initiatives in India have been instrumental in improving the quality of healthcare services and strengthening the healthcare system's capacity to respond to health challenges. By enhancing the skills and knowledge of healthcare professionals, the WHO is contributing to the development of a competent and skilled healthcare workforce in India that can effectively deliver high-quality health services to the population.

Advocacy and Awareness:

To further expand on the role of the WHO in advocacy and awareness campaigns, it is important to note that the organization has worked closely with the government of India to raise awareness of a variety of health issues. One example is the promotion of the National Tobacco Control Program (NTCP), which was launched in 2007 to address the high prevalence of tobacco use in India. The WHO has provided technical assistance to the government of India in the development and implementation of the NTCP, and has also supported advocacy and awareness campaigns to promote the program.

The WHO has also supported advocacy and awareness campaigns in other areas, such as mental health. In 2014, the organization launched a campaign called "Depression: Let's Talk" in India to raise awareness of depression and promote access to treatment. The campaign included social media outreach, public service announcements, and other activities to promote dialogue and reduce stigma around mental health issues.

Additionally, the WHO has supported advocacy and awareness campaigns related to vaccination. For example, the organization has collaborated with the government of India to promote the importance of vaccination and to address vaccine hesitancy. As part of these efforts, the WHO has worked to increase access to accurate information about vaccines, and has supported the development of targeted communication strategies to promote vaccination.

Overall, the WHO's role in advocacy and awareness campaigns has been crucial in promoting healthy behaviors and addressing health issues in India. The organization's collaborations with the government of India and other stakeholders have helped to improve public health outcomes and reduce the burden of disease in the country.

Research and Innovation:

The WHO also supports research and innovation in India's healthcare sector. It collaborates with the government of India and other stakeholders to identify research priorities, promote research initiatives, and disseminate research findings. The WHO also provides technical assistance and guidance on research methodologies and ethics.

One example of the WHO's support for research and innovation in India is the India Country Cooperation Strategy (CCS) for 2019-2023. This strategy includes a focus on strengthening research and innovation in the healthcare sector, with a particular emphasis on addressing the burden of non-communicable diseases (NCDs). The strategy outlines several objectives related to research and innovation, including:

- Strengthening the research capacity of the Indian Council of Medical Research (ICMR) and other research institutions in India
- Promoting the development and implementation of innovative technologies and interventions for NCD prevention and control
- Supporting the dissemination of research findings to improve health policies and programs
- Strengthening health research ethics in India

The WHO has also supported research initiatives in India related to tuberculosis (TB) and malaria. For example, the WHO has collaborated with the government of India and other stakeholders to conduct research on the effectiveness of new TB drugs and to develop new malaria diagnostic tools. Through these research initiatives, the WHO aims to contribute to the development of evidence-based policies and programs to improve health outcomes in India.

XIV

Community Services in Rural,Urban and School

In India, healthcare services for rural, urban, and school populations are provided through a combination of government-run and private healthcare facilities. The government has implemented various national health programs to provide accessible and affordable healthcare services to the population.

Rural Health Services

Healthcare infrastructure in rural India comprises three levels of healthcare facilities: Sub-Centers, Primary Health Centers (PHCs), and Community Health Centers (CHCs). These healthcare facilities are managed by the government of India and are supported by various national health programs.

Sub-Centers: Sub-Centers are the first point of contact between the community and the healthcare system. They provide basic healthcare services to the community and are the primary healthcare infrastructure in rural India. The primary focus of Sub-

Centers is on maternal and child health, family planning, immunization, and basic healthcare services. Sub-Centers are staffed by a female health worker (Auxiliary Nurse Midwife) and a male health worker (Multipurpose Health Worker).

Primary Health Centers (PHCs): PHCs are the second level of healthcare infrastructure in rural India. They provide essential primary healthcare services to the community and are equipped with basic diagnostic facilities. PHCs are staffed by a Medical Officer, a Pharmacist, and a team of healthcare workers. The main focus of PHCs is on preventive healthcare, maternal and child health, family planning, and treatment of common illnesses.

To further elaborate, PHCs provide a range of healthcare services including antenatal care, immunization, laboratory tests, minor surgeries, and treatment of communicable and non-communicable diseases. They also play a crucial role in health promotion and disease prevention through community-based programs and awareness campaigns.

For example, in the state of Karnataka, the government has implemented a program called "Usha Kirana" to improve the maternal and child health outcomes in rural areas. Under this program, PHCs conduct regular health check-ups and provide essential maternal and child healthcare services such as antenatal care, immunization, and nutrition counseling. The program has shown significant improvements in maternal and child health indicators in the state.

Another example is the "National Rural Health Mission" (NRHM) which was launched by the government of India in 2005 to strengthen the healthcare infrastructure in rural areas. The NRHM aims to provide equitable and affordable healthcare services to the rural population by strengthening the PHC system, providing essential drugs and diagnostics, and improving the quality of healthcare services. The program has contributed to significant improvements in maternal and child health outcomes in rural areas.

Overall, PHCs play a critical role in providing basic healthcare services to the rural population and are an essential component of the healthcare infrastructure in rural India.

Community Health Centers (CHCs): CHCs are the third level of healthcare infrastructure in rural India. They provide comprehensive healthcare services to the community and are equipped with diagnostic facilities and specialist doctors. CHCs are staffed by Medical Officers, Specialists, and a team of healthcare workers. The main focus of CHCs is on providing specialized healthcare services, including obstetrics and gynecology, surgery, medicine, pediatrics, and dental care.

Challenges: The healthcare infrastructure in rural India faces various challenges, including inadequate funding, shortage of healthcare workers, inadequate infrastructure, and lack of access to diagnostic facilities. The government of India has implemented various initiatives to address these challenges, including the National Rural Health Mission (NRHM) and the Ayushman Bharat scheme, which aim to improve the quality and accessibility of healthcare services in rural areas.

In conclusion, the healthcare infrastructure in rural India is critical in providing basic healthcare services to the community. The government of India has implemented various national health programs and initiatives to improve the quality and accessibility of healthcare services in rural areas. However, there is still a need for sustained efforts to address the challenges faced by the healthcare infrastructure in rural India.

Sub-Centers

Sub-Centers are an essential component of the rural healthcare infrastructure in India. They act as a vital link between the community and the formal healthcare system, particularly for those residing in remote and underserved areas. Sub-Centers provide a wide range of services to the community, including health promotion, disease prevention, and basic curative services.

Maternal and Child Health: Maternal and child health services are the primary focus of Sub-Centers. They provide antenatal care, postnatal care, and immunization services to pregnant women and children. Female health workers at Sub-Centers play a critical role in promoting safe motherhood practices and educating women about the importance of maternal health. They also provide counseling and support to women during and after childbirth.

Family Planning: Sub-Centers also provide family planning services to couples. Health workers at Sub-Centers counsel couples on various family planning methods and help them choose the most suitable method based on their needs and preferences. They also provide contraceptives and conduct follow-up visits to ensure the continued use of family planning methods.

Immunization: Sub-Centers are responsible for organizing and conducting immunization programs in their catchment area. They provide immunization services to children and pregnant women against various vaccine-preventable diseases such as measles, polio, and tetanus. Sub-Centers also maintain immunization records and conduct outreach activities to ensure maximum coverage.

Basic Healthcare Services: Sub-Centers provide basic curative services to the community. They treat minor illnesses and injuries, manage common childhood illnesses, and provide first aid in emergencies. Health workers at Sub-Centers also conduct health check-ups and screening for common non-communicable diseases such as diabetes and hypertension.

Despite their importance, Sub-Centers face various challenges such as inadequate infrastructure, shortage of staff, and limited resources. However, several initiatives such as the National Rural Health Mission (NRHM) have been launched to address these challenges and improve the functioning of Sub-Centers in rural India.

For example, the NRHM has supported the development of sub-center infrastructure, including the provision of essential equipment and supplies. The NRHM has also provided training and capacity building for health workers, which has improved their skills and knowledge in providing quality healthcare services. Additionally, the NRHM has introduced performance-based incentives for health workers, which has helped to improve their motivation and commitment to their work.

In conclusion, Sub-Centers are an essential component of the rural healthcare infrastructure in India. They play a crucial role in providing basic healthcare services to the community and improving health outcomes, particularly for women and children. Despite the challenges they face, several initiatives have been launched to improve the functioning of Sub-Centers, which has helped to strengthen the rural healthcare system in India.

UPHC in Hyderabad

Primary Health Centers (PHCs):

PHCs are the second level of healthcare infrastructure in rural India. They provide essential primary healthcare services to the community and are equipped with basic diagnostic facilities. PHCs are staffed by a Medical Officer, a Pharmacist, and a team of healthcare workers. The main focus of PHCs is on preventive healthcare, maternal and child health, family planning, and treatment of common illnesses.

PHCs provide a range of healthcare services including antenatal care, immunization, laboratory tests, minor surgeries, and treatment of communicable and non-communicable diseases. They also play a crucial role in health promotion and disease prevention through community-based programs and awareness campaigns.

For example, in the state of Karnataka, the government has implemented a program called "Usha Kirana" to improve the maternal and child health outcomes in rural areas. Under this program, PHCs conduct regular health check-ups and provide essential maternal and child healthcare services such as antenatal care, immunization, and nutrition counseling. The program has shown significant improvements in maternal and child health indicators in the state.

"National Rural Health Mission" (NRHM) which was launched by the government of India in 2005 to strengthen the healthcare infrastructure in rural areas. The NRHM aims to provide equitable and affordable healthcare services to the rural population by strengthening the PHC system, providing essential drugs and diagnostics, and improving the quality of healthcare services. The program has contributed to significant improvements in maternal and child health outcomes in rural areas.

PHCs play a critical role in providing basic healthcare services to the rural population and are an essential component of the healthcare infrastructure in rural India.

Community Health Centers (CHCs)

Community Health Centers (CHCs) are the third and final level of healthcare infrastructure in rural India, and they serve as the referral centers for Primary Health Centers (PHCs). CHCs provide comprehensive healthcare services to the community and are equipped with diagnostic facilities and specialist doctors. They are typically located in district headquarters and larger towns and have more advanced equipment and resources than PHCs.

The primary focus of CHCs is on providing specialized healthcare services, including obstetrics and gynecology, surgery, medicine, pediatrics, and dental care. They also provide preventive healthcare services, including immunization, health education, and disease surveillance. CHCs are staffed by Medical Officers, Specialists, and a team of healthcare workers, including nurses, pharmacists, and laboratory technicians.

One of the major challenges in providing healthcare services in rural India is the shortage of specialist doctors. To address this issue, the government has launched various initiatives to attract and retain doctors in rural areas, such as the "National Rural Health Mission" and "Rural Health Practitioners' Program." Additionally, CHCs have been equipped with telemedicine facilities, which enable doctors to remotely diagnose and treat patients using video conferencing technology.

Despite these efforts, there are still significant gaps in healthcare infrastructure and services in rural India. For example, there is a shortage of healthcare workers, and many rural areas lack basic diagnostic and treatment facilities. This has led to poor health outcomes and a high burden of disease in rural communities. However, the government of India continues to invest in improving healthcare infrastructure and services in rural areas, and there is hope that with continued efforts, access to quality healthcare will improve for all rural residents.

An example of a successful CHC in India is the Aundh Civil Hospital in Maharashtra, which provides a wide range of healthcare services to the local community. The hospital has a team of doctors and healthcare workers who are trained to provide specialized care, including surgeries and emergency services. The hospital also runs outreach programs to educate the community about various health issues, and it has implemented innovative programs to improve access to healthcare, such as the use of mobile clinics to reach remote communities. These efforts have led to improved health outcomes and increased access to healthcare services for the local population.

One of the major challenges in rural healthcare is the shortage of healthcare professionals, which has resulted in uneven access to healthcare services. The government has launched several initiatives to address this issue, such as the National Rural Health Mission (NRHM), which aims to improve the availability and quality of healthcare services in rural areas. NRHM has also focused on strengthening community participation and improving the accountability of healthcare providers.

Urban Health Services

In urban areas, the healthcare infrastructure is typically made up of Community Health Centers (CHCs) and Primary Health Centers (PHCs), which provide essential healthcare services to the population.

Community Health Centers (CHCs) in urban areas are similar to those in rural areas but with more specialized services. They provide comprehensive healthcare services, including outpatient care, inpatient care, and emergency care. CHCs in urban areas are equipped with more advanced diagnostic facilities, including X-ray machines, ultrasound machines, and laboratory services. They are also staffed by specialist doctors in areas such as gynecology, surgery, medicine, and pediatrics.

Primary Health Centers (PHCs) in urban areas are similar to those in rural areas but are typically smaller in size and scope. They provide essential primary healthcare services, including immunization, maternal and child health, family planning, and treatment of common illnesses. PHCs in urban areas are staffed by Medical Officers, Nurses, and a team of healthcare workers. They are equipped with basic diagnostic facilities, such as blood pressure monitors and thermometers, and may also offer laboratory services.

Both CHCs and PHCs in urban areas play a critical role in providing accessible and affordable healthcare services to the population. They provide a range of healthcare services that are essential for maintaining good health and preventing the spread of diseases.

For example, in the city of Mumbai, the Municipal Corporation of Greater Mumbai operates a network of primary healthcare centers that provide essential healthcare services to the population. The centers offer a range of services, including immunization, family planning, antenatal care, and treatment of common illnesses. The centers also provide referral services to higher-level hospitals for patients who require specialized care.

In Delhi, the government has implemented the Mohalla Clinic program, which aims to provide accessible and affordable healthcare services to the urban population. Under the program, primary healthcare centers, called Mohalla Clinics, have been set up in densely populated areas. These clinics provide basic healthcare services, including consultation with a doctor, laboratory services, and medicines. The program has been successful in providing accessible and affordable healthcare services to the urban population.

School Health Services

School Health Services aim to promote the health and well-being of school-aged children by providing preventive and promotive health services. The Government of India has implemented several school health programs, including the National School Health Program (NSHP) and Rashtriya Bal Swasthya Karyakram (RBSK).

The NSHP provides health services to school children through regular health check-ups, immunizations, health education, and nutrition services. The program is implemented through the education system, with school teachers, school health nurses, and health workers providing health services to school children. The program also includes the provision of safe drinking water and sanitation facilities in schools.

The RBSK is a comprehensive health program that provides services to children aged 0-18 years in both rural and urban areas. The program aims to screen children for common health conditions, provide early identification and management of diseases, and refer children to higher levels of care when necessary. The program includes the provision of health services such as health check-ups, immunizations, and nutrition services, as well as services for children with disabilities.

Under the RBSK program, children are screened for various health conditions, including birth defects, developmental delays, nutritional deficiencies, and common childhood diseases such as malaria, tuberculosis, and pneumonia. The program provides early identification and management of diseases through the provision of essential drugs, diagnostic tests, and referrals to higher levels of care when necessary.

The RBSK program also provides services for children with disabilities, including early identification, assessment, and management of disabilities. The program provides assistive devices such as hearing aids, spectacles, and wheelchairs to children with disabilities, as well as rehabilitation services such as physiotherapy and speech therapy.

Overall, the School Health Services aim to promote the health and well-being of school-aged children through the provision of preventive and promotive health services. The programs are implemented through the education system and provide essential health services to children in both rural and urban areas.

Examples and Case Studies:

The NRHM has led to significant improvements in maternal and child health indicators in rural areas. The program has focused on improving access to maternal and child health services and increasing the availability of skilled birth attendants.

The Ayushman Bharat scheme has provided financial protection to millions of families in urban areas, leading to improved access to healthcare services and reduced financial burden.

The NSHP has led to increased awareness of health and wellness among school children, resulting in improved health outcomes and reduced absenteeism.

The RBSK has led to early identification and management of several health conditions in children, leading to improved health outcomes and reduced morbidity and mortality.

Primary health centers (PHCs)

Introduction: Primary Health Care (PHC) is an essential element of the healthcare system in India. It is the first point of contact between individuals and the healthcare system. PHCs provide a range of healthcare services that are accessible, affordable, and of good quality. The PHC system in India plays a crucial role in addressing the healthcare needs of the population, particularly in rural areas where access to healthcare services is limited.

Functions of PHC:

Prevention and control of communicable diseases:

PHCs play a vital role in the prevention and control of communicable diseases. They provide immunization services to prevent the spread of infectious diseases like polio, measles, and tetanus. PHCs also conduct surveillance and control measures for diseases like tuberculosis, malaria, and HIV/AIDS.

For example, in the state of Odisha, the government has implemented a program called 'Dastak,' which aims to improve immunization coverage in rural areas. The program uses mobile vans to reach remote areas and provide immunization services to children.

Maternal and child health services:

PHCs also provide maternal and child health services, including antenatal care, postnatal care, and child health services. They provide immunization services to children, including vaccination against measles, polio, and other childhood diseases. PHCs also provide family planning services and promote the use of contraceptives.

For example, the Janani Suraksha Yojana (JSY) is a national program that provides cash incentives to women in rural areas who give birth in a health facility. The program aims to reduce maternal and neonatal mortality rates by encouraging women to seek maternal and child health services at PHCs.

Treatment and management of non-communicable diseases:

PHCs also provide treatment and management services for non-communicable diseases like diabetes, hypertension, and cancer. They provide diagnosis, treatment, and follow-up services to patients with chronic diseases.

For example, the government of Tamil Nadu has implemented a program called the 'Non-Communicable Disease Control Program' to prevent and control non-communicable diseases. The program includes screening and treatment services for diabetes and hypertension at PHCs.

Health education and promotion:

PHCs play a crucial role in health education and promotion. They promote healthy behaviors and provide information on disease prevention and management. PHCs also conduct health education campaigns on various health issues, including nutrition, hygiene, and sanitation.

For example, the government of Kerala has implemented a program called 'Arogyakeralam' to promote health education and awareness among the population. The program includes various activities like health camps, health education campaigns, and training programs for healthcare professionals.

Referral services:

PHCs also provide referral services to higher-level healthcare facilities for patients who require specialized care. They refer patients to district hospitals or medical colleges for specialized treatment.

For example, the government of Maharashtra has implemented a program called 'Maha Arogya' to provide a seamless referral system for patients. The program includes a toll-free number that patients can call to get information on healthcare services and referral to higher-level healthcare facilities.

Disease Control and Prevention:

PHCs play an important role in the control and prevention of communicable diseases like tuberculosis, malaria, and HIV/AIDS. They provide immunization services, conduct screening and surveillance programs, and offer treatment and counseling services to control the spread of these diseases.

Examples of PHC functions in action include:

In the state of Kerala, PHCs have played a crucial role in the prevention and control of communicable diseases such as malaria, tuberculosis, and HIV/AIDS. PHCs in Kerala have implemented various strategies such as community-based surveillance, health education programs, and distribution of insecticide-treated mosquito nets to control the spread of malaria.

In the state of Rajasthan, PHCs have focused on maternal and child health services. PHCs in Rajasthan provide antenatal care, safe delivery, and postnatal care services to pregnant women and newborns. They also conduct immunization drives to ensure that children receive their vaccines on time.

In the state of Tamil Nadu, PHCs have implemented health promotion and education programs to raise awareness about various health issues. PHCs in Tamil Nadu conduct health camps and workshops to educate people on topics such as hygiene, sanitation, and healthy lifestyle habits. They also provide counseling services to patients and their families on managing chronic diseases like diabetes and hypertension.

PHCs play a critical role in providing healthcare services to the population, particularly in rural areas. They provide a range of services, including disease prevention and control, maternal and child health services, treatment and management of non-communicable diseases, health education and promotion, and referral services. PHCs are an essential component of the healthcare system in India and are vital in addressing the healthcare needs of the population.

XV

Improvement in Rural Sanitation

Sanitation is a critical component of public health, and poor sanitation can lead to the spread of diseases, especially in rural areas. In India, the government has implemented several rural sanitation programs to address this issue, including the Total Sanitation Campaign (TSC) and the Swachh Bharat Mission Gramin (SBM-G).

The Total Sanitation Campaign (TSC)

It was one of the most significant rural sanitation programs in India, launched by the Government of India in 1999. The program aimed to provide access to sanitation facilities for all rural households in the country. At the time of the launch of the program, only 22% of households in rural India had access to proper sanitation facilities.

The TSC had a two-pronged approach to increase the percentage of households with access to sanitation facilities.

First, it aimed to create awareness about the health hazards associated with poor sanitation practices, and second, it sought to promote the adoption of safe sanitation practices through community-led approaches. The campaign focused on behavior change communication to encourage people to adopt safe sanitation practices.

One of the notable figures associated with the TSC is Bindeshwar Pathak, the founder of Sulabh International, an NGO that works towards providing sanitation facilities to the underprivileged in India. Bindeshwar Pathak was awarded the Gandhi Peace Prize in 2016 for his contributions to the field of sanitation.

One of the significant challenges faced by the TSC was the prevalence of open defecation in rural areas. According to studies, nearly 80% of infections in rural areas were caused by fecal matter. To tackle this issue, the TSC promoted the use of various types of toilets, including Sulabh Sauchalaya, dry toilets, close pit toilets, and others. The use of these toilets helped reduce the prevalence of open defecation in rural areas.

In 2014, the Government of India launched the Swachh Bharat Mission Gramin (SBM-G), which aimed to provide access to toilets to all households in rural areas. The SBM-G has been successful in achieving significant progress in the area of rural sanitation. As of 2021, over 110 million toilets have been built in rural areas, and the percentage of households with access to proper sanitation facilities has increased to over 99%.

TSC was a significant initiative in the field of rural sanitation in India, and its success paved the way for further programs such as the SBM-G. The adoption of safe sanitation practices has had a significant impact on the health and wellbeing of the rural population in India.

Nirmal Bharat Abhiyan (NBA):

The NBA was launched in 2012 to continue the efforts of the TSC and provide universal access to sanitation facilities in rural areas. The goal of the NBA was to eradicate open defecation by 2022, which was later advanced to 2019 under the Swachh Bharat

Abhiyan (SBA) campaign. The NBA aimed to promote hygiene practices, construct household toilets, and ensure the sustainability of sanitation facilities through behavior change communication and community mobilization. The NBA also provided financial incentives to households to construct toilets and promoted the use of innovative technologies such as twin pit toilets and bio-toilets.

Incentives for toilets: Under the NBA, financial incentives were provided to households to construct toilets. The incentives varied depending on the location and the type of toilet constructed. For example, in plain areas, a household could receive up to Rs. 10,000 for constructing a toilet, while in hilly and difficult terrain areas, the incentive amount was up to Rs. 12,000. The NBA also provided additional incentives for households who constructed toilets with improved designs such as twin pit toilets, bio-toilets, and composting toilets. The financial incentives were provided to households in installments based on the progress of toilet construction.

Hygiene promotion: The NBA also emphasized hygiene promotion to ensure the sustainability of sanitation facilities. The campaign focused on behavior change communication to promote the adoption of safe sanitation practices and the maintenance of sanitation facilities. The hygiene promotion activities included community mobilization, training of community volunteers, and the use of media campaigns to spread awareness about safe sanitation practices. The NBA also aimed to integrate hygiene promotion activities with other development programs such as water supply, health, and nutrition.

The TSC and the NBA played a significant role in promoting sanitation in rural areas of India. The campaigns emphasized behavior change communication and community mobilization to promote the adoption of safe sanitation practices and ensure the sustainability of sanitation facilities. The campaigns also provided financial incentives to households to construct toilets and promoted the use of innovative technologies to improve sanitation facilities. The Swachh Bharat Abhiyan (SBA) campaign, launched in 2014, built upon the efforts of the TSC and the NBA and aimed to achieve the goal of a clean and open defecation-free India by 2019.

Swachh Bharat Mission Gramin (SBM-G)

Swachh Bharat Mission Gramin (SBM-G) was launched on October 2, 2014, with the aim of making rural India open defecation-free (ODF) by October 2, 2019. The mission has been successful in improving sanitation coverage in rural areas and reducing the incidence of open defecation.

Under SBM-G, individual household toilets (IHHLs) are constructed in households without toilets, and community toilets are constructed for those who cannot afford to construct their own. The mission also promotes behavior change by focusing on the importance of safe sanitation practices and hygiene promotion.

To achieve its goal, SBM-G has implemented various strategies, including:

1. Community-led total sanitation: This approach focuses on community engagement to identify and address the open defecation practices in the community.
2. Information, education, and communication (IEC) activities: SBM-G uses various IEC activities to create awareness among the community about safe sanitation practices and the importance of toilet usage.
3. Incentives: SBM-G provides financial incentives to households to construct IHHLs and to local governments to achieve ODF status.
4. Capacity building: SBM-G provides training to masons and other stakeholders on toilet construction techniques and quality standards.

The SBM-G has made significant progress towards achieving its goal of making rural India ODF. As of March 2020, more than 10 crore IHHLs had been constructed, and over 6 lakh villages and 699 districts in India had been declared ODF.

The success of SBM-G can be attributed to the strong political will, community participation, and the use of innovative strategies like behavior change communication and financial incentives. The mission has not only improved sanitation coverage in rural areas but has also contributed to improving the overall health and well-being of rural communities.

Sulabh Sauchalaya

Dr. Bindeshwar Pathak, the founder of Sulabh International Social Service Organisation.In the year 2016, Sulabh International was honored with the **International Gandhi Peace Prize** for its efforts in improving sanitation conditions in India and liberating manual scavengers.

Sulabh Sauchalaya is a sanitation system developed in India by Sulabh International, a non-governmental organization established in 1970 by social activist **Dr. Bindeshwar Pathak**. The organization aims to promote human rights, environmental sanitation, and social reforms through the construction of low-cost sanitation facilities. The Sulabh Sauchalaya is a unique and innovative approach to sanitation, which addresses the problem of open defecation and lack of proper sanitation facilities in rural and urban areas of India.

The Sulabh Sauchalaya is a cost-effective and environmentally friendly solution that is based on the concept of twin-pit pour-flush toilets. The system includes two pits that are alternately used for collecting human waste. When one pit becomes full, the other one is used, and the full pit is left to decompose for several months. The decomposed waste is then used as fertilizer for plants, which promotes sustainable agriculture.

The Sulabh Sauchalaya has several advantages over traditional pit latrines and flush toilets. It requires less water than flush toilets and is more hygienic than pit latrines, as it prevents the spread of diseases and reduces the risk of contamination of groundwater sources. It is also easy to construct and maintain, making it suitable for use in rural and remote areas where resources are limited.

Sulabh International has constructed over 1.5 million Sulabh Sauchalayas in India and other countries, providing improved sanitation facilities to millions of people. The organization has also implemented several programs to promote hygiene and sanitation awareness, including the construction of community toilets and public health campaigns.

The Sulabh Sauchalaya has received international recognition for its innovative approach to sanitation. It has been praised by the United Nations and received several awards, including the Stockholm Water Prize in 2009 and the Energy Globe Award in 2013. The Sulabh International Museum of Toilets, located in New Delhi, is dedicated to showcasing the history and evolution of toilets and sanitation systems, including the Sulabh Sauchalaya.

The number of people using Sulabh Sauchalayas on a daily basis varies depending on the location and demand for the facility. In urban areas, where there is a high population density and limited access to sanitation facilities, the number of users can be quite high. In rural areas, the usage may be lower due to the availability of other sanitation options such as open defecation or traditional pit latrines. However, it is estimated that millions of people use Sulabh Sauchalayas across India every day. The organization reports that they have constructed over 1.5 million toilets and serve around 15 million people daily through their various sanitation projects.

The Sulabh Sauchalaya is an innovative and effective solution to the sanitation challenges faced by India and other developing countries. Its cost-effectiveness, sustainability, and ease of construction and maintenance make it a suitable option for providing improved sanitation facilities in rural and remote areas. The success of the Sulabh Sauchalaya in India and other countries is a testament to the importance of innovative and community-led approaches to addressing sanitation and hygiene challenges.

Dry toilets

Dry toilets, also known as ecological toilets or composting toilets, are an innovative approach to sanitation that can be particularly useful in areas where water is scarce or where there is no access to sewage systems. In dry toilets, the urine and feces are kept separate to prevent the formation of harmful compounds such as ammonia, and to facilitate the conversion of feces into fertilizer.

One type of dry toilet is the urine-diverting toilet, which separates urine from feces using a specially designed toilet bowl. The urine is collected separately and can be used as a fertilizer, while the feces are mixed with a dry carbon-rich material such as sawdust or peat moss to promote decomposition. This process kills harmful pathogens such as roundworm eggs and produces a nutrient-rich fertilizer that can be used for gardening or farming.

Dry toilets have several advantages over traditional flush toilets, including lower water consumption, reduced pollution, and reduced energy requirements. They also provide a solution for areas where there is no access to sewage systems or where the cost of building and maintaining traditional sewage systems is prohibitive.

The use of dry toilets has been promoted by organizations such as Sulabh International, which has developed a low-cost, ecological toilet system that is suitable for rural areas. The Sulabh Sauchalaya system is a self-contained unit that uses a composting process to convert human waste into fertilizer. The system is easy to install and maintain and has been widely adopted in rural areas in India and other countries.

It is difficult to estimate how many people use dry toilets on a daily basis, as their use is not yet widespread in many parts of the world. However, the use of dry toilets is growing in popularity, particularly in areas where water is scarce or where there is no access to sewage systems.

Closed pit toilets

Closed pit toilets, also known as dry pit toilets or pit latrines, are a type of non-flush toilet that rely on the natural decomposition of human waste in a pit located below the toilet. These toilets have been widely used in rural areas of developing countries where access to water and sanitation facilities is limited.

Closed pit toilets typically consist of a simple hole or pit dug in the ground, lined with bricks or stones, and covered with a platform or slab for sitting or squatting. The waste deposited in the pit is allowed to decompose naturally over time, with microorganisms breaking down the waste into compost-like material.

However, closed pit toilets can pose health and environmental risks if they are not managed properly. The pits can overflow, contaminating the surrounding soil and groundwater with pathogenic microorganisms, including bacteria, viruses, and parasites. Moreover, the decomposing waste emits foul odors, and can attract flies and other disease-carrying insects.

To mitigate these risks, it is essential to maintain the pit toilets properly, including regular cleaning and emptying of the pit, proper disposal of the waste, and ensuring adequate ventilation to prevent odors and gas buildup. Additionally, promoting the use of alternative sanitation technologies, such as composting toilets or eco-san toilets, can help address the environmental and health concerns associated with closed pit toilets.

Impact of Rural Sanitation Programs:

Rural sanitation programs in India have had a significant impact on public health. According to the World Health Organization, around 80% of infections in India are transmitted through fecal matter, highlighting the importance of improved sanitation. The TSC and SBM-G have contributed to reducing the incidence of open defecation and improving access to sanitation facilities in rural areas, thereby reducing the spread of diseases. Additionally, these programs have also improved the dignity and safety of women by providing them with access to private and safe sanitation facilities.

Rural sanitation programs in India have played a crucial role in improving public health and reducing the spread of diseases. The efforts of individuals like Bindeshwar Pathak and the implementation of initiatives like the TSC and SBM-G have contributed to improving sanitation facilities in rural areas. However, there is still a long way to go in ensuring universal access to safe and hygienic sanitation facilities in rural India.

XVI

National Urban Health Mission

I. Introduction

A. Overview of NUHM

The National Urban Health Mission (NUHM) is a flagship program launched by the Government of India in 2013 to improve the health status of the urban poor in the country. NUHM aims to provide equitable and quality healthcare services to the urban poor, including the slum dwellers and migrants. The mission is implemented through the state governments and Union Territories and is funded by both the central and state governments.

B. History of NUHM

NUHM is a part of the National Health Mission (NHM), which was launched in 2005 to address the health needs of underserved areas in the country. The NHM is divided into two sub-missions: the National Rural Health Mission (NRHM) and the National Urban Health Mission (NUHM). The NRHM focuses on improving the health status of rural areas, while NUHM aims to improve the health status of urban areas.

C. Objectives of NUHM

The primary objective of NUHM is to improve the health status of the urban poor by providing them access to basic healthcare services, including maternal and child health, family planning, and non-communicable diseases. The secondary objectives of the mission are to reduce infant mortality rate and maternal mortality rate among the urban poor, promote health-seeking behavior among the urban poor, improve the availability and accessibility of quality healthcare services for the urban poor, and strengthen the health system and infrastructure in urban areas.

D. Components of NUHM

Strengthening of the healthcare system: This component focuses on strengthening the healthcare system in urban areas by improving the infrastructure of urban health centers, providing equipment and supplies, and training health personnel.

Maternal and Child Health: This component aims to reduce maternal and infant mortality rates by improving access to maternal and child health services, including antenatal care, postnatal care, and immunization services.

Family Planning: This component focuses on improving access to family planning services and increasing the awareness of family planning methods among the urban poor.

Non-communicable Diseases: This component aims to prevent and control non-communicable diseases, such as diabetes, hypertension, and cancer, among the urban poor by promoting healthy lifestyles, early detection, and management of these diseases.

Communicable Diseases: This component focuses on preventing and controlling communicable diseases, such as malaria, dengue, and tuberculosis, among the urban poor by improving the surveillance and management of these diseases.

II. Health Facilities Under NUHM

The National Urban Health Mission (NUHM) aims to provide access to basic healthcare services to the urban poor, including the slum dwellers and migrants. The mission is implemented through the state governments and Union Territories and is funded by both the central and state governments. The health facilities under NUHM are designed to cater to the needs of the urban population in different areas.

A. Primary Health Centers (PHCs)

Primary Health Centers (PHCs) are the first point of contact for the rural and urban population seeking healthcare services. PHCs under NUHM are designed to provide primary healthcare services to the urban poor. Each PHC caters to a population of around 30,000 in urban areas. The services provided at PHCs include maternal and child healthcare, family planning, immunization, and treatment of minor ailments.

B. Urban Primary Health Centers (UPHCs)

Urban Primary Health Centers (UPHCs) are the equivalent of PHCs in urban areas. UPHCs under NUHM are designed to cater to the health needs of the urban population. The services provided at UPHCs include outpatient services, maternal and child healthcare, family planning, immunization, and treatment of minor ailments. Each UPHC caters to a population of around 50,000.

C. Community Health Centers (CHCs)

Community Health Centers (CHCs) are designed to provide secondary healthcare services to the urban population. CHCs under NUHM are equipped with specialist doctors, diagnostic services, and inpatient facilities. Each CHC caters to a population of around 1 lakh.

D. Sub-District Hospitals

Sub-District Hospitals under NUHM are designed to provide tertiary healthcare services to the urban population. These hospitals are equipped with specialist doctors, diagnostic services, and inpatient facilities. Each Sub-District Hospital caters to a population of around 5 lakhs.

E. District Hospitals

District Hospitals are the highest level of healthcare facilities under NUHM. These hospitals are equipped with specialist doctors, diagnostic services, and inpatient facilities. Each district hospital caters to a population of several lakhs.

The NUHM focuses on strengthening the healthcare infrastructure in urban areas to provide equitable and quality healthcare services to the urban poor. The mission aims to reduce infant mortality rate, maternal mortality rate, and the incidence of communicable and non-communicable diseases among the urban poor.

III. Human Resources for Health Under NUHM

A. Medical Officers in Charge (MOICs)

MOICs are responsible for overseeing the functioning of the health facilities at the urban primary health center and community health center level.

They are required to have a degree in allopathic medicine and have experience in managing healthcare facilities.

Their duties include ensuring the availability of medicines and medical supplies, supervising staff, and ensuring that the health facilities provide quality healthcare services to the urban poor.

B. Auxiliary Nurse Midwives (ANMs)

ANMs are responsible for providing primary healthcare services at the urban primary health center and community health center level.

They are required to have completed a diploma in nursing and midwifery and are trained in providing basic maternal and child health services, family planning services, and basic healthcare services.

ANMs are responsible for conducting home visits to pregnant women and newborns, promoting health-seeking behavior, and providing health education to the community.

C. Accredited Social Health Activists (ASHAs)

Accredited Social Health Activists (ASHAs)

Accredited Social Health Activists (ASHAs) play a crucial role in the implementation of the National Urban Health Mission (NUHM) in India. ASHAs are community health workers who act as a link between the community and the healthcare system. Their main role is to provide healthcare information and services to the community, with a special focus on the urban poor, slum dwellers, and migrants.

The role and responsibilities of ASHAs in NUHM are as follows:

1. Health Promotion and Education: ASHAs are responsible for promoting health and hygiene practices in the community

through health education sessions. They educate the community on topics such as family planning, nutrition, sanitation, and prevention of communicable and non-communicable diseases.

2. Identification of Health Risks: ASHAs identify health risks in the community by conducting regular surveys and screening programs. They identify high-risk groups such as pregnant women, infants, and the elderly and refer them to the nearest health facility for appropriate care.
3. Referral Services: ASHAs refer community members to health facilities for preventive, promotive, and curative services. They also accompany patients to the health facility to ensure that they receive the required care.
4. Tracking of Health Services: ASHAs track the health status of the community by maintaining records of births, deaths, and immunizations. They also monitor the treatment adherence of patients with chronic diseases such as tuberculosis and diabetes.
5. Support for Maternal and Child Health: ASHAs play a crucial role in promoting maternal and child health. They conduct home visits to pregnant women and newborns and provide them with information on antenatal care, delivery, and postnatal care.
6. Provision of Family Planning Services: ASHAs provide information on family planning methods and services. They also distribute contraceptives and refer women to health facilities for long-term contraceptive methods.

In summary, ASHAs are an important link between the community and the healthcare system in India. They provide a range of services to promote health and prevent disease, especially among the urban poor, slum dwellers, and migrants.

D. Mahila Arogya Samiti (MAS)

MAS is a community-based organization responsible for promoting maternal and child health in urban areas.

It is a group of women volunteers who are trained to provide health education to the community, conduct home visits to identify health issues, and create awareness about the importance of antenatal care, immunization, and other health issues related to women and children.

MAS also plays a role in monitoring the quality of healthcare services provided at the urban primary health center and community health center level.

The main activities and functions of MAS (Mahila Arogya Samiti) include:

1. Community Mobilization: MAS helps in mobilizing the community for health promotion and disease prevention activities. It creates awareness among the community members about the importance of personal hygiene, sanitation, and immunization.
2. Health Education: MAS conducts health education sessions on various topics related to maternal and child health, family planning, nutrition, and hygiene. The sessions are conducted in the community or at the health facility, depending on the convenience of the members.
3. Monitoring of Health Services: MAS members monitor the quality of health services provided by the ANMs and other health workers in the area. They also keep track of the immunization status of children and pregnant women and encourage them to complete their vaccination schedule.
4. Referral Services: MAS members refer pregnant women and sick children to the nearest health facility for further treatment. They also follow up with the women and children to ensure that they have received proper care.
5. Coordination with Health Workers: MAS members coordinate with the ANMs and other health workers to ensure that the health services are delivered effectively. They also assist the health workers in conducting health camps and other outreach activities.
6. Record Keeping: MAS members maintain records of the health-related activities conducted in the area, such as the number of health education sessions conducted, the number of people

attending the sessions, and the number of referrals made.

IV. NUHM Programs and Services

The National Urban Health Mission (NUHM) offers a wide range of programs and services to improve the health status of the urban poor in India. Some of the key programs and services under NUHM are:

A. Maternal and Child Health

NUHM gives special attention to maternal and child health, aiming to reduce maternal and infant mortality rates. Services provided include antenatal care, institutional deliveries, postnatal care, newborn care, immunization, and family planning.

B. Family Planning

NUHM aims to promote family planning and provide accessible contraceptive services to urban poor families. It focuses on creating awareness about family planning methods, ensuring the availability of contraceptive methods, and providing counseling to couples.

C. Non-Communicable Diseases

NUHM has initiated programs for the prevention and control of non-communicable diseases such as hypertension, diabetes, and cancer. It focuses on creating awareness, early detection, and treatment of these diseases.

D. Communicable Diseases

NUHM also aims to prevent and control communicable diseases such as malaria, tuberculosis, dengue, and hepatitis. It focuses on creating awareness, early detection, and treatment of these diseases.

E. Health Promotion and Education

NUHM has initiated programs to promote health and hygiene among the urban poor. It focuses on creating awareness about healthy living, personal hygiene, and sanitation.

F. Urban Health Infrastructure Development

NUHM aims to strengthen the health infrastructure in urban areas. It focuses on creating new health facilities, upgrading existing facilities, and providing basic amenities such as clean water and sanitation facilities in health centers.

V. NUHM Achievements and Challenges

A. Achievements

1. Improved access to primary healthcare services for the urban poor
2. Reduction in infant mortality rate (IMR) and maternal mortality rate (MMR) among the urban poor
3. Increased awareness and utilization of family planning services among the urban poor
4. Strengthening of urban health infrastructure and facilities
5. Reduction in the prevalence of communicable diseases such as malaria, tuberculosis, and dengue fever

B. Challenges

1. Limited funding and resources for NUHM implementation
2. Inadequate health workforce and training programs for NUHM
3. Difficulty in reaching out to the most marginalized and vulnerable urban populations
4. Limited community participation and engagement in NUHM programs and services
5. Need for greater coordination and collaboration among different stakeholders involved in NUHM implementation

XVII

Health Promotion and Education in School

I. Introduction

A. Overview of health promotion and education in schools

India is a country with a population of over 1.3 billion people, and a significant proportion of the population is comprised of children and adolescents who attend school. Health promotion and education are crucial components of ensuring the wellbeing and future success of this young population.

In India, health promotion and education in schools aim to empower students to adopt healthy behaviors and practices, develop positive attitudes towards health, and acquire knowledge and skills to make informed decisions about their health. The primary focus of health promotion and education in schools is on the prevention of health problems and the promotion of positive health outcomes.

Health promotion and education in schools in India cover a wide range of topics, including personal hygiene, physical activity, nutrition, mental health, and sexual and reproductive health. Schools play an essential role in promoting health and preventing illness among children and adolescents, as they are not only educational institutions but also places where students spend a significant amount of their time.

B. Importance of health promotion and education in schools

Health promotion and education in schools in India are essential for several reasons. Firstly, children and adolescents are particularly vulnerable to a range of health problems, and schools provide an ideal setting to address these problems. Secondly, schools can provide a platform for reaching a large number of students and can help to address health inequalities that exist across different sections of society.

Moreover, health promotion and education in schools can have a positive impact on students' academic performance and their overall quality of life. For example, research has shown that physical activity can improve academic performance, and mental health problems can negatively impact academic achievement.

Health promotion and education in schools can also help to promote a culture of health and wellbeing among students, which can have far-reaching benefits beyond their school years. By promoting healthy habits and behaviors, schools can help students to develop healthy habits that can last a lifetime.

II. Understanding Health Promotion and Education

A. Definition of health promotion and education

Health promotion and education are processes that aim to improve the health and wellbeing of individuals, communities, and populations. Health promotion involves creating conditions that enable people to achieve their full potential for health, while health education focuses on providing individuals with knowledge, skills, and resources to make informed decisions about their health.

In schools, health promotion and education involve a range of activities and strategies designed to promote positive health outcomes among students. These may include classroom-based education, health and wellbeing programs, physical activity and sports, and the provision of healthy food options in school canteens.

B. Benefits of health promotion and education in schools

1. Health promotion and education in schools have numerous benefits for students, teachers, and the wider community. Firstly, they can help to prevent a range of health problems, such as obesity, poor mental health, and substance abuse, which can have long-term negative effects on individuals' health and wellbeing.
2. Health promotion and education can improve academic performance and attendance rates, as students who are healthy and well-nourished are better able to concentrate and learn. Additionally, health promotion and education can contribute to the development of positive social skills and attitudes, which can help students to build positive relationships and succeed in their future careers.
3. Health promotion and education in schools can have a positive impact on the wider community. By promoting healthy habits and behaviors among students, schools can help to create a culture of health and wellbeing that extends beyond the school

gates and into the wider community.

C. Key principles and strategies of health promotion and education

Health promotion and education in schools are based on several key principles and strategies.

1. They should be evidence-based, meaning that interventions and programs should be based on scientific evidence and best practice. Secondly, they should be tailored to the needs and characteristics of the school community, taking into account cultural and social factors that may influence health behaviors.
2. Health promotion and education in schools should be participatory, meaning that students, teachers, and other stakeholders should be involved in the planning, implementation, and evaluation of programs. Programs should also be sustainable and long-term, with a focus on building capacity and creating a culture of health and wellbeing.
3. Key strategies for health promotion and education in schools include creating a supportive environment for health, developing life skills and social competence, providing accurate health information and education, and promoting healthy policies and practices. These strategies should be implemented in a holistic and integrated manner, with a focus on addressing thethe multiple determinants of health and wellbeing.

III. Health Issues in Schools

A. Common health problems among students

Students in India face a range of health issues, both physical and mental. Some of the most common health problems among students include malnutrition, obesity, poor dental health, respiratory infections, and mental health problems such as anxiety and depression. Additionally, many students in India are at risk of contracting communicable diseases such as malaria, dengue, and tuberculosis.

B. Contributing factors to poor health among students

There are several factors that contribute to poor health among students in India. These include poverty, inadequate access to healthcare and sanitation, poor nutrition, lack of physical activity, and exposure to environmental pollutants. Additionally, students in India may be at increased risk of poor mental health due to factors such as academic pressure, family conflict, and social isolation.

C. Impact of poor health on learning and academic performance

Poor health can have a significant impact on students' learning and academic performance. Students who are malnourished or have poor dental health may experience physical discomfort and pain, which can affect their ability to concentrate and participate in school activities. Additionally, students who are obese or have low levels of physical activity may have reduced fitness and energy levels, which can impact their ability to engage in physical education and sports.

Poor mental health can also have a significant impact on students' academic performance. Students who experience anxiety, depression, or other mental health problems may have difficulty concentrating, remembering information, and completing schoolwork. Additionally, poor mental health can contribute to absenteeism, social isolation, and poor relationships with peers and teachers.

Poor health among students in India can have significant negative effects on their learning and academic performance. Addressing the underlying factors contributing to poor health, and promoting positive health behaviors and practices, is essential for ensuring the wellbeing and academic success of students in India.

IV. Policies and Frameworks for Health Promotion and Education in Schools

A. Overview of national policies and frameworks for health promotion and education in schools

In India, there are several national policies and frameworks that guide health promotion and education in schools. These include the National Health Policy 2017, the National Education Policy 2020, and the Rashtriya Kishor Swasthya Karyakram (RKSK) program. These policies and frameworks emphasize the importance of promoting health and wellbeing among children and adolescents, and provide guidance on strategies for achieving this goal.

B. Role of schools and teachers in promoting health

Schools and teachers play a critical role in promoting health and wellbeing among students. They can provide students with information, resources, and opportunities to develop positive health behaviors and habits. Schools can also create a supportive environment that promotes healthy lifestyles and behaviors, such as providing healthy food options in school canteens and promoting physical activity through sports and recreation.

Teachers can play a key role in health promotion by incorporating health education into their curriculum and teaching practices. They can also act as role models for healthy behaviors and attitudes, and provide individual support and guidance to students who may be struggling with health issues or challenges.

C. Approaches and best practices for implementing health promotion and education in schools

There are several approaches and best practices for implementing health promotion and education in schools.

These include:

Creating a whole-school approach: A whole-school approach is an approach to health promotion and education that involves the whole school community - including students, teachers, parents, and other stakeholders - in promoting health and wellbeing. It recognizes that health is not just the responsibility of individuals, but is also influenced by the broader social and environmental contexts in which people live, learn, and work.

A whole-school approach involves addressing different aspects of health - such as physical, mental, and emotional health - through a range of strategies and interventions that are integrated into the school's policies, programs, and practices. It also involves creating a supportive and inclusive school culture that promotes positive health behaviors and attitudes, and fosters a sense of belonging and connectedness among students.

Examples of whole-school approaches to health promotion and education might include:

Providing students with access to accurate and age-appropriate health education, covering topics such as nutrition, physical activity, hygiene, sexual health, and mental health.

Creating a healthy and safe physical environment that supports physical activity, healthy eating, and access to clean water and sanitation facilities.

Encouraging students to take an active role in promoting health and wellbeing, by organizing health campaigns, clubs, and events.

Engaging parents and the wider community in health promotion and education, by providing information and resources, and encouraging them to support healthy behaviors and practices at home.

Providing students with access to healthcare services, such as vaccinations, screening tests, and mental health support.

A whole-school approach recognizes that health promotion and education is a shared responsibility that involves everyone in the school community, and that the most effective strategies are those that are integrated, coordinated, and sustained over time.

Providing comprehensive health education: This involves providing students with accurate and age-appropriate health education, covering topics such as nutrition, physical activity, hygiene, sexual health, and mental health.

Promoting physical activity: Schools can promote physical activity through sports, recreation, and physical education classes. This can help students to develop fitness, coordination, and social skills, as well as improving their overall health and wellbeing.

Providing access to health services: Schools can provide students with access to healthcare services, such as vaccinations, screening tests, and mental health support. This can help to identify and address health issues early, preventing them from becoming more serious problems.

Engaging parents and the wider community: Schools can engage parents and the wider community in health promotion and education, by providing information and resources, and encouraging them to support healthy behaviors and practices at home.

Implementing health promotion and education in schools requires a collaborative and holistic approach, involving teachers, students, parents, and the wider community. By promoting positive health behaviors and attitudes, and addressing the underlying factors contributing to poor health, schools can help to improve the wellbeing and academic success of students in India.

V. Strategies for Implementing Health Promotion and Education in Schools

A. Building partnerships and collaborations

Building partnerships and collaborations between schools and other stakeholders, such as health organizations, community groups, and local government agencies, is an important strategy for implementing health promotion and education in schools. These partnerships can provide schools with access to expertise, resources, and funding, as well as opportunities for joint planning and implementation of health programs.

B. Developing comprehensive school health programs

Developing comprehensive school health programs is another important strategy for promoting health in schools. These programs should be based on a whole-school approach and should encompass a range of strategies and interventions that address different aspects of health, including physical, mental, and emotional health.

Comprehensive school health programs should include the following components:

Health education: Providing students with accurate and age-appropriate health education, covering topics such as nutrition, physical activity, hygiene, sexual health, and mental health.

Health services: Providing students with access to healthcare services, such as vaccinations, screening tests, and mental health support.

Healthy environment: Creating a school environment that supports healthy behaviors and attitudes, such as providing healthy food options, promoting physical activity, and addressing environmental factors that can impact health, such as air pollution and unsafe water.

Family and community involvement: Engaging parents and the wider community in health promotion and education, by providing information and resources, and encouraging them to support healthy behaviors and practices at home.

C. Engaging students, parents, and the community in promoting health

Engaging students, parents, and the community in promoting health is a key strategy for creating a culture of health and wellbeing in schools. This can involve a range of approaches, including:

Student-led initiatives: Encouraging students to take an active role in promoting health and wellbeing, by organizing health campaigns, clubs, and events.

Parent and community involvement: Engaging parents and the wider community in health promotion and education, by providing information and resources, and encouraging them to support healthy behaviors and practices at home.

Social media and technology: Using social media and technology to promote health and wellbeing among students, such as by sharing information and resources, or by creating online support groups for students who may be struggling with health issues.

VI. Addressing Challenges and Barriers

A. Common challenges in implementing health promotion and education in schools

There are several challenges that schools in India may face in implementing health promotion and education programs. These may include:

Limited resources: Many schools may not have adequate funding, staff, or infrastructure to implement comprehensive health promotion and education programs.

Lack of trained personnel: Schools may not have trained teachers or healthcare professionals who can deliver health education or provide healthcare services.

Cultural barriers: Some communities may have cultural or religious beliefs that may hinder the implementation of certain health promotion and education programs.

Resistance to change: Some schools or individuals may resist implementing health promotion and education programs due to a lack of understanding or willingness to change.

Lack of community support: Some communities may not prioritize health promotion and education programs, or may not see them as relevant to their needs.

B. Strategies for overcoming challenges and barriers

To overcome these challenges, schools may consider the following strategies:

Collaborating with external partners: Schools can partner with community organizations, non-profits, or government agencies to provide resources, funding, or technical support.

Investing in training: Schools can invest in training for teachers or other staff to build capacity for delivering health education or providing healthcare services.

Engaging with communities: Schools can engage with parents, students, and community leaders to understand cultural and religious beliefs and identify ways to adapt health promotion and education programs to meet their needs.

Creating a supportive environment: Schools can create a supportive environment that fosters a culture of health and wellness, and encourages individuals to adopt healthy behaviors and practices.

Advocating for policy change: Schools can advocate for policies at the local or national level that support health promotion and education programs in schools.

VII. Evaluation and Monitoring

A. Importance of evaluation and monitoring in health promotion and education programs

Evaluation and monitoring are essential components of any health promotion and education program. They help to assess the effectiveness and impact of the program, identify areas for improvement, and ensure that the program is meeting its goals and objectives.

B. Key indicators for evaluating health promotion and education programs in schools

Some key indicators for evaluating health promotion and education programs in schools may include:

1. Student attendance and academic performance
2. Rates of absenteeism due to illness or health issues
3. Rates of chronic diseases or conditions, such as obesity or diabetes
4. Changes in student knowledge, attitudes, and behaviors related to health

C. Tools and techniques for monitoring and evaluating programs

There are several tools and techniques that schools can use to monitor and evaluate their health promotion and education programs. These may include:

1. Surveys and questionnaires to assess student knowledge, attitudes, and behaviors related to health.
2. Focus groups or interviews to gather feedback from students, parents, and other stakeholders about the program.
3. Health screenings or other assessments to measure the physical health of students.

4. Analysis of school attendance and academic performance data to identify trends and patterns related to health.

XVIII

References

1. https://www.nhp.gov.in/healthprogramme/national-health-programmes
2. https://www.ncdc.gov.in/index4.php?lang=1&level=0&linkid=35&lid=95
3. http://nrhm.gov.in/nhm/nrhm.html
4. https://dghs.gov.in/
5. https://www.who.int/health-topics/severe-acute-respiratory-syndrome#tab=tab_1
6. https://www.cdc.gov/
7. https://nhm.gov.in/index1.php?lang=1&level=1&sublinkid=150&lid=226
8. https://idsp.mohfw.gov.in/
9. https://www.nhp.gov.in/pulse-polio-programme_pg
10. https://dghs.gov.in/content/1364_3_NationalVectorBorneDiseaseControlProgramme.aspx

9 798890 024589

Printed by Libri Plureos GmbH in Hamburg,
Germany